WELL HELLO

In 2014, two of Australia's most high-profile journalists sat at a kitchen table, hit record on a phone and started a rambling conversation that's still going on (and on). From books to TV, music to cooking, friendship to films, there's little cultural terrain Annabel Crabb and Leigh Sales haven't traversed in their oddly named but nonetheless wildly popular podcast *Chat 10 Looks 3*.

Now, in their first book together, the pair takes a stroll through some of the issues of our time, offering advice for would-be writers, thoughts on developing a rich reading life, tips for navigating the perilous world of social media, and the secrets of a great friendship, all with the digressions that listeners of their podcast have come to love. Here Crabb and Sales discuss kindness, success and failure, and not taking yourself – or others – too seriously, with a liberal sprinkling of fairy-wrens, granny pants, show tunes, creative insults, diabolical mum bags and CLANGs.

Whether you're a devoted listener of *Chat 10 Looks 3*, curious as to what all the fuss is about, or simply looking to cry-laugh on public transport, *Well Hello* is the book for you.

Leigh Sales AM is a frustrated musical theatre star and wannabe undercover operative who instead fills her days posing as one of Australia's highest-profile journalists. For the past decade, Sales has hosted the ABC's flagship nightly current affairs program *7.30*, a role that has had her interview everyone from Hillary Clinton to Bill Gates to Paul McCartney (about whom she will not stop banging on). She is also the anchor of the ABC's federal budget and election night broadcasts. Sales is a former foreign correspondent based in Washington, DC, and is the author of three books: *Detainee 002: The Case of David Hicks*, *On Doubt* and *Any Ordinary Day*. She has three Walkley Awards for journalism and an Order of Australia medal that she likes to position prominently in the background of Zoom calls with Annabel Crabb, just to rub it in. She is the mother of two gorgeous boys and in her spare time . . . haha, gotcha – as if she has any spare time! Salesy is a monster who culls books as soon as she has read them; regifts presents if she doesn't want them; and unapologetically uses margarine. She likes cats, but not *Cats*.

Annabel Crabb **OAZ*** is an ABC writer and presenter with a 20-year career covering Australian politics for various organs. With catlike stealth, she has incorporated her hobby (cooking) into her day job and in 2011 devised *Kitchen Cabinet*, a kitchen-based political interview program that has either offered an intriguing glimpse into the characters of our political leaders or destroyed democracy as we know it, depending on whom you ask. Yes, she has fewer Walkleys than Sales. Amazing how frequently this comes up. But she's written more books, so suck on that, Ginger . . . *Losing It: The Inside Story of the Labor Party in Opposition, Rise of the Ruddbot, Stop at Nothing: The Life and Adventures of Malcolm Turnbull, The Wife Drought, Special Delivery, Special Guest* and *Men At Work*. For the ABC, she has written and presented *The House*, a documentary series on the inner workings of Parliament, and *Ms Represented*, about Australian women in politics, as well as presenting the popular history series *Back in Time For Dinner*. She also appears on *Insiders*, budget and election coverage, and writes a weekly politics newsletter for the ABC. Annabel lives in Sydney with her partner Jeremy and their three children, all of whom can spot a Chatter at ten paces. ('She's going to stop and talk for a gazillion hours, isn't she.') Team Butter. Of course.

*   Orders of Australia: Zero

Annabel Crabb
- AND - Leigh Sales
with Miranda Murphy

WELL HELLO

Meanderings from the world of Chat 10 Looks 3

PENGUIN BOOKS

PENGUIN BOOKS

UK | USA | Canada | Ireland | Australia
India | New Zealand | South Africa | China

Penguin Books is part of the Penguin Random House group of companies whose
addresses can be found at global.penguinrandomhouse.com

Penguin
Random House
Australia

First published by Penguin Books in 2021

Cover design and illustrations by Boxer & Co.
Internal illustrations by Boxer & Co.
Internal design by Adam Laszczuk © Penguin Random House Australia Pty Ltd
and Boxer & Co.
Typeset by Post Pre-press, Brisbane, Australia
Printed and bound in China by 1010 Printing International Ltd. Co.

A catalogue record for this
book is available from the
National Library of Australia

ISBN 978 1 76104 152 5

penguin.com.au

contents

just two chicks chatting into the same phone

the chat 10 looks 3 story

🐦 'Pre-emptively – it's not an audition for a show and it's not an ABC thing. It's just us mucking around for a few weeks.'

Tweet by Leigh Sales announcing that she and buddy Annabel Crabb were launching a little podcast, November 2014.

Picture: Stephen Blake

When podcast anthropologists eventually study the phenomenon of *Chat 10 Looks 3* they'll quickly deduce that Episode 1 laid down all the signposts for what was to come: piss-poor audio quality; Leigh luring Annabel into a room that just happened to have a grand piano in it; an immediate, gregarious launch into a show tune; the first hero-worship of Yotam Ottolenghi ('constantly in my top 1 of cookbooks') and Helen Garner ('the best living Australian writer'); shameless name-dropping and clock-watching; and Sales giving Crabb the wind-up at the 30-minute mark – all inside a barely planned conversation held together by a string of creative yet affectionate insults.

'We might leave it here for this week, and then we'll see how it goes. And if we've got time, we'll do it again next week. Thanks for listening to us,' wrapped up Leigh, casually. 'Oh, Crabb just fell over.'

Annabel: 'It's my physical grace you admire.'

Yet somehow this shambolic and deeply self-indulgent opener became a hit with listeners. Perhaps they had come for the serious Leigh Sales of *Lateline* and *7.30* and stayed for the daggy, potty-mouthed Queenslander with unfulfilled dreams of stage musical stardom. Or maybe they'd tuned in for the wit and warmth of Annabel Crabb and got sucked in by her outlandish vocabulary and anecdotes of unwieldy length and dubious merit.

By Episode 2, our bumbling bibliophiles realised people would actually tune in to two chicks chatting into the same phone about what they'd 'read, watched, cooked or been irrationally interested by' that week. Leigh's then husband Phil Willis – later to become known as 'Brendan' due to an erroneous iTunes review – was producing the podcast and had supplied them with a hand-held microphone, which quickly became the victim of a power struggle between Crabb and Sales. Leigh revealed herself to be a monster who discards unwanted books – even inscribed ones; Annabel called a man who'd ineptly tried to insult her on social media a 'prong'. Cake was discussed and eaten; bookshelf organisation was compared; fantasy memoir names were tossed about; and a frankly disturbing tale of jellied breastmilk was allowed to air.

Certain motifs emerged as more episodes were somehow recorded despite the hosts' galactic ineptitude with the audio equipment. Various interruptions – planes, dogs, kids – in the recording became the norm. Leigh said unprovoked, rude things about tuba players. Competitive baking ramped up and the compliment 'smug bundt' was bandied about. Sales droned on and on about music but tapped her watch impatiently when Annabel launched into one of her shaggy-dog stories. Celebrity names were dropped with suspicious regularity, causing the hosts to shriek 'CLANG!' each time. And almost every episode was derailed at some stage by the pair collapsing into cry-laughing at something absurd the other had said.

It became frighteningly apparent that yes, people were listening. The hard-to-classify and cryptically named *Chat 10 Looks 3* had become an unlikely smash, as Annabel and Leigh discovered. Fans – who had started to self-identify as 'Chatters' – seemed not to mind about the slapdash structure and inconsistent release schedule, sometimes waiting weeks before Crabb and Sales hit the mic once more for a shoddy recording session in a cupboard, or the ladies' loos, or a car.

And the podcast that had ostensibly started out about books and movies and cooking had unintentionally revealed itself (or, at least, by Episode 25, as follows) to be about something else: friendship.

a I have to say, one of the nicest things is, ==I've met some incredibly excellent people who really I only know because they have listened to the podcast== and come up and say 'Hello' or hand over cakes. And you can really tell a podcast listener because they'll just come up and give you a giant hug. It's a really interesting thing, isn't it?

L Well, it's interesting for me because previously, because of my *7.30* persona, people tended to be somewhat scared of me, and give me a wide berth, or approach me with some level of trepidation. Whereas the *Chat 10* listeners barrel up like they're my best friend and want to have a chat, which is really, really lovely. One of the greatest compliments, actually, that I look at occasionally, on the iTunes reviews that Brendan's always directing people into ...

a The best one ever is that lady who said, 'God, it's the greatest podcast, I just love it, it's so cool, I've just never heard anything like it! Two out of five.' Two stars! She is excellent.

L I liked the one that was the construction worker: 'Yeah, look, I started listening to this because I needed to drown out the noise of an angle grinder, and all I knew was that Sales was some harpy that rips into politicians and Crabb is something or other else and yeah, it's actually pretty good!'

a That was my dad.

L The thing that I've seen multiple people say is ==they feel like they're hanging around with us, and like they're trying to get a word in edgeways== but they can't. Which I think is a really, really nice compliment – that you actually feel like we're your friends, that we're hanging around with you. So that makes my heart glad.

> **The best one ever is that lady who said, 'God, it's the greatest podcast, I just love it, it's so cool, I've just never heard anything like it! Two out of five.' Two stars! She is excellent.**

A horde of Chatters keen to join the conversation needed an outlet, thought Sales and second producer Cathy Beale, aka Brenda 1.0, and so the behemoth *Chat 10 Looks 3* Community Facebook group was spawned, becoming a vast locality of like-minded, interesting, kind folk with a subculture of its own that we definitely avoid calling a cult, because, well . . . cults. A *Chat 10* merchandise shop sprang up, fuelled by consumer demand for fairy-wren regalia and insults-based kitchenware. More on all that later.

More on this later, too: the decision of two already overstretched women on the verge of a nervous breakdown to embark on live podcast shows, selling out theatres across Australia to audiences who paid 40ish bucks to watch them not only sit around gasbagging about books but also sing, dance, dress up in idiotic costumes, quiz guests, accidentally insult their hosts and generally make arses of themselves.

But a multi-pronged media and entertainment empire needs a support crew, and Crabb and Sales roped in a gang of pals and partners to help run it. Phil uploaded the first podcasts, and started the indispensable podcast notes; Leigh's ABC pal Cathy succeeded him and added Facebook wrangler to her job description; neighbour Gwen Blake handled the merch and the marketing and the design and just about everything else; Crabb's partner Jeremy Storer came on board as the details and logistics bloke and revealed a hitherto untapped skill as a theatre impresario; old chum Miranda Murphy whipped up a sporadic email newsletter; Chatter Bec Francis turned into Brenda 2.0 and took over as Facebook shepherd with the help of a flock of Brendalings; and Antony Stockdale took time out of his busy *Betoota Advocate* schedule to be brought on as partnerships and podcast production guy.

To the undoubted astonishment of audio engineers everywhere, *Chat 10 Looks 3* was even a double winner at the 2019 Australian Podcast Awards, managing to cover the gamut of culture from low to high by being recognised in the categories of TV, Film & Pop Culture AND Literature, Arts & Music.

That's what happens when Leigh Sales and Annabel Crabb 'just muck around for a few weeks'. The 'itinerant podcast in which they discuss what they're reading, watching, cooking, listening to or irrationally exhilarated by' found a niche and then lodged itself under the skin of thousands of new friends.

'I like that we have a space where it says: you know what it is okay to be in life? Smart, well-read and a nice person,' Sales said in a Fairfax newspaper profile of *Chat 10*. 'Because I think for women the messages that you get elsewhere are usually not that. The messages you get are it's good to be skinny, to not have wrinkles and to look amazing. And we never talk about any shit like that. We don't care about that.' (More on that later, too.)

To mark the 100th episode of *Chat 10 Looks 3*, Leigh got uncharacteristically sappy, posting this photo and message in the Facebook group. *Picture: Miranda Murphy*

'Having this community with all the listeners has been the most unexpected and amazing thing and thank you to all of you for the gift you've given to Annabel Crabb and me. We really do feel the love. And thanks to Annabel Crabb for the unbelievable number of laughs, her generosity of spirit, her brilliant mind and the non-stop interesting conversation. Love that turnip-obsessed, Brian May-haired, Ottolenghi-stalking freakshow of a person.'

chapter 1

the odd couple

songs of chat 10

'Chat 10 Looks 3: The Song'

It's entirely possible this podcast owes its existence to Leigh's ridiculously-close-to-the-surface obsession with musical theatre. In the very first episode she monstered a piano to belt out an explanatory reworking of the song 'Dance: Ten; Looks: Three' from *A Chorus Line*, Sales's favourite musical before *Hamilton* rushed the stage. After hitting a slightly mistimed key, Leigh insisted,

> **'That missed note there at the end is the only reason I've not been able to make a career in musical theatre. The ONLY reason.'**

Crabb established herself as the Rex Harrison of the partnership, merely required to contribute the occasional spoken lyric. Take it away . . .

Picture: Madeleine Hawcroft

well hello

Sales:
Chat: Ten; Looks: Three,
Well it sure beats unemployment,
Chatting for our own enjoyment.

Crabb:
Least they won't care
About our bad hair.

Sales:
Chat: Ten; Looks: Three,
Give us a spin,
Can't be that hard,
Pretend it's Hansard,
In case your boss wanders in.
Crabb and Sales,
Books and arts and polity—

Crabb:
Slightly crappy quality—

Sales:
This ain't mission creep—

Crabb:
It's just super cheap!

Sales:
Crabb and Sales,
Come and join us banging on,
Anything from canapés to crime.

Crabb:
Nice.

Sales:
Crabb and Sales,
Won't change your life,
We'll just waste time.

how we met

Ⓛ *When I was a child,* I used to tell my younger brother that my parents had found him in a rubbish bin and took him home because they felt sorry for him. The indignation on Glen's face as he insisted that this was untrue is sometimes what I think of when I see Crabb's expression as I tell my version of the origin story of our friendship and the *Chat 10 Looks 3* podcast.

In *my* memory, the first encounter I ever had with Crabb was when she cold-called me sometime around 2009 to ask my thoughts on joining the ABC, as I was anchoring the late-night news program *Lateline* at the time. She said she felt like she knew me, as we had many mutual friends, and could she pick my brains? We talked for a while and I said that if she ended up joining the ABC, there was an empty desk near me and she should try to secure herself a berth there – which she did.

At some point after that, I invited Annabel to my house for morning tea. She showed up and we got on fabulously but as the hours passed, I started to get somewhat anxious and wondered if she was ever going to leave. She'd arrived at about 10.30 am and somewhere around 4.30 pm she looked at her watch and declared she'd lost track of time and had a live radio cross to do, so raced up to my bedroom for a quiet spot. She finally went home and we've been firm friends since, although these days I prefer to go to her house for the obvious reason that I can control the departure time and bring the rendezvous to an end in under 6.5 hours.

The podcast came about because we found our conversations so stimulating and engaging that I was constantly saying things like, 'Do you know what we

Teeny Leigh with younger brother Glen.

well hello

should do – write a book together!' or 'I think we could write a really great sitcom together.' And Crabb would always say, 'Well, when do you think *we would have time to do this*?' Finally, in 2014, after one too many of these conversations, we sat down and pondered,

'Okay, how much free time do we actually have and what could we realistically commit to doing?'

Podcasts had just started to become a thing and we figured we could maybe dedicate an hour to recording it every few weeks – but with the understanding that we could let that slide out to longer if we were busy. We'd discuss things we never got to mull over in our day jobs – notably literature, the arts and cooking. We had no sense whatsoever of whether anyone beyond ourselves would listen; and it seemed somewhat self-indulgent, frankly, to imagine that our conversations were worth recording. Still, we just started doing it and, to our amazement, *Chat 10 Looks 3* turned into something huge. We realised after a while that it wasn't just a podcast about culture, it was a podcast about friendship.

I try to keep Crabb on her toes by never saying anything complimentary to her, but the truth is she's incredibly interesting and hilarious and I am amazed sometimes by how her brain works and the connections she makes. I usually can't wait to hear her take on everything – from the latest political scandal to what she thinks of a new custard bun at the local bakery.

'This podcast is getting increasingly filthy and I blame you.'

what the heck is with that stupid podcast name?

Well, thanks for asking, you and almost every single listener we have! In the musical *A Chorus Line*, there's a showstopper of a song called 'Dance: 10; Looks: 3'. It's sung by aspiring star Val, who tells the tale of constantly auditioning and missing out. One day, she swipes a look at her dance card and notes the casting folk give her a 10 for her dance skills, but only a 3 for looks. So she heads off to a plastic surgeon for 'tits and ass' and then, 'Suddenly I'm getting national tours!'

Sales, and Crabb's partner, Jeremy, are giant fans of *A Chorus Line* and around the time the podcast was hatching they'd dragged a bunch of people to see a production of it in Sydney. One of those was Miranda Murphy, who was later sitting at Crabb's kitchen table when options for the podcast name were being brainstormed. Fresh from *A Chorus Line*, she said, 'How about *Chat 10, Looks 3*?' and everybody fell about laughing . . . and it stuck. Would Crabb and Sales have gone with that ludicrously obscure name had they known their podcast would amount to a lot more than a dodgy recording listened to by only themselves and their immediate families?

Hard to know, but, like fellow branding giants Coke or Nike, it would seem foolhardy to change it now. (Which megalomaniac wrote that sentence? You be the judge.)

well hello

how we really met

(a) *I remember when I first met Leigh Sales.* It was at Aussies cafe at Parliament House in Canberra in 2008. I was working for the *Sydney Morning Herald*, having freshly returned from London, and Sales was hosting the ABC's *Lateline*. I thought that she was an excellent interviewer, and when I saw her in Aussies I went over and said so.

Naturally, Sales has no recollection of this interaction. Either because she receives praise so lavishly that my low-grade fawning did not make much of an impression, or because I was generally unmemorable as a person at the time. I'm not sure which it is. But in 2009, when I left the *Herald* and went to work for the ABC, I rang her and asked where I should sit. She said, 'Why don't you come and sit near me?'

A decision she now sorely regrets, I imagine.

One day she invited me over to her house for a cup of tea. I turned up late in the morning and we started chatting. After a while, my phone rang. It was the 4.30 pm radio spot I was supposed to be doing. I could not believe that so many hours had passed. At the time, I was thrilled to have found such a fascinating new friend but, looking back, I am thrilled for entirely different reasons. I picture the scene: me breezing in with a cake, then plonking myself down and gibbering happily for five hours, while Sales moves politely through all her normal wind-up tricks (glancing at the clock, bringing conversation topics to a close with an elegant summary, the discreet reference to the pile of work yet to be done) to absolutely no effect whatsoever. I imagine her, as I cheerily leave, double-bolting the door and then sliding down it to collapse on the floor in a puddle of disbelief and frustration.

Lord, it makes me laugh.

The thing about Sales, though, is she has an extremely interesting brain.

I used to read her column 'Well-Readhead' and marvel at the breadth and oddity of her cultural consumption. She can effortlessly switch between political philosophy and RuPaul, and draw pleasure from each.

Conversations can be wearing if you're having them with a person who's over-anxious for you to know how great they are, or who wants to chivvy you into something. But there is nothing quite so energising as talking with someone who grips her topic lightly, has read and thought about things you haven't even considered, and who is endlessly willing to duck down byways with you just for the fun of it.

And that, people, is the strength of the Leigh Sales conversation.

Unsurprisingly, we disagree on how the podcast got started. We had multiple small children at that point, and were doing the typical thing that many working parents of young kids do, which is forgo pleasant, non-essential child-free activities. I seem to recall that we decided to do a podcast because it would mean we'd be less likely to neglect catching up. I legitimately cannot recall why Sales reckons we decided to start it. Sorry, luv. I'll read your bit after I've finished this.

But either way, we did start a podcast, and our friend Murph said, 'You should call it *Chat 10 Looks 3*,' because we'd just been to see, at Sales's hysterical insistence, her favourite musical, *A Chorus Line*. I remember that we couldn't work out if anyone was listening to it at first, and then we suddenly realised that HEAPS of people were listening to it.

Since then, it's grown like a bizarre and fabulous weed. We've had live shows and made countless new friends and I still can't quite believe that people would download and listen to the audio of two fortysomething slappers crapping on in an entirely unstructured fashion. It's never boring, and it never feels like work. And by far the best thing is when we hear from people who are in hospital, or far away from their friends and family, or looking after someone who's unwell, or spending long hours on the road or working night shifts, who get in touch to say we've made them feel a bit less lonely, or a shade less downcast.

That is even more rewarding than annoying Leigh Sales.

dear sir/madam

(aka Common complaints)

Hey, look, sometimes we stuff up. Deeply suspect research suggests that Sales is about 92.3 per cent perfect and Crabb a smidgen less perfect than that. So, in the interests of disclosure and self-flagellation, here's  a truncated list of things that have – mostly justifiably – got people's goats over the years.

Demonstrating the advantage of good lighting.

- irregular (we prefer 'peripatetic') podcast schedule
- crappy audio
- incessant interruptions/aircraft noise
- Crabb interrupting Sales to tell an anecdote
- Sales cutting off Crabb at 30 minutes
- Crabb wanting to discuss something that Sales has already exhaustively talked about in previous episodes
- episodes too short
- talking too fast
- audible chewing or sipping
- too many in-jokes
- too many nicknames
- too much cry-laughing
- too much *The Americans*
- too much *Hamilton*

- too much baking
- not enough baking
- no structure/too much rabbiting on
- accidentally spoiling endings
- accidentally offending or triggering
- too female
- too white
- too privileged
- too ABC
- too lightweight
- too earnest
- not earnest enough
- too much politics when we're not allowed to discuss politics on the Facebook group.

classic episode 5

a unicorn in your backyard

This is taken from Episode 5 of the podcast, and captures the moment at which the adorable fairy-wren became the unofficial ornithological mascot of *Chat 10 Looks 3.* Crabb and Sales are at Leigh's house, blithely podcasting in the backyard without a thought for aircraft or traffic noise. Sales is trying to keep the conversation about TV shows on track but Annabel has excitedly spotted a trophy bird.

a Look at that beautiful little wren!

L Some people knocked on my front door about that and said that it's a really rare bird that just happens to be in the backyard.

a They are so beautiful. So we're looking at . . . it's like a superb blue wren but it's not blue. So it's a little grey wren and—

L The blue ones do come in.

a All right. So you've got blue?

L Yeah.

a That is a very lucky thing.

L Okay, you're a birdwatching freak. I didn't know this. So people knocked on the front door and they didn't show any sign that they knew who I was but then I got a letter at work, which was sent to my producer, to say, 'We're putting in a press release about Sydney's native bird thingies and we know that Leigh Sales has got them. So can she please be at our press release about how much she likes the birds?' And I'm like, 'Well, I don't think I can because I—'

a 'I don't endorse bird species.'

L I don't endorse birdwatching, okay? I just can't encourage that.

(a) *Not A Twitcher: The Leigh Sales Story*. I'm constantly thinking up titles for memoirs.

(L) I know. You said about three things today that I think could be a title for the podcast. *Not A Twitcher* is probably going to be it.

(a) So these tiny little wrens are just jumping around in that little wren-y way that only really a creature with a thoroughly flexible tail can. Animals that express themselves through their tails are just so cool.

(L) I'm so sorry, listeners, that you have come to this podcast thinking that it's going to be books and films, and now it's birdwatching.

(a) Oh, no – come on.

(L) *Birdwatching, with Annabel Crabb*.

(a) Right. I'm about to read out your address so that everybody can come and enjoy these damn birds because I think they're wasted on you.

(L) Now can I tell you my favourite TV?

(a) You must never get a cat.

(L) No, that's a good point, actually. But enough of the birds. My favourite TV. They were both things to which I was a reluctant convert and had to be talked into watching. And I thought they were both fantastic. One was *Masters of Sex* and the other was *Please Like Me*. So, starting with *Masters of Sex*, which is a drama . . . it stars the guy who always plays Tony Blair, Michael Sheen.

(a) Michael Sheen.

(L) And it's basically— No, she's still looking at birds, everyone.

(a) I'm listening with my left ear to you. They're nesting, look, Sales, they'll even have babies!

(L) Are they really nesting?

(a) Oh my god. There could be a bloody Tasmanian tiger in your backyard and you'd be like, 'But anyway, back to me and what I like to watch on television . . .'

(L) Crabb would be like, 'There's a unicorn. There's a unicorn in your backyard.' And I'm like, 'But I read a fantastic book by Steve Toltz.'

(a) Sorry, now I'm going to shut up and not even look at the incredibly adorable bird. I mean, I'll be focused on you.

(L) You can look at the bird as long as I can just keep talking.

glossary

Here is a compendium of idiosyncratic terms or in-jokes thrown up by the show, based on the sterling glossarising of long-time Chatter and Brendaling Caroline Braithwaite.

9 pm: Leigh's bedtime and thus time for all dinner guests to leave her house.

ABC Fat Cats: A term that originated in a newspaper article about ABC stars' salaries, now used liberally by Annabel and Leigh to mock themselves, e.g. 'ABC Fat Cat Moans About Being Invited to Opening Nights and Lovely Parties'.

***The Americans*:** A TV show about Russian spies living in America with which Leigh became obsessed and endlessly badgered Annabel into watching until she also became equally obsessed. It was then supplanted by French spy thriller series *The Bureau*, which Annabel is still holding out on watching purely to exasperate her friend.

Annabel's boyfriend/The Boyfriend: Yotam Ottolenghi. Attractive and brilliant chef who has published several cookbooks favoured by Chatters. Unofficial icon of *Chat 10* and a terrifically good sport who remains the only guest invited on the podcast, for its CLANGtastic 100th episode.

'Are you my driver?' An unintentionally obnoxious question once asked by Leigh in relation to transportation options, which she has never lived down.

Audio quality: A hallmark of the podcast. Traditionally absolutely woeful – through no fault of the producers. Decent audio equipment (see **Medieval Contraceptive Device**) was eventually purchased but Annabel and Leigh were too bumbling to use it properly, thus perpetuating the terrible audio quality.

Boob cabbage: Refers to an act of mega-kindness (see page 44) that typifies how wonderful Chatters are. The *Chat 10 Looks 3* Community Facebook group now hands out Cabbage Awards to recognise acts of kindness and, really, should have shares in cabbages because the Chatters are an extremely kind bunch.

Brenda: A nom de plume for former podcast producer/show notes compiler/ official Facebook group founder Cathy Beale (**Brenda 1.0**) and current social media manager/moderator Bec Francis (**Brenda 2.0**). Why 'Brenda', though? Phil Willis, Leigh's then husband, was *Chat 10*'s first podcast producer, and when an iTunes reviewer erroneously referred to him as **Brendan**, the name stuck. When Cathy succeeded Phil, 'Brendan' became 'Brenda' . . . and when Bec took over the social side of things, she became Brenda 2.0. Simple!

Brendalings: A term used to describe the magnificent gang of volunteer moderators of the *Chat 10 Looks 3* Community Facebook group over the years.

Bundt: Unofficial cake mascot of the podcast. No one can really remember why.

Chat 10 Looks 3: Possibly the worst podcast name ever. Must be constantly spelled out and explained. Everyone regrets it.

Chatters/Chatterati/Chatterkin: Affectionate terms for fans of the podcast and members of the *Chat 10 Looks 3* Community Facebook group. A lovely collection of kind, creative and generous people.

CLANG!: The sound of name-dropping from a great height and a charming interruption to any anecdote involving someone of note.

Crack: Aka Chatters' Crack. An insanely delicious and punworthy substance that's a slice-style snack consisting of salty crackers topped with caramel and melted chocolate. The recipe WENT OFF among Chatters and is helpfully reproduced on page 57.

Crack Wax: A *Chat 10 Looks 3* branded beeswax wrap to keep your Crack in, *obviously*.

Diabolical Mum Bag: See page 152. An incredibly capacious and practical bag Leigh bought that was subsequently ridiculed by the Chattersphere, much to her indignation.

Fairy-wren: Avian mascot of the podcast. First discussed when Annabel noted that Leigh had lovely blue wrens in her backyard, a revelation to which Sales was utterly indifferent. There are now fairy-wren lapel pins to help spot Chatters in the wild.

Flora's Fancies: A ridiculously overwrought gothic novel written by 13-year-old Leigh, which she reads aloud over several episodes to a delighted Crabb. Oh yes, we've extracted it at length in this book.

Frump nightie: Incredibly unattractive albeit comfortable nightwear favoured by Crabb.

Gwen Blake: Aka the Merch Queen. A fearsomely organised friend of Leigh and Annabel who's also creator of the *Chat 10* branding and graphics, and all the merchandise. She can also do a shockingly funny impression of a horse.

Hamilton: The musical by Lin-Manuel Miranda and with which Crabb and Sales are unscratchably obsessed – so much so that they promised to stop blathering on about it after complaints from listeners.

Helen Garner: Renowned Australian author whose work Leigh and Annabel worship. Rarely an episode goes by without a Garner reference.

Interruptions: It wouldn't be an episode without one or several, ranging from children to plane noises to phone calls to dogs chewing the audio equipment.

Kate Pritchett: Platinum Chatter. Cake-baking wonder woman. Owner of Momo, an exceedingly fluffy and cheerful Samoyed much loved by the Facebook group.

Kenny Family Christmas Day Organisational Chart: A laughably detailed flowchart (see page 50) by one Brett Kenny that divvied up his family's Christmas Day tasks. It was shared with the Facebook group by his bemused sister Pee-Wee Lewis and subsequently became *Chat 10* folklore.

Malcolm Turnbull: The baffling safe word Annabel suggests for Leigh after they watch the film *Fifty Shades of Grey*. No explanation is ever offered as to why.

Medieval Contraceptive Device: A fiendish electrical device on which the podcast was for a time recorded, acquired after constant complaints about bad audio quality.

Monster: A term of affection, but also a way to describe someone (Leigh Sales) who regifts books with reckless abandon.

Moral High Grounds: The Crabb-described smug feeling one gets from using a reusable cup that's almost as if the coffee is made from the moral high grounds. Immediately turned into a merchandise opportunity by Gwen, Moral High Grounds reusable cups were snapped up by Chatters.

Murph: Old friend of Crabb and Sales who rags them more than they rag each other. Author of the *Chat 10 Looks 3* email newsletter and co-writer of this book – and the one who came up with that stupidly obscure name for the podcast.

Powder my bundt: Obviously refers to a technique involving putting flour on your bundt tin before baking your bundt, to enable a smooth dismount (de-tinning of the cake).

Priest hole: Tiny, inexplicable crawlspace tucked into a corner of Crabb's ABC office that's used as a quiet location for podcast recording, much to the discomfort of the rather taller Leigh Sales. So named after 'medieval hiding holes down the sides of chimneys and places where you could stuff a priest while the priests were being murdered,' according to Annabel. 'So if anyone from Accounts is ever looking for me . . .'

Redacted: A brand of oven that caused Crabb much rage. The name has been redacted.

Show tunes: Possibly Leigh's second love – behind her children but ahead of everything else. Leigh gleefully torments Annabel by bursting into song at every opportunity.

Smug Bundt: A person who's just as smug as someone who feels smug because the bundt cake they baked perfectly dismounted from its tin.

Sport: Not a big interest of Leigh's, as evidenced by once having to look up 'who is Justin Langer' when informed she was interviewing the Aussie cricketing great in five minutes' time. Yet she suddenly became an unbearable cricket know-it-all after interviewing Shane Warne, and a basketball know-it-all after watching the doco series *The Last Dance*.

Strobe Cream: A highlighting cream that Crabb and Sales google how to use when they are applying their make-up together, in a classic episode.

Tubas/tuba players: An instrument and a group of musicians about which Sales is excessively and inexcusably unkind.

Uncle Ian: Poor unsuspecting Ian. There he was, just going about his business when he became suddenly famous thanks to the *Chat 10 Looks 3* Community Facebook group juggernaut (see page 52).

Yoghurt: A substance that was thrown at Leigh during a book festival talk. Also a substance that she managed to drop all over herself just a couple of weeks later backstage at a *Chat 10* live show in Adelaide. Avoid.

chapter 2

the group

don't call it a cult

The official Chat 10 Looks 3 Community Facebook group could be one of the friendliest internet postcodes. With a membership north of 40,000 people, it rivals the population of a regional city – a Tamworth's-worth of lovely, clever, funny and mostly like-minded people who come together to talk about the kinds of things discussed by Leigh and Annabel on the podcast. (This analogy falls over only once we acknowledge that, at last glance, Tamworth doesn't have a demographic breakdown of 85 per cent female residents ... but do stick with us.)

It might well also be the only place where kindness and smugness peacefully co-exist; where people can share their minor or major triumphs, or post their hilarious failures and receive support and encouragement. Because let's admit it – we've all been there when a birthday cake fails or loo paper sticks to the back of our pants or a small victory is had or an act of decency adds joy to someone's day.

The Facebook group has become such an unexpected phenomenon and so central to the *Chat 10* experience that it's perhaps surprising to discover it wasn't officially hatched until almost three years in. Producer Cathy Beale ('Brenda 1.0') set it up after suggesting casually to Sales that it might be nice to have somewhere that fans of the podcast can get together. Here's the big introduction, from Episode 60:

🅛 I've got some happy news – we've set up a group on Facebook.
🅐 It's like a mosh pit, that place.
🅛 We have come to realise that *Chat 10 Looks 3* is a cult.
🅐 It's so good, though. But I've been losing so much time because I go in there early in the morning, and someone's already always just posted something hilarious.

well hello

Leigh

L In good news, this seat seems to come with extra recline!

L We get a lot of feedback from women who are at home looking after young kids. And they often say we help them get through, and whatnot. I would recommend that you take a look at this Facebook group because I think it's a very good source of support and encouragement and a good community of people. And also the recipe for that Crack – that Salada biscuit Crack stuff is there.

a Saladas would be, like, disappearing off shelves because of so many sales, along with that brand of margarine that you favour.

L 'Brought to you by Western Star and Saladas.'

A hat tip here to much-loved Chatter Jane Britt, who'd already created a Facebook fan group that cheerfully migrated to the new mothership. Another Chatter created and posted a global map on which listeners could drop pins to show where they were and an astonished Crabb and Sales – still stunned that anybody listened at all – **gave a shout-out to the people in South Sudan! Iceland! Tanzania! Hobart!** Member numbers multiplied like rabbits into the many thousands.

The group provides Sales with a receptive forum for trolling Crabb.

Prospective Chatters were greeted with a mission statement that went something like this:

f Hello, fans of Yotam Ottolenghi, Helen Garner, and tuba players with sound personal hygiene: welcome to the official *Chat 10 Looks 3* podcast community group. This is a safe forum for listeners to share interesting articles, photos of cooking, or recommendations about books, TV, film, and recipes. We are into manners, kindness, and good humour so please be nice to each other. Anybody found being a pest will be subjected to Salesy singing the entire soundtrack of *Cats*.

Cathy heroically handled the increasingly brontosaurean task of running the Facebook group and moderating members' comments – a tough gig for a card-carrying introvert who for a long time kept her identity hidden behind the pseudonym 'Brenda Chats'. The all-powerful Brenda became the greatest anonymous enigma since The Stig – even sparking *Chat 10* merchandise mogul Gwen Blake to create an 'I am Brenda' T-shirt for Chatters to wear to confuse each other with.

But for a job that big, a Brenda's gonna need some help – and that's where the Brendalings came in. Cathy gathered a small posse of volunteer moderators, quickly dubbed the Brendalings (and sometimes just 'Blings') from among the most switched on, sensible, generous Chatters to help wrangle what is, admittedly, a mostly self-wrangling group. Over the years, at least 20 Brendalings across Australia and elsewhere have had a calm hand in keeping the juggernaut running smoothly, kindly, and safely for everyone.

So, is anything off-limits? Well, Leigh and Annabel insisted on a politics-free zone from the get-go because of their day jobs as journalists. Also, no medical advice! No financial advice. No selling your stuff. No getting snippy with other Chatters. There's a few more thoroughly reasonable rules in the fine print somewhere. And, as Sales periodically reminds a group of 40,000-plus punters, if you wouldn't feel comfortable saying it onstage at Wembley Stadium, it's probably not a good idea to post it.

Bec Francis (Brenda 2.0), Cathy's successor as social media manager, puts it thus:

We're all adults here, and we expect all Chatters to make their own decisions about what to contribute to and what to scroll on by. Our posts run the gamut from reviews and recommendations for all sorts of media, celebrations of bundts baked, calls for help or commiseration, to pictures of wrens (lots and lots of pictures of wrens). Plus all sorts of inspired madness in between. We love the ramshackle nature of our community. We share things that are funny, enlightening, inspiring, vulnerable, and sometimes rage-inducing. We seek and receive advice and support, and we try to do it with a spirit of kindness.

Frankly, it's now so much bigger than the podcast, which really could be considered just a beard for the many activities of the Facebook community. Chatter book clubs and social clubs have been set up all over the shop. There are no official spin-off Facebook groups at *Chat 10*, but its creative and diverse community has set up loads of independent Chatter-adjacent groups that cater for more niche interests. There are hangouts for cat people, dog people, trashy-TV people, book clubs, local residents' groups, *Dr Who* fans, Chatters with cancer, knitters, crocheters, cross-stitchers, sewing buffs, poultry fanciers, students, politics discussers, LGBTQIA+ers, bendy yoga types, cooks, bakers, gluten-free folk, vegans, Thermomixers and more.

Just a couple of Brendas and Brendalings unmasked. From second-left: Bec Francis, Cathy Beale, Deepa Srinivasan, Kerry Hogan-Ross and Jane Britt.

Chatters are relentless in their efforts to help their chatmates feel better in tough times. Funny threads, relatable musings, daily photo posting, group games, inspiring tales and of course the annual enormous, sustainability-themed Secret Santa exchange that's so well run that actual Santa takes notes on logistics.

And then there are the legendary random acts of kindness, now almost an Olympic event. Chatters finding themselves in a jam come to seek help, and generous, inventive Chatters give them help. They love to fix things, find things and ferret things out for those in need – one only need ask and seconds later the Chatter hive mind is on the case.

Crabb and Sales pop in regularly for a chinwag or to, inevitably, share pictures of their food. Leigh memorably busted open a can of worms when she asked: do any Chatters talk back to them when listening to the podcasts? The responses were swift and wide-ranging, from supplying helpful answers for the memory-challenged, to shouts of 'You've talked about this before!' and sighs of 'Oh, you didn't' to that perennial *Chat 10* chestnut:

'CHECK THE AUDIO LEVELS!'

> ## 'SHE'S NOT AS GOOD AS YOU ALL THINK SHE IS.'
>
> *Elliott, Annabel's then-nine-year-old son*

They've both posted numerous odd videos: gonzo baking in their homes; getting ready for live shows; annoying each other while on aeroplanes; and broadcasting several bumbling shows on Facebook Live during the 2020 lockdown to replace their cancelled stage events.

But possibly the best thing to ever happen in the group – in a very crowded field – was the day Annabel's then-nine-year-old son Elliott memorably hacked her Facebook to declare that 'SHE'S NOT AS GOOD AS YOU ALL THINK SHE IS'. Undetected for some time and with the wind at his back, Elliott then engaged with gleeful Chatters to reveal a catalogue of complaints, chiefly that 'she makes me do homework and she always stops on the street to talk to random people and she takes one trillion years', before being discovered by Annabel and sent off to live on a lovely farm.

It was a majestic example, like the group itself, of the rarely seen positive power of social media; a place we can all gather – a town square, if you will – to freely take the piss out of Annabel Crabb.

5 questions for...
social media wrangler Bec Francis

(Brenda 2.0)

1. Anyone who's listened to the pod knows how shambolic Crabb and Sales are. Given that, what made you decide, 'Sure, I'd love to be involved in this ramshackle operation and take over the thankless role of Brenda 2.0'?

Shambolic is a feature, not a bug! So much of our lives is governed by rules and processes and the 'right way' to do things. I love that *Chat 10* can let that go. And really, you know the 'shambles' thing is an act, don't you? It takes discipline to be this shambolic.

How did I get here? I don't remember when I first heard about the podcast. I'm sure Sales's and Crabb's egos will withstand my saying that I wasn't really a fan of either of them before I started listening. My own Facebook profile was gathering dust in some corner of my phone so I have no idea what possessed me to join the group. But I found something in this community that I wasn't expecting. You hear a lot about the hellscape social media can be and that's true. But this group ... I remember I was going through some stuff at the time, and I posted asking for ideas just to help get me through. And the group members were so kind and supportive and they didn't even know me. So I began engaging more. I organised a Secret Santa that year and I started going to live shows. I was a single mum with two tiny children; I used travelling to the live shows as my way of escaping my life for a couple of days and figuring out who I was. I offered in the group to buy merchandise for people who couldn't get there. That's how I met Brenda 1.0, Cathy Beale. I turned up at the merch store at a Canberra show with a list: 16 fairy-wren pins, 12 tea towels ... she was still trying to be secret squirrel about her real identity but she gave me that half-eyebrow raise Cathy does and I figured out who she was.

Later, I got a call from Cathy: did I want to be a volunteer moderator for the group? Then when Cathy was stepping down I wrote to Leigh and Annabel saying, 'I'm a lawyer. I have no experience in social media, or promotions or any of that. You may want someone who is more professional and closer to home. But if you want someone who's woefully underqualified but knows the group and the ethos of the place ... well, I'm keen.' And they said yes. So I guess *Chat 10*'s shambolic nature is really why I have this role.

2. The Facebook group associated with the podcast is huge and very active. What are the challenges involved in moderating a group like that?

It's a juggernaut of a thing and everyone has Very Important Opinions. The challenge, then, is to maintain our status as the hyperbolically named 'Kindest Place on the Internet'. I like to say that our group is like a giant cocktail party, where almost anything goes, but in the end what we want is kindness. This is a big and important question because kindness can be used to shut down minority voices, and I am very aware of constant pull towards the tyranny of the majority. But kindness isn't the same as 'niceness' and we don't need to silence people to be kind. I try very hard to give everyone a space to say what they need and I assume the best of Chatters. I think that in general Chatters moderate themselves. They are an extraordinary bunch of people and mostly I just give them a nudge now and then and the group sorts itself out. Also, I couldn't possibly do this on my own. I am so fortunate to have the best group of volunteer moderators on the planet to keep things in check. Brenda and the Brendalings - we may sound like a '60s mod band but we are a formidable team.

3. What have you liked most about your involvement with
Chat 10 Looks 3?

I've met my closest friends through my involvement. I've connected
with strangers and seen the bright side of the internet. You know, we get
so scared of digital communities because we worry that we are losing
real community but these are just methods of communication. You
build community where you can. Truthfully, my favourite parts are the
tiny serendipitous moments I get to be part of. It's meeting people with
whom you never thought you'd have anything in common.

> It's snort-laughing on the bus on the way to work.
> It's watching someone in the group post a cry for help into the ether
> and seeing dozens of people surround them with love and care.
> That's my favourite thing about being part of this group.

4. Like Sales, you are a musical theatre tragic. What's your
favourite musical?

Don't make me choose between my children! I've loved musicals
since I was five years old, when I saw *Annie*. Apparently – thank god –
the theatre was two-thirds empty because I kept leaping up to sing
along, and at one point Mum had to physically prevent me from
joining the orphans onstage.

There are musicals that have meant something to me at different
times in my life. In the 2000s I worked in the box office for Marriner
Theatres in Melbourne, and there I must have seen Jonathan Larson's
Rent dozens of times. As a queer girl just coming into herself, I felt like
Rent spoke directly to me and I'll always love it for that. That said, a
couple of years ago I saw a revival – and I have to say, the bohemian
aspects of young kids running around New York and refusing to pay
their rent seemed somewhat less empowering than it once did!

I've of course been mainlining *Hamilton* and I am so pleased that
Leigh has finally seen the show so we can stop hassling her about it.

5. Like Crabb, you are a crumpet tragic. Why go to the effort of making a crumpet when you can buy a packet of them and spread them with some delicious margarine straight from the shop? [*It's clear who wrote these questions – Ed.*]

Stop it, Sales! I made a recipe for crumpets because I had two small children and I wanted something a bit special that I could put together at night in between nappy changes and bath time, and make in the morning while putting on episodes of *Bluey*. That's the magic of cooking. You can create tiny moments of joy in the midst of mundanity. And you can't get that in plastic from the shop.

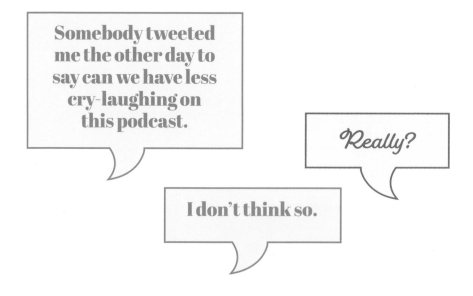

Somebody tweeted me the other day to say can we have less cry-laughing on this podcast.

Really?

I don't think so.

what's with the cabbages?

Are you sponsored by Big Cabbage?

The heartwarming tale of Jacqui Kennedy on page 44 has helped the cabbage throw off its hitherto unglamorous reputation and become a symbol of generosity among the Chatters. After Leigh quipped, 'Do you need a cabbage?' as a Chatter way of asking if someone needed help, the Cabbage of Kindness was born.

And there are so many worthy examples. Here's just the teensiest tip of the iceberg (oh wait, that's a lettuce):

Thanks!

Chat 10 Looks 3 Kindness Award

operation chatter-care

The epic Victorian lockdown of 2020 sent the Kindness-O-Meter to 11. Caring Chatters from all over Australia sent hundreds of care packages to others stuck at home: cards, chocolate, tea, crafts, textiles, books, biscuits, fairy-wren stuff…Much of it was through an ingenious formal registry called Love to Lockdown, run by Sally Gardner, Danielle Crismani and Reilly Case to match gift-givers with receivers. Enthusiasm was so high that the Love to Lockdown project organised *three rounds* of pressie-sending, and more than 600 gifts were given. This outpouring of good-heartedness deserved an extra Cabbage of Kindness for everyone involved.

from break to mosaic

Kate Slapp was crying on the kitchen floor after she accidentally broke her treasured baking dish that had belonged to her grandmother. 'I wish I could get a hug from her to tell me it's okay that I broke her casserole dish – because it doesn't feel okay,' she told the Chatters. As well as a virtual hug, Kate received solutions from the 'fix-it'-minded, including a tutorial on how to use ceramic glue and an offer to send a replica … but then thoughtful Clare Green took the pieces and turned them into a very special mosaic that even incorporated a photo of Kate's nanna. 'The mosaic still has pride of place in my kitchen,' says Kate. 'I look at it often and am reminded of that kindness.'

honey, I forgot the gifts

Allison Patrick drove from Canberra to country Victoria for Christmas but left a stack of presents at home! She was looking at a pretty sad Yuletide, but asked Chatters for a holiday miracle: was anyone driving that way who might have room for the gifts? Adrienne Picone to the rescue! She delivered the pressies, they had a lovely chat and the nightmare before Christmas had a fairy-tale ending.

go go flamingo

Natali Pearson's eight-year-old daughter lost her beloved Gilda the Flamingo and was absolutely devastated, as well as worried about her stuffed toy being out in the big world by herself. Now Gilda, being a Beanie Boo, is a not-uncommon creature, so Natali asked the Chatters 'with a Gilda in your life, to share a photo of Gilda doing something fun' for her daughter. What followed was a flood of hilarious and heartwarming photos of Gildas living their best lives – at the beach, by the pool, at parties, with minor celebrities, even watching Leigh Sales on *7.30*. Natali and her daughter were amazed and very grateful, and they received a – *shhh!* – replacement Gilda courtesy of the Chattersphere, too.

#BringBackTheDress

Chatters do a good line in 'lost and found' and #BringBackTheDress shows their collective supersleuthing in full flight. In short, Alise Hardy posted a challenge: her sister-in-law Eleanor Russell had lost a much-treasured vintage dress, so Alise wanted to make her a replacement – but the distinctive fabric (a 'barkcloth that was quite possibly a curtain or tablecloth in a former life') was proving devilishly difficult to track down. Enter an absolute ARMY of people getting on the case in various online groups, including *Chat 10 Looks 3*. Someone, somehow, found the exact same '70s tablecloth and clever Alise secretly remade it into a replica dress for her delighted relative.

white-tie madness

Johanna Wicks panicked when she had to attend a white-tie event on the same evening as a 5 pm *Chat 10* live show in Melbourne. Would she have time to go home and change? What would she wear? What even is 'white-tie', anyway? Shit, it's a ballgown! Chatters rubbed their hands in anticipation of getting to dress up Johanna at the venue and Augusta Zeeng lent her a stunning original 1950s Harrods gown. No good deed goes unpunished, though, and a gleeful Crabb insisted the gorgeous, frocked-up Johanna get onstage to show the Chatters before she headed off to the ball in a cabbage-shaped carriage. Okay, we made up the carriage.

Chatter Yersheena O'Donoghue probably summed it up best when she observed,

'There are the big acts of kindness, but sometimes it's the little things. A high five for trying, a suggestion of a way to support someone, words of encouragement. The small acts are so meaningful because it lets a stranger know that someone took time to care.'

conversation

the group

a giant, beautiful spiderweb

a Can I just say that, as we record this, you're sitting at your kitchen table with a knee rug, wearing the most frankly preposterous slippers I've ever seen. They're kind of hand-tooled leather slides with owls and bugs on them.

L I'm hiding my cold, purple feet.

a They are actually fantastic shoes.

L My friend Sabra gave them to me. They're awesome slippers.

a Don't tell me that Sabra Lane hand-tools leather slippers in her spare time?

L No, she bought them at some market in Canberra, but I really like them. She's an amazing friend. If you go, 'My house is really cold and my feet are freezing,' three days later you get a package in the mail, and she will have gone and bought slippers for you. She's a lovely person. Never forgets a birthday. Always sends a present. Let me tell you, it's a lot of pressure being mates with her.

a I love that we've sat down to talk about the podcast and **we're already totally off track.**

L But we're talking about something that I've learned more about on the podcast and that's friendship. The first thing I was going to ask you, before you so rudely interrupted about my choice of throw rug and slippers, is about the journey this podcast's taken us on, and *god knows I hate the word 'journey'*. It's been so unexpected – what are your reflections on that, on the journey, what do you mostly think about?

a Well, I think—

L Can I just interrupt there again?

a All right, yeah, sure, go ahead.

It feels like we plugged something in to the wall and simply hit the power switch.

L For anyone reading this, that question I just asked would be a masterclass in how NOT to craft a question, if you're ever interviewing somebody. That was the worst, broadest, waffliest question ever, but I'm just going to leave it there because it's instructional.

a Just leave it dangling out there, an unflushable turd of a question. Thank you.

L Carry on.

a What I marvel at is the independent life the *Chat 10 Looks 3* listener community has developed, that is so far from being run or orchestrated by us. It was a community begging to establish itself and I feel like all we did was – completely unwittingly – offer a little anchor point and then suddenly there's this giant, beautiful spiderweb.

L It feels like we plugged something in to the wall and simply hit the power switch and this huge thing lit up.

a Yeah. And a lot of that is traceable to our own incompetence, I think, because when we first were doing the podcast, more people were listening to it than we realised. The number of times people would come up in the street and say, 'I'm a Chatter' – I don't think that word was even invented in the early days, but that's how we realised a lot of people were listening.

L That there was a community that sprung up around it, who share these in-jokes and language and interests. When I consume podcasts or TV shows or whatever, I tend to view myself as a member of an audience, not as a member of a community. That's why it caught me by surprise.

a There was this awkward phase when there were quite a lot of people listening and then people would write in and say, 'Can you talk about this?' It seemed like there were audience members who were really hanging out to be connected to each other in some way.

Ⓛ **I remember a penny-dropping moment** when we did an event for the Sydney Writers' Festival together. It sold out really fast and the audience was very engaged – this was well before the Facebook group – and people were bringing us cakes and books and relishes, and somebody even brought us a salad that became known as 'The Salad'.

Ⓐ From Kate Knott!

Ⓛ And you happened to need to go out to Homebush for something straight afterwards and you ate The Salad on the way. I remember somebody overheard you asking me for directions to Wynyard Station so you could get the train to Homebush, and then a Chatter who lived out that way interrupted and said she'd give you a lift.

Ⓐ She made that up. This was a cop and her girlfriend and the mum who overheard me talking about how I had to get to a netball game with my daughter. And they're like, 'Jump in. We're going that way.' And of course, I'm like, 'Really?' And on the way there, I'm like, 'Where do you live?' They're like, 'Homebush Heights.'

Ⓛ They just wanted to hang out with you for a bit longer.

Ⓐ Yeah. They actually lived in the Shire or somewhere!

What is this 'Facebook'?

Ⓛ I reckon that was one of the first occasions where I realised, 'Hang on a minute, this is a huge, invested audience for this thing, what's going on? They're all really lovely and friendly and they seem really keen to have a chat.' But at that time, it was like the spokes on a wheel. Everyone was only connected to us in the centre, the spokes weren't connected to each other – maybe the spokes needed to be connected up. And so Cathy Beale started the official Facebook group to give people an exchange point.

Ⓐ And neither of us is very good on Facebook. I am a member of that group and that's about it.

Ⓛ No. I actually don't go on Facebook that often. I don't think anybody had a sense that it was going to become as big as it did.

🅐 Also, poor Beale, a mild-mannered librarian, in really quick succession became our producer – putting up the podcast and editing the links and doing all of that – and then a social media moderator as well, which was full-on because the group grew really quickly and it's hard work.

🅛 That's right. And now Brenda 2.0, Bec Francis, is paid to manage that, because it's such a big undertaking.

🅐 There are volunteer moderators in the group too, the amazing Brendalings. They've got this kind of 'cultural icon' significance there as well. They're the most engaged members and put a lot of work into just keeping the place rolling along. It's been amazing to witness how the group has taken on a life on of its own. People have their own friendships and stuff that have been sparked by this thing they have in common, which is listening to *Chat 10 Looks 3*.

Oi! This is a politics-free zone!

🅐 I think a lot of the tone is influenced by one of the rules we made when we were talking about, 'Can we have a Facebook group?' There are obviously some issues there, more about your job than about my job, but if there's a Facebook group that's got your name on it, then what happens if something blows up in that group? Especially a political discussion. We bounced this around because obviously we don't often talk about politics on the podcast, but what happens if there's a big blow-up in a group that's got our names on it? Does it reflect badly on the ABC? That's always something we need to take into account.

So we decided that if we were going to set up this forum, for essentially other people to talk to each other, it would need some rules about political discussion. That's essentially what the moderation of the group amounts to. It's dealing with any complaints, but also keeping politics out – because god knows there are a hundred million places on the internet where you can go to argue about politics. Obviously everyone's entitled to their own opinions, but please just take it elsewhere because we can't have this group otherwise. That has actually had a really interesting effect, I think, in that I suspect people sometimes use the group as a bit of a shelter from the more politicised debates of the day.

L I'm sure some people probably feel a bit irritated that they can't have political discussions in there because there are a lot of like-minded people.

a Oh, totally, it would be annoying.

L And some people would possibly view our quite hardline stance about this and our own silence in that space as its own form of activism. Obviously, silence can send a message as well, but it's just that the kind of journalism you and I choose to do means that we don't wish to be advocates in any sort of political sense. I think the effect on the group is that people are able to focus more on what they have in common as human beings, rather than their differences.

a There's also another reason behind it, which you haven't outlined, which is that you in particular have an incredibly demanding professional life where most minutes of the day are accounted for, so you don't really have a lot of time to hose down bushfires that might break out.

L Oh yeah, totally. Also, I'm immersed in politics all the time for work and I have zero interest or bandwidth for it outside of work. I'm usually not even interested at dinners with my friends, really, in hearing about politics.

a You're quite boring at dinners.

It's all about the kindness

L Another thing that I've found really heartening about that group is its contrast with the way the internet can be such a shouty, unpleasant place. It's wonderful to see a space where people are actually kind to each other and nice and pleasant. Something that makes me feel great is that I see acts of kindness strangers do for each other because of that group, and I think without what we've done, that wouldn't exist.

One of my favourites of those kinds of incidents was a woman who posted in the group that she had to go to a wedding in Melbourne – she was in her 50s and she was feeling frumpy and awful. She wasn't looking forward to going and she didn't know what to wear and so was asking for advice. Then a woman on the group said, 'Look, I'm in Melbourne, I'm a make-up artist. I can meet you at the airport if you want, and do your make-up for you. It might make you feel a

well hello

bit better.' And the first woman said, 'That would be fantastic.' So they met and they had a fun time.

Afterwards the woman posted a shot of herself, ready to go to the wedding, and she looked lovely. She said, 'I didn't say this in the original post, but the reason I was feeling so "blah" is because my partner died last year and this is the first time I've had to go off to something by myself. And it really helped having the support. It made me feel like I could do it. And I had, actually, a really nice time. And thank you very much.' That's so fantastic.

a I think there's so much on the internet that's sort of competitive in a bad way. On Twitter and social media, there's no downside to elevating a dispute or being cruel to someone, particularly for people who operate anonymously. Even though I know that there are people who are anonymous on public social media for good reasons, it kind of unclips a sense of human restraint, sometimes, to the interactions.

But one thing that I notice about the group is that if there is a competitive element, it's competing in kindness. It's not what's driving people, trying to outdo each other, but there is a baseline assumption that people will be good to each other. That Facebook group doesn't serve every purpose that you need in life or even in your online life. It doesn't supply everything that a full human being requires, but sometimes it can be a little bit of a respite.

L There's a rule in it I like. I can't remember if it was Cathy Beale or Bec Francis who instigated it, but it's 'scroll on by'. When you see a post that annoys you, instead of jumping on someone and going, 'That's a ridiculous thing to ask about, check your privilege,' just scroll on by. Ignore it and move on to the next thing. It doesn't always happen. But I think that that's a good lesson and it's something that I've taken into my online life outside of *Chat 10*. I think it's a really good way to view the internet.

a It's heartening to see all the acts of kindness in the group. Sometimes it's easy to forget how many lovely people are out there in the world.

It's okay, we're all friends here

Ⓛ I notice when people interact with us in the real world, I find if someone comes up to me and says, 'I'm a Chatter,' or whatever – they are the easiest people to talk to. I don't know if it's the shared sense of humour or the mutual interest in books and arts. I was at a cafe the other day waiting outside for a sandwich and this woman left the cafe and as she walked past, she said, 'Hi, I'm a Chatter and a big fan,' etc. And then we just stood there talking until my sandwich was ready. It was like chatting to an old buddy. It was so easy.

Ⓐ Don't you reckon that's because there's this weird circumstance where because they've been a part of our friendship it feels like you don't have to do all the introductory awkward talk?

Ⓛ Yeah, true.

Ⓐ One of the things that really surprised me about the way that people listen to the podcast is when we first did it I thought people would be interested because they like reading or cooking or culture or films or music or whatever. But actually it became really clear after we had interactions with a lot of people who were listening to it that the thing they really liked was the friendship bit of it. Or they really like it when we slag each other off, which is funny and interesting. One of the real threads is that people are listening to it when they're by themselves. We hear a lot from people who are working shift work or sick or in hospital, or have a newborn baby, or who are really sad for some reason or looking after somebody else. They listen to us and they feel better.

Ⓛ They get the same hit that you get when you see your friends.

Ⓐ Yeah. And plenty of people who've been listening on public transport have told us they've embarrassed themselves because they've said something out loud, because they're kinda jumping into the conversation. Or they've laughed a lot out loud.

Ⓛ Often when we have a discussion and it hits a note with people, a lot get in touch with me on social media, or sometimes people even email me to connect over it. We had an episode about bad earworms sparked by *Hamilton* and I reckon half a dozen people emailed me directly to say, 'Excuse me, I'm sorry to jump straight into your inbox but I listened to *Chat 10*, and oh my god, the *Hamilton* earworms, they're so bad!' That's always really funny when you feel like people reach out for that point of common connection over something we've discussed.

a It's not always good, though. There was that woman who said in the group that her husband has ruined *Hamilton* by pointing out that 'Alexander' scans perfectly to 'Adam Sandler'. So the lyrics are ruined. 'Go home, Adam Sandler. That's an order from your commander.'

L 'At night, I dream of Adam Sandler's eyes.' That really made me laugh.

a Thanks very much for that. Thanks for your feedback.

I'm Annabel and she's Leigh

L As you said before, it's actually about friendship. That's what people are listening for. They're not necessarily listening because they want to know about Helen Garner's new book. They want to hear how we interact with each other when we're talking about Helen Garner's new book.

The friendship aspect of it is really obvious at the live shows because people come with their friends. It's a night out with the person you feel is your Annabel Crabb or your Leigh Sales. People come up to me at the end at the book signings and they'll go, 'I'm Annabel and she's Leigh.' And they sort of see themselves in us.

a That's quite terrifying.

L People even dress like you, I've noticed. Which is lovely. Such a nice homage.

a And then sometimes you really banana-skin them by dressing as me, and that freaks everybody out.

Chatters do love a chase

L This is weird, but I sometimes have this sense of safety from Chatters.
I feel like, at any time, I'd be able to get on the Facebook *Chat 10* group and go,
'I'm lost in Paris' or 'I'm somewhere and I don't have anywhere to stay' or
'I've locked my keys in my car, is anyone within five minutes of Homebush?'
And I feel like a Chatter would come to my rescue wherever I was, because
the evidence of the group is that they always do.

a Jacqui Kennedy is the absolute ultimate example of that.

Jacqui and the Boob Cabbage of Kindness

There have been some Olympic feats of crowdsourced kindness in our
Facebook group and this one was the first gold medallist. In November
2018, member Jacqui Kennedy found herself suddenly in a small
country hospital in an unfamiliar town far from home with a breast-
cancer-related infection, and desperately needed to procure a cabbage
to help relieve her painful boobs. Uber Eats? Woolies delivery? Hell
no – Chatters!

'Are there any Moruya NSW Chatters out there? I need some help,'
posted a ginger Jacqui on Facebook . . . and 23 MINUTES LATER she had
a soothing brassica in her hands. Huge props to the network of Moruya
Chatters who not only came through with an urgent boob cabbage
delivery but also sent along flowers, coffee, smoothies and food,
gave Jacqui company over her week-long hospital stay and even
did her washing.

'Arriving in a town not knowing a soul, having been
adopted by strangers and shown love and kindness over
an extended period of time has made my medical hiccup
stress-free and less lonely. So much love for Chatters,'
wrote Jacqui after she'd been released.

well hello

Jacqui is a tremendous sport, coming to the Canberra live show just weeks later and frankly brought the house down recounting her now-legendary story onstage.

Jacqui, in her favourite T-shirt, and one of the helpful Moruya Chatters, Kim Small – the hits of the 2018 Canberra show. *Picture: Jacqui Kennedy*

Ⓛ Amazing.

ⓐ Of course, they're still friends.

Ⓛ Those stories make me so happy when I see them.

ⓐ There's nothing that focuses that Facebook group like the chase. They love a chase. Remember when that chick in Broome lost her spectacles?

Ⓛ Yep.

ⓐ Such a funny, ridiculous story.

Wake Up, Amanda!

You really couldn't make this one up and it does raise the unsettling spectre of the *Chat 10* Facebook group possibly possessing magical powers.

In late 2018 Chatter Amanda Burton posted one of the longest of long shots when she asked if anyone in Western Australia had seen her glasses, in a reasonably distinctive case, which she'd lost in Broome the previous week. Gobsmackingly, within an hour, Broome dweller and Brendaling Alice Best replied with a picture of said glasses, asking, 'Do these look familiar?'

Meanwhile, the rest of the Chatter nation was on tenterhooks as NSW-based Amanda had gone to bed by then, sparking an avalanche of comments sporting the hashtag #WakeUpAmanda. Come morning, an amazed Amanda confirmed ownership and Alice explained she'd asked on a Broome Facebook group, where two minutes later a police sergeant messaged to say they were at Broome Police Station.

Despite an excellent suggestion that the glasses go on a victory tour from Broome 'passed Chatter-hand to Chatter-hand like the Olympic flame', they were popped into the post and before too long ended up back on Amanda's face for bedtime reading.

Crabb demanded this saga be made into a play but Chatter Ann Petrou arguably went better by making a mock movie trailer, while Claire McGlew wrote and recorded a whole song titled 'Wake Up, Amanda'.

Alas, no one's yet been able to help the Chatter who said she'd left George Clooney in Broome and could anyone assist, or the one who said she'd lost her virginity on Lord Howe Island in the 1980s, so if anyone happened to be in the area . . .

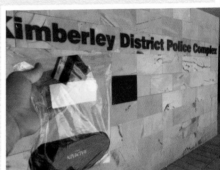

Amanda's glasses, as retrieved by Alice's husband Franque. *Picture: Alice Best*

Ⓛ Everyone activates and tries to fix it. And often they succeed. I mean, that stuff makes me really happy because I feel like *Chat 10* has helped put something tangibly positive into the world.

ⓐ It doesn't address the major structural wrongs of society.

Ⓛ No.

ⓐ I think probably what it does is give people who want to opt in to it a bit of an opportunity to have a little break.

Ⓛ It's just small.

ⓐ Every now and again: 'Isn't that a nice small thing to do?'

Ⓛ It's not Oprah giving everyone a car, it's just that some random stranger might drop you a cabbage.

ⓐ Yeah, we've never given anyone a car. What kind of ABC Fat Cat are you?

well hello

Like a dog who keeps coming back

Ⓛ There are very few downsides to the Facebook group. But there is one of them that I worry about and it's related to what you said before about keeping people company or helping them if they're sick or in remote locations or whatever. I do feel a little bit of pressure, like what would happen if we wanted to stop doing it? I feel worried that we would be letting people down.

Ⓐ The podcast?

Ⓛ The podcast and the group, all of it. If we just said, 'Okay, we're ready to do new things.' Or if we had a massive falling-out.

Ⓐ Imagine that.

Ⓛ I'd feel like, 'Everybody thinks we've let them down.' So, I feel a little bit of pressure around that.

Ⓐ You may be overestimating your own centrality to the experience, love. I mean, they're all grown ups.

Ⓛ True. And as you said before, we don't really drive a lot of the interaction.

Ⓐ Right. Also, if we left the equation, it'd be interesting because there wouldn't be the rule prohibiting political debate anymore.

Ⓛ That's true.

Ⓐ So maybe it would become like 4Chan.

Ⓛ That would destroy it, I reckon. I've always said – and I never have changed my mind on this – that if you died or left or whatever, I wouldn't keep doing it. I couldn't replicate it with somebody else.

Ⓐ Why is that, really? Because we do both have other friends, you know.

Ⓛ I can't explain it, but I think there's a very unique quality to our interaction that I don't have with any other friends. I have friends with whom I have hilarious conversations, of course.

Ⓐ So, you're just saying that those friends are less interesting than I am?

Ⓛ Mostly they just lend themselves less to having the piss taken out of them.

Ⓐ I'm like a dog who just keeps coming back, no matter how often the Sales boot is sunk into my hairy arse. I just come back and keep kissing yours, smoochie-woochie.

L I think it's a unique thing that exists around you and me. When one or the other of us departs, it will cease to exist. I mean, it might spring up in a new form, it might be called *Chat 9 Looks 4,* with a different person, who knows? But this would not be easy to replicate in any way.

a And the funny thing about that is that it was so completely random that it happened.

L You easily could have ended up starting it with somebody else.

a We would have been haunted by the ghost of a smelly ginger with terrible slippers. No, they're lovely slippers.

Je ne regrette rien

L Do you have any regrets about starting it?

a No. None at all.

L Same. And the upside has been huge. Even when I say, 'Oh, the one downside is I'd worry we would be letting people down,' that feels like 0.2 per cent and that the whole rest of it, 99.8 per cent, has been awesome.

a It's just been this kind of completely random outbreak of joy, really, and an opportunity to meet incredible people and hear great stories and be a bit reassured about the essential goodness of human nature. That's always useful.

L Totally. It sounds like a bit of a wank, but I want to take this opportunity to thank everybody who's been part of it, because I feel like I've been given so much from it, from this network of amazing people and their interesting recommendations and just the laughs I've had from them.

a They don't mind getting into some really random shit. And I like that.

L Remember that conversation at the live show in Newcastle, where I absolutely shit-canned that really popular book *Where the Crawdads Sing*? We took some questions at the end, and this woman took the microphone and she said, 'I disagree,' and she went on about what she felt was good about it, like, 'It was full of lovely descriptions of nature.' And I was just, 'Oh, yawn.' But even though she was a stranger and I was a stranger, and I was teasing her by pretending to yawn, you can have a conversation like that and it feels like you're with a buddy, not like anyone's attacking anyone or anything.

ⓐ I've never thought of that, but actually, because we're constantly attacking each other in a fond way, maybe it's like a sort of homeopathic remedy for instant offence-taking. I don't know.

Apparently none of us is perfect

ⓐ The other thing about – now that I'm addressing my brain to it – what makes that online *Chat 10 Looks 3* group very strong is that it's not ever about perfection. I just don't think I ever really see people posting 'This is why I'm so fabulous', or selfies where they look amazing or whatever. There's not really a big sort of humblebrag culture. I suspect that's probably because when we're talking about things going on in our own lives, it's often just that we've fucked something up, or that life is chaotic, you know?

ⓛ The way people post things is like, 'Look, I just feel really happy with myself because it was my daughter's 13th birthday and she asked me to make a Harry Potter cake and I feel like it turned out all right.'

ⓐ 'Because I suck at this and this has been less bad than I anticipated.'

ⓛ It's never, 'Look at my perfect life and look at my perfect children and look at my amazing stuff.' The vibe to me usually feels like, 'I'm shuffling along as best I can. And sometimes I need a bit of support, and sometimes I do something good and I like sharing it with the group, so that everyone can share a bit of my sense of things going well.' So yeah. I never go in there and feel like I'm inadequate or, 'Oh, I really suck, everyone else has their shit together, much more than me.' It makes me feel the opposite, which is really fantastic.

suddenly famous:
chatterstories

the Kenny family Christmas Day organisational chart

Days before Christmas 2017, Andrea – aka Pee-Wee – Lewis posted a very complicated-looking organisational diagram on the *Chat 10* Facebook group with this simple explanation: 'I have three brothers and this year it's my oldest brother's turn to host Christmas Day. We received these instructions by email yesterday. And yes, he IS an accountant.'

Since then, countless Chatter-hours have been spent poring over and laughing at one of the best *Chat 10 Looks 3* Facebook group posts ever: the priceless document that is the Kenny Family Christmas Day Organisational Chart.

'In charge' Brett has divvied up his large family's Chrimbo meal contributions in the most hilarious and intriguing way. Sharon Francis is assigned 'Girly shit, candles, crap on tables, useless stuff on tables but looks pretty' along with a number of other tasks. Lucy Kenny must do all the internal cleaning herself. Tony Ng can provide salads #1 and #3 – but, inexplicably, not salad #2, which is Paul Kenny's job. Kenny parents Eeni and Trev are bringing the 'cheap red', there is a range of four 'deserts', including one from Lucy's 'vegan assessment'. Liam Kenny has a range of odd jobs, including 'heaters'.

Chatters had SO MANY QUESTIONS about all of this – division of labour being high on the agenda. Brett copped a bit of early flak for giving himself responsibility solely for condiments, bottle openers and music – though Pee-Wee explained he was recovering from knee surgery. Also, what were 'cheese and greens' and 'Kaiser rolls'? Melbourne things? What did 'white wine (base only)' mean? And would there be a post-Christmas performance review?

Brett's chart brought many Chatters much-needed comic relief from the pre-Christmas grind. Annabel and Leigh loved it so much they created a *Chat 10 Looks 3* Melbourne Live Show Org Chart, and dragged Brett onstage for a debrief.

Kenny Family Christmas Day – Org Chart

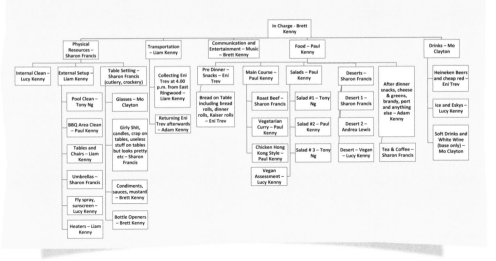

🎧 The legend himself Brett Kenny is here! Poor Brett had never listened to the podcast, was not a fan of the podcast.

Brett: Or read a book.

🎧 Or read a book, or had anything to do with it. And suddenly – much like Hot Callum – found himself a cult figure in it. I mean, Brett, how do you feel about becoming a cult figure in a podcast you'd never heard of?

Brett: Well, my wife said, I've got the perfect face for podcasting. So that wasn't a problem.

And had the famous flowchart led to a smooth running of Christmas Day?

Brett: It went seamlessly. I mean, at one point the gas heater caught on fire and luckily we just went to the Organisational Chart. My son Liam was in charge of that, so he picked it up and threw it in the pool and that was the end of that problem.

Fair to say after that the Kennys became the First Family of *Chat 10 Looks 3* as Chatters followed Pee-Wee's ever entertaining posts and then more poignant updates about her mum Eeni and dad Trev's move to supported care facilities across the road from each other. Hong Kong-based brother Paul Kenny was even a Brendaling for a time!

Uncle Ian, who is very loved

A classic of the *Chat 10* Facebook group sleuthing genre that's also weapons-grade delightful. In early 2020, Fiji resident Polly Henry was fossicking around in her local op shop, as you do, when she ferreted out an interesting T-shirt. It sported a photograph of a man's face, with the touching words 'I am Uncle Ian. I am very loved'.

Intrigued, Polly posted, 'Chatters, a somewhat fanciful yet entirely life-consuming request for you to do your magic: help me find Uncle Ian (who is very loved). I want to, nay I NEED to, know who he is and how this shirt came about. I need to know if Uncle Ian is out there and that he's okay and still very loved. Maybe he is a Chatter? A friend? Your delightful neighbourhood wine-shop owner who likes fun shirts?'

It's true – he is. *Picture: Polly Henry*

The Chatterverse immediately warmed to this challenge and – and stop us if you've heard this before – BINGO! Brisbane-based Dr/Uncle Ian Davis was identified and located *within the hour* by his work colleague Emelie Dahlsköld, who then had a bit of explaining to do for an amused and no doubt rather perplexed Uncle Ian, who had been going about his business until he suddenly found himself with thousands of new friends. He quickly joined the Facebook group to explain the backstory of the T-shirt, opening with this masterpiece of understatement: 'This certainly is an odd day indeed ...'

During a visit home to the UK, Uncle Ian's family and friends had thrown him a small party at which he was touched to find them all wearing custom-printed Uncle Ian T-shirts. 'How loved did I feel,' he wrote. 'I had a stack of T-shirts to take home, so I gave a couple to an op shop and that is how it ended up with you, Polly, and I am very glad it did. One thing this proves is something done with love resonates beyond that one moment or act.' An obliging Ian posted some pictures of the party and hundreds of Chatters found themselves with a speck of dust in their eye.

CSI: Chat 10 had done its mind-boggling work yet again. As one commenter remarked, **'Now, does anyone else have an international manhunt with minimal clues they want resolved in under two hours?'**

Annabel, who'd been on a flight in the hours that this short saga unfolded, turned her phone back on to a fusillade of text messages from Leigh ordering her to self-isolate from any Uncle Ian-related threads until she could tell the story at the Brisbane live show the following week – at which Uncle Ian was secretly slated to appear. Alas, that got canned by lockdown (leading to Crabb and Sales's bumbling foray into broadcasting live on Facebook . . . a story for another chapter. Chapter 8, to be exact).

Kate of the cakes . . . and the plates

Now to the chick we call 'Platinum Chatter Kate Pritchett'. It's difficult to choose the greatest aspect of her fame in the Facebook group – though she'd no doubt cringe at us mentioning any of it. But let's have a stab, anyway.

1. Momo's mum

In 2018 Kate began posting photos and sweet tales of her dreamy Samoyed, Momo, gaining such a following that 'Momo Mondays' were established by popular demand. It's hard to overstate what an adorable doofus that dog is, but **there was a time when Momo was bigger than Crabb or Sales** (can confirm: they were deeply jealous). Kate's lovely husband, Michael, was even CLANG'd in the street as 'Momo's dad'. Momo makes guest appearances at park-based Chatter events, to much eye-rolling from his sister dogs Rosie and Bella.

Momo, in all his fluffy majesty.
Picture: Kate Pritchett

2. Crazy-arse cakes

Kate creates gobsmackingly beautiful and clever cakes for lucky friends, colleagues and strangers. Often they come about because she's been mucking around in her magic kitchen at 5 am, whipped up something preposterous with ingredients you've never heard of, and then offered it for free in the Facebook group. Pritchett outdid herself and even got on American TV with a showstopping Harry Potter book cake topped by a *levitating, rotating* Golden Snitch (magnets involved, science). That one was merely a 'practice' cake for a child's birthday party, so Kate gave it to a children's charity *LOUD APPLAUSE*. In 2020, she had a crack at creating a loo-roll cake, which turned out so realistic that Michael asked why there was toilet paper in the fridge. Also, Kate does not eat cake.

3. Cuisine queen

Cake not your bag? No worries, Pritchett also posts pictures of meticulously prepared and plated Asian fusion dishes that she's made for, oh, breakfast or something. It's food and art, displayed on something stunning from her collection of ceramics. Deep sigh. She's also highlighted great chefs, suppliers and producers of fresh, diverse ingredients and inspired Crabb, Sales and others to learn more.

4. The Great Fall of China

But ... crockpocalypse! In 2020 a shattered Pritchett wrote of her anguish after a kitchen shelf collapsed, smashing her most treasured ceramics. Gifts and offers of help flowed to a grateful Kate from Chatters, ceramicists and wider internet good-sorts. Among the hundreds of messages, Crabb wrote, 'I think you know how much you're loved here ... it's about the deep recognition of how much love and care you show for others, and our collective sense of outrage that the cosmos could hurt you in any way. The experiences and impulses that made those objects irreplaceable to you, make you irreplaceable to us.'

recipes

Chatters' Crack

A gnawingly addictive, super-sweet salty-crunchy treat that made people lose their tiny minds, Chatters' Crack became the fledging Facebook group's first craze – and its high sugar content is probably partially responsible for the joint becoming as bonkers as it is.

It began innocently enough when podcast listener Claire Valtwies dropped off a book for Crabb and Sales at the ABC, along with a box of an enticing chocolatey-toffeey-crackery snack. Alas for Leigh, Annabel swooped in, scoffed the lot with her editing team, and then gibbered about it on the podcast, possibly high as a kite on sucrose.

Desperate for her next bite, Crabb immediately worked on reverse-engineering what appeared to be Saladas covered in a hard caramel and then coated in shiny dark chocolate and crushed nuts and cracked into (theoretically) shareable shards.

Legend has it, Claire's concoction was based on a recipe from SmittenKitchen.com, and an Aussie metric-measurement version was promptly posted to the *Chat 10 Looks 3* Facebook group by Jo Waugh. Quickly dubbed Chatters' Crack, it WENT OFF. People posted their crisp triumphs and soggy failures. They experimented with toppings: toasted nuts, slivered pistachios, freeze-dried berries, sprinkles (for that 'unicorn Crack' effect), silver balls, popping candy, salt, coconut, dried fruit, crumbled Peppermint Crisp . . .

Leigh

Longtime listener, first time Crack maker. I've gone toasted nuts on top.

Hundreds of people have sent us photos of their crack.

Crabb and Sales watched agog, and sniggeringly began to tap the rich vein of 'crack' puns it opened up.

ℒ We're sort of feeling our way a bit with what we're doing with *Chat 10*. We're doing some live shows and we've got this gigantic Facebook group now and are just sort of a bit shocked by how big it all is. Salada sales have apparently increased 15 per cent since March, according to Coles.

a You just love being right about this, don't you. Leigh Sales was onto this a while back, she's like: 'I reckon Salada sales are gonna go through the roof.'

ℒ SBS Food have done a piece about it going viral. Hundreds of people have sent us photos of their crack.

a Um, you might like to rephrase that.

Chatters' CRACK

Ingredients:
1 pack Salada biscuits
1 cup brown sugar
1 tsp vanilla essence
200g butter (Not margarine. Sales. Not this time.)
200g dark chocolate, chopped
Big pinch of salt

Method:
Have your **driver** TAKE YOU to the shops to retrieve ingredients.

Chat affably to wild-eyed fellow shoppers fighting you for Saladas. **PREVAIL.** RETURN TO BASE AND PREHEAT OVEN TO 180C.

Rummage swearingly through oven-tray cupboard to find one that will fit three Saladas one way and four the other way. LINE IT WITH FOIL AND THEN WITH BAKING PAPER, AND THEN LAY OUT THE SALADAS SNUGLY.

Snap them to fit if **ABSOLUTELY** *unavoidable.*

In a saucepan, melt butter and sugar together over a moderate heat.

⏱ Cook for about five minutes

Add vanilla, salt & stir.

Take the toffee off the heat & immediately pour over the Saladas. Smooth with an offset spatula if you have one. If you don't have one, send your driver out immediately.

INTO THE OVEN FOR **15 MINS**

Or until the toffee has darkened to a deep gold.

Maybe listen to a good podcast? Don't get caught up though: **CRACK CAN BURN**

FOR REAL an offset spatula will change your life.

Sprinkle the chopped choc over the hot toffee & leave for a minute until melted. Spread evenly with the spatula.

Congratulations!
You have made crack.

YOU MAY ENHANCE IT WHILE THE CHOCOLATE IS STILL WARM BY ADDING VARIOUS TOPPINGS:

Christmas Crack: Slivered toasted pistachios and dehydrated raspberries.

Nutcracker: Chopped toasted nuts. Upside is your kids can't take it to school.

Builders' Crack: Crumbled chocolate biscuits.

Sarah Wilson's Crack: Substitute biscuits, butter and sugar for half a raw carrot.

Thanks to: Crabtree Claire. Vultured for first delivering crack to Leigh and Annabel. See you in rehab, Chatter.

Crabb's Chatters' Crack recipe was printed on a *Chat 10* tea towel, and the joke was flogged further on the release of *Chat 10* beeswax food wraps – named Crack Wax, obviously because they're good for keeping Crack in. Never mind.

well hello

Crabb's Chatters' Crack

Ingredients:

1 x 250g pack of Salada-style biscuits
200g butter (Not margarine, Sales.)
185g (1 cup) soft brown sugar
1 teaspoon vanilla essence
big pinch of salt
200g dark chocolate, chopped
topping of choice

Method:

1. Have your driver take you to the shops to retrieve ingredients. Chat affably to wild-eyed fellow shoppers fighting you for Saladas. Prevail.

2. Return to base and preheat oven to 180°C. Rummage swearingly through oven-tray cupboard to find one that will fit three Saladas one way and four the other way. Line it with foil and then with baking paper, and then lay out the Saladas snugly. Snap them to fit if absolutely unavoidable.

3. In a saucepan, melt butter and sugar together over a moderate heat. Cook for about five minutes. Add vanilla and salt, and stir.

4. Take the toffee off the heat and immediately pour it over the Saladas. Smooth with an offset spatula if you have one. If you don't have one, send your driver out immediately. For real, an offset spatula will change your life.

5. Put the tray in the oven for 15 minutes or until the toffee has darkened to a deep gold. Maybe listen to a good podcast? Don't get caught up, though: CRACK CAN BURN. Sprinkle the chopped chocolate over the hot toffee and leave for a minute until melted. Spread evenly with the spatula.

6. Congratulations! You have made Crack. You may enhance it while the chocolate is still warm by adding various toppings (see Chatters' suggestions earlier). When cool, snap into pieces and scoff.

Alice Ryan's glass potatoes

There's a recipe that Crabb enthuses about as 'the best use of a carb and a fat that I have yet encountered'. It's Glass Potatoes, a dish now so beloved of Chatters that on one Easter weekend at least 80 people posted about cooking them. They're roasted spuds with bottoms that are 'a translucent, crackling, toffee-coloured brittle delight' and one of Broadsheet's most popular recipes of the decade.

Crabb invited the woman she credits for Glass Potatoes, long-time mate Alice Ryan, to a Melbourne show to 'acknowledge her contribution to the potato and oil industry' and recount their delectable genesis.

'It was a dish that was born of my inability to cook and drink at the same time,'

Alice explained to 2500 Chatters, who were probably jotting down notes. 'So it was a dish that you could put in the oven. Forget about it. Get a little bit buzzed with your friends, go back an hour and a half later and they were crispy. It's an accidental dish, but very popular. It's kind of like the best chips in the hot chip packet.'

And as Annabel advises in *Special Delivery*, her cookbook written with dear friend Wendy Sharpe, if you're planning to skimp on the oil or salt, then just don't bother.

Leigh

Chalk up another victory for glass potatoes, served up at the yummiest lunch by my friend Melanie Andersen.

well hello

Glass Potatoes

Serves 6

Ingredients:

2kg large potatoes (ideally kestrel), skin on
250ml olive oil
1 tablespoon salt flakes

Method:

1. Preheat your oven to 220°C (200°C fan) and dig out a suitable roasting tin. The heavy cast-iron type is ideal, but use what you have; no ceramics, though, please. My 40cm x 28cm tin fits 2kg of potatoes nicely.

2. Put the potatoes, whole, into a large saucepan and cover with water. Bring to the boil and cook for about 30 minutes, or until the potatoes are soft and a knife goes to the heart with ease. The skins will have split a little. Drain and tip into your *unoiled* roasting tin.

3. Okay. With a big spoon, press down on each potato to crush it slightly. What you're looking for is a big dent in the top of each spud, which will obligingly split a bit. Now pour over your scandalous, Exxon Valdez quantity of oil, sprinkle with the salt flakes and put the whole thing into the oven. After 10 minutes, turn the oven down to 200°C (180°C fan), and let the potatoes go for another hour. Don't poke or baste or shake or otherwise interfere with them.

4. The ancillary beauty of these spuds is that they are very laid-back. If an hour goes by and you suddenly remember that you need to make a salad and you haven't yet, or you were going to cook some steaks and were so busy chatting that you plain forgot, just turn the oven temperature down to 180°C (160°C fan) and the potatoes will coast along for another half an hour while you catch up.

the '70s called and they want that recipe for Nuts and Bolts

Crabb caused kitsch cooking consternation among the *Chat 10 Looks 3* Facebook group when she idly asked about making Nuts and Bolts, `a truly horrifying snack food of the late '70s`.

'I remember an Easter holiday when we went to stay with family friends who had a place at the beach. They'd give us Nuts and Bolts – a salty–sweet blend of peanuts, Nutri-Grain cereal and . . . I think curry powder was involved. Super oily. So, here's my confession: I want to make some. I procured Nutri-Grain

and peanuts but the recipes I see online are wildly variant. One suggests 250g of BUTTER, for pity's sake. Some say paprika. Some say curry powder. Some say powdered cream of chicken soup (WHAT?). I'm frightened. But determined to continue.'

`Chatters fretted. Was this to be the New Crack Craze?` Still, Annabel's plea sparked more than 500 replies, from nostalgia to bafflement to horror. Chatters dug out handwritten recipes – even a version by the late, great Margaret Fulton. Annabel went mad and shoved all sorts of stuff in: '500g Nutri-Grain, 500g Nobby's peanuts, 125g butter, ⅓ cup olive oil, 3 tsp cumin, ½ tsp cinnamon, 1 tsp curry powder, 1 tsp cayenne, 1 crumbled Massel chicken stock cube, 1 tsp celery seed. Warm oil and stir all spices through. Then pour over Nutri-Grain and mix well, stir nuts through and spread on a tray to bake in a 160°C oven for . . . I don't know how long.'

For the record, Nutri-Grain does offer a recipe, and we're sure it was a coincidence but shortly afterwards Kellogg's launched 'Nuts & Bolts Trail Mix, inspired by the original Nuts & Bolts snack recipe'.

5 questions for...
Callum Denness

aka *Hot Callum*

Christmas treat for the chatters – me and Callum, who just made us walk around the office looking for better lighting 'because I'm Hot Callum, it's a lot of pressure to live up to this'.

1. Had you ever heard of *Chat 10 Looks 3* before you arrived to work as a producer with Leigh Sales at *7.30* (for that matter, had you ever even heard of Leigh Sales)?

I had listened to a couple of episodes of the podcast before joining *7.30*. In fact, it may have been a decisive factor in getting the job. I had an interview over Skype with a selection panel, and felt horrendously underprepared. One of the questions Leigh asked was about what podcasts I was listening to, probably expecting I'd answer with something actually relevant to the job. The only thing I could think of was *My Dad Wrote A Porno*, which was discussed on one of the *Chat 10* episodes I'd listened to. It made Leigh laugh and made me way more relaxed.

2. How did you learn that you had become a cult figure known as Hot Callum in a podcast mostly listened to by bookish women who wear cardigans?

The origin story is that Leigh and Annabel were recording an episode in a green room at the ABC. I needed to speak to Leigh on urgent *7.30* business, so I busted into the room unaware I was interrupting. They encouraged me to say hi to the audience and dragged me to the mic. I said the first thing that popped into my head – which was a shout-out to the gay audience, letting them know I was single.

I want it on the record that I did not come up with this nickname.

Once I left, Annabel talked me up to potential suitors, which is how the Hot Callum name came about. I was a bit mortified to learn of the nickname because of the instant pressure of high expectations. Later I was told there was a bit of a frenzy on the Facebook page, including a lot of Chatters keen to set me up with their daughters. Sorry to disappoint, again.

3. How has that affected your life?
Mostly it's just my sisters informing me when I've gotten a mention on the podcast, or the occasional sneaky DM on Twitter. There are worse nicknames to be known by but, it's sometimes awkward and you can encounter Chatters in surprising places. Rod Sims, chairman of the Australian Competition and Consumer Commission, once addressed me as Hot Callum before a *7.30* interview which is ... weird, because not even my boyfriend calls me that.

4. Sales wants it on the record that Crabb is the one who came up with the nickname, while Leigh always felt slightly alarmed that it was inappropriate, given that if (her predecessor) Kerry O'Brien had referred to a female producer as Hot Mary-Ellen, all hell would have broken loose. Why did you never report Sales and Crabb to ABC Human Resources for a bit of re-education on appropriate workplace behaviour?

I assumed that as powerful ABC Fat Cats they were untouchable.

5. For a few years, you spent more time with Sales than anyone else in her life. Tell us something about her that would surprise us.

Initially I was surprised to learn that Leigh is a High Priestess of the Illuminati. But now I realise it's not so surprising because, if you pay attention, she gives away extremely subtle clues when she's presenting 7.30. Leigh would love to receive handwritten correspondence on the topic. Please ensure all letters are written entirely in capital letters on pages torn from the Bible, with random words highlighted.

I think you haven't gone to Hamilton because you've been told so many times. I've seen you do this before. You've got this little set to your jaw where everyone's just gone, **'Oh, oh, the *Hamilton* musical, you've gotta see that,'** *and you're like,* **'Mmm-hmm, nuh-uh.'**

songs of chat 10

'It's a cult, you're all in it'

This is a song Sales performed at the first ever live *Chat 10 Looks 3* show in Melbourne in November 2017. She was accompanied on guitar by her old friend Chris, from Breakthru, the *Christian rock band in which Leigh used to play keys as a teenager.* 'We used to drive around with our instruments in Chris's white Kombi van, it was … very cool,' she told the audience. Chris reports that Leigh 'had a very low tolerance for jamming in band practices'. Anyway, they cranked out this pearler to the tune of 'Bitch' by Meredith Brooks:

> *That was possibly the most humiliating thing I've seen you ever do,'*

reported Annabel, deeply unaware that live vocal performances – even involving herself – would become a fixture at future *Chat 10 Looks 3* live shows.

Leigh with former bandmate and very good sport Chris.

well hello

I went to work one day
And I downloaded a podcast on the way
It was called Chat 10 Looks 3
There's lots of people just like me
They're really fun
And they seem so nice and friendly.
So I joined their Facebook page
15,000 people claim it's all the rage
But I start to feel alarmed when I scroll back
And see that they're all into Crack
And 18 women all named Donna have strong thoughts on the Oxford comma.

CHORUS

It's a cult, you're all in it
When you write a book, I'll bin it
And we fight about small birds
But we love all you book nerds
We mock tubas, we say **CLANG**
In a compound we should hang
We worship Annabel's clothes and her curly hair.

I hop in bed one night
And I think that I should just turn off the light
But instead I take one last look at the group
And then I'm sucked into a loop
And when I next look at the time it's fucking 11.59.

CHORUS

It's a cult, you're all in it
When you write a book, I'll bin it
And we fight about small birds
But we love all you book nerds
We mock tubas, we say **CLANG**
In a compound we should hang
We worship Annabel's clothes and her curly hair.

chapter 3

how to read

conversation

how to read

Crabb and Sales have discussed hundreds of books over the life of the podcast – some of them multiple times when they forget they've already been talked about (a laughably regular occurrence). A question they get asked a lot by listeners is: how do they find the time to read so much? Short answer: brutal Leigh gallops through a book at a time, scans for plot and chucks it in early if she's not digging it. More casual Annabel has a few books on the go at once but sometimes forgets what she's reading. Crabb hoards books she's read, Sales moves 'em on – even ones lovingly inscribed by the giver. And worst of all, Leigh dog-ears the pages *of library books*. What is wrong with her?!

L Do you feel like you read a lot?

a Yes, I do. My fantasy is to have an entire day where I don't have to do anything except lie on a bed and read. I'm happy to read sitting up but ideally I would be lying on a bed. And in my mind's eye, this bed is in a clearing in a lovely forest and there's a bit of a breeze blowing and the bed's got lots of fluffy pillows, but it's also got that kind of weird netting stuff. It's somehow a four-poster bed.

L Oddly, when I was a child, I also wanted a four-poster bed.

a No, I want to be completely clear about this. I did not want a four-poster bed as a child. It's the bed that I'm reading on in my fantasy clearing. I don't want a four-poster bed in any other element of my life. I also know, deep in my heart of hearts, that this shit will never happen. So I think the four-poster bed is an embroidery. Maybe there's also a unicorn gazing from the Henri Rousseau-style undergrowth, peering at me.

L You are giving me some good ideas for your 50th birthday present, I'm not going to lie. I think Gwen Blake could make that happen.

a It'd just involve you all leaving me alone for a week.

L Imagine how terrified you would actually be if we put you in the car, took you out to the bush in the middle of nowhere, and there was just a big bed there and a stack of books and we threw you out of the car and went, 'Okay, see you in a week.' You would be crapping yourself.

a I'd be torn apart by wild animals in short order.

L So the fantasy doesn't really hold up.

a And to be honest, within 20 minutes I'd feel so guilty that I was not achieving anything or about what was happening in my absence and who I was letting down by not being there. I'd be back in 35 minutes.

ReKindle my love

L What about phone withdrawal?

a Oh, fine. I'd have no problem with that whatsoever.

L I suspect for a lot of people checking their phone and disappearing down a phone rabbit hole is perhaps a thing that takes them away from time they could use reading.

a That's true. It depends, I guess, on what use you make of the shortened attention span that we've all got, thanks to those devices. I find that it actually does allow me to jump in and out of books with great facility. Possibly that's about the way I read as well – I read fast.

L Do you read books on the phone now?

a I do. I remember when I was on the book tour for *The Wife Drought* in 2014, maybe 2015. And I was travelling with a publicist and I noticed she was on her phone, seemingly reading huge amounts of texts. I said, 'What's going on?' And she said, 'I've got the Kindle app on my phone.' And I said to her, 'I would never do that.' Yet I do now, because it's an economical way to carry a lot of books around with you.

L Definitely so. I went through a phase where if I couldn't read something on my Kindle, which I use on my iPad, I used to feel annoyed. In the olden days when I'd go on holidays, my suitcase would weigh a tonne because I was so scared that I might run out of books. I'd take, like, ten books on holidays. And so I love the idea that when you're travelling it's all on your iPad or you can download. But I must admit that in recent times I've gone back to preferring a hard-copy book just because of the feeling of the uniqueness of each book. The thing with the Kindle is that everything is texturally the same.

How about that tiger in the boat

Ⓛ I read a lot, although maybe not as much as people think.

ⓐ Yeah. That's because you're brutal. You read four pages and you're like, 'I don't like you – in the bin.' So you've got plenty of titles to reel off.

Ⓛ You can give the appearance of having read them because you can go, 'Oh yeah, *Life of Pi*, how about that tiger in the boat?' But you've only read a fraction of it.

ⓐ I've never read that book.

Ⓛ When I was a kid, I could not go to sleep unless I read. And that's still, at night, the most efficient way for me to get to sleep.

ⓐ Me too, absolutely.

Ⓛ I'm a really fast reader as well. I get through stuff quite quickly.

ⓐ But do you then have to read it back to absorb it more? I mean, sometimes I feel bad about the fact that I will quite often gallop through a book and then friends of mine – who are much more cautious or slow readers but really imbibe and absorb a lot more – say, 'What did you think about that thing that happened on page 35, that glance that Eleanor shot to Jack where it silently revealed so much about the contextual business of their relationship?' And I think, 'What?'

Ⓛ Definitely. I gallop through often for plot because I want to know what's going to happen, what's happening next. I do sometimes find that when I'm reading really good writers – Gerald Murnane springs to mind – the quality of the writing forces me to slow down. Some writers you can't read quickly. Or *Far From the Tree* by Andrew Solomon, that non-fiction book that I banged on about a lot.

ⓐ Oh yeah, yeah, yeah. It's enormous and my copy has such tiny, tiny text. It makes my eyes cross a bit. Maybe I should read that on Kindle.

ⓛ But I totally agree with you, I think I miss a lot of things because usually I just rattle through too fast.

ⓐ One thing that bothers me about reading things on Kindle is – and this sounds so stupid – is that sometimes I can't remember the title of the book I'm reading. This is where the old adage about not judging a book by its cover is a bit misleading, because a book cover can contextualise a book for you, help you remember it. I mean, to remember the title and the author's name. Sometimes when I'm burning through a bunch of books simultaneously on an ebook app, I think, 'What the hell was the title again?' I'm reading this fantastic book at the moment and I can't remember the title or the author's name.

ⓛ When *Any Ordinary Day* came out, I was thrilled with the cover because I felt it so perfectly, in an abstract way, captured the theme of the book. The cover was dandelions floating through the air. It's a really beautiful-looking cover, but it also just captures the ephemeral nature of the subject I was writing about. Another book cover I totally loved was the first edition of Helen Garner's *The First Stone*, which is a sort of grey-green colour and shows a fist clenched around a stone. It's immediately arresting.

ⓐ The other thing about ebooks is that you can't spy on what people are reading on the train.

ⓛ On a plane, if the person next to me has an electronic book device, I will still attempt to look. Sometimes I like to see if I can guess the book from the text without seeing the title.

ⓐ I have done that to the point of being a bit weird.

'What did you think about that thing that happened on page 35, that glance that Eleanor shot to Jack where it silently revealed so much about the contextual business of their relationship?' And I think, 'What?'

Don't tell me what to read, dammit

L   I don't often take a recommendation from somebody, but do you?

a   Of course you don't. That's so deeply typical of you. In fact, sometimes I think if I recommend something, that will cause you to just mildly avoid it.

L   Oh – pot, kettle! I like the chain-reaction kind of approach. I remember years ago I read *The God of Small Things* by Arundhati Roy and I loved it so much that it sent me on an Indian literature binge. And then I went through a patch where I read a Chekhov short story that I liked and that led me off to the Russians.

a   Oh god, I'm glad I wasn't around then. I read all of the Russians when I was 15, of course.

L   Mostly, I just wander into a bookshop and I grab something because it takes my eye or often a favourite author has a new book out. Sometimes if everybody's talking about something or I've read an article about it, I might pick it up. More often it will be that I've read something about, say, the Churchills, and it'll refer to Diana Mitford so then I'll be like, 'Oh yes, I must go and get a Mitford book.'

a   So it's basically the literary equivalent of that basketball documentary series *The Last Dance* making you order a thousand books on basketball strategy, which I hope has proved as disappointing as I suspected it would.

L   Exactly. Is that how you do it as well?

a   One of the great things about the podcast is that sometimes publishers will send books, and so I probably get to read more new books now than I ever did. I used to be left to my own devices. But I'll still come across books by accident. One of my very favourite things to do is walk into a remainder bookshop and pull out something I didn't know I'd been needing my whole life. I quite like the randomness. I like the little added chocolate-wheel element of people sending books in. And it makes me feel like I'm probably more up to date with present literary trends than I've ever been in my lengthy career of reading lots of books.

L   It's really scaring me, now that you've said this, that your house is about to be buried under industrial truckloads of books being dumped on your doorstep.

a   Good point. Well, yeah – book management is an issue because I don't have your habit of just clearing them out.

well hello

🅛 It sounds, though, based on your fantasy of spending your days lying in the bush reading books on a bed, that if you couldn't die while doing that, probably from being attacked by, what are they called, red ants?

🅐 Soldier ants! I was just talking about soldier ants with my son! They keep marching and killing everything in their path and picking the bones clean of whatever. Elliott said, 'How long does a queen ant live for?' And so I googled it – how long do you think a queen ant can live for?

🅛 No idea. Five years?

🅐 Up to 90.*

🅛 What? That's incredible!

🅐 And there was some queen ant that lived in captivity for 30 years. How weird, right? Anyway, where were we?

🅛 I was saying that your preferred manner of death, if not by a platoon of soldier ants on a four-poster bed, would possibly be being buried alive in your own house when a truckload of books gets dumped on you.

Crabb is a keeper, Sales is a culler

🅐 I get very sentimentally attached to books. I panic that one day I'll need a particular book, and life proves me right often enough to make me very worried about turfing books. It happened to me just yesterday. There was a book I didn't really like about a politician and I've thought about throwing it out a bunch of times. I thought, 'Oh, I wonder if I'll ever I need that.' Sure enough, yesterday I needed an anecdote from it that I so clearly remembered, I even knew how far into the book it was. I do remember a lot about books that I read, including which page, left or right, was the relevant detail that I'm looking for and so on. I know that that essentially means I am a hoarder and that one day you'll hear me defending the fact that I've got eight plastic bags full of odd jar lids. I just don't ever want to be without a book in which I urgently need to find something that I half remember.

---

* Tragically for listeners who rely on me for their entomological updates, scant evidence can be found for an ant living for 90 years. Thirty years, yes. And, to be honest, if Elliott is not impressed by that, then he can go look for a new mum.

🅛 Fair enough. That happened to me this week as well. I was looking for the book *Musicophilia* by Oliver Sacks and I had recycled it in one of my culls.

🅐 Why would you recycle that? Like, that's one of the books that I would've thought you would hang on to your whole life.

🅛 I know. Every now and again there'll be a book where I'll just think, 'Why on earth did I get rid of that?'

🅐 I remember a few years back receiving a call from your then husband seeking a copy of your own book, *Detainee 002*. And I said, 'Hang on, sorry – do you not have a copy in your house?' And you did not.

🅛 I can only presume it must've been in a box somewhere or something. I would have had one.

🅐 I really don't think you did.

Eclectic tastes and lost teeth

🅐 How were your reading patterns formed? Looking at my kids and how they read, I kind of remember the stuff that started me reading. I guess it was primary school stuff, but then in late primary school and early high school I had this bizarre habit where I mainly read *Reader's Digest* magazines. I remember my mum at some point having a word to my English teacher about it and saying, 'Is this weird?' And my teacher said, 'Look, it doesn't matter, as long as she's reading.' I would carry them around with me and go to country fetes and buy a stack of 20 *Reader's Digest* magazines for five cents each or whatever.

🅛 Oh my god, I just scooted my child's tooth off the table onto the floor!

🅐 Oh my lord. Okay.

🅛 He lost his first tooth yesterday. I meant to put it in a glass and I left it on the table and now I've bloody swept it somewhere onto the floor!

[*Both pause important discussion about books to get on their hands and knees to scour the floor for said tooth.*]

🅐 And you're going to send this to Vinnie's as well? Another treasured thing that you're binning?

well hello

🅛 Oh good, you've got it – ugh, gross. Hang on, let me put it in a glass of water.

🅐 **You are a very weird unit.**

🅛 Sorry, where were we? Oh yeah – how do you think the evolution of your reading was affected by being heavily into *Reader's Digest*?

🅐 Well, at the end of chapters, they have these little, kind of, 'Life's Like That' – jokes and added notes and things that were short and funny. And you could get something like 50 bucks for writing the best entry for that month. I did entertain fantasies of taking home the bacon for that prize. But I think it tells me, now, something about the kind of reader that I was and that I still am, which is a bit eclectic. I like to jump around between books that each tell me something different or offer something new in terms of enjoying the way a writer writes or just learning something bizarre and fresh about another area of life. I think that's something that influenced me in choosing the career that I have as well. My worst nightmare is being stuck doing the same job every single day – I mean, I could only do your job for about two weeks. The idea of skipping between subjects and getting revelations and, 'Oh my gosh, isn't that incredible?' For a curious person, I think that's a great way to consume.

🅛 **My reading life started heavily with Enid Blyton because I was sick in Grade One and I was home a lot.**

🅐 So you were like *What Katy Did?*

🅛 Yes! And that's one of my favourite books from childhood. *Secret Seven, Famous Five, The Enchanted Wood* – I was heavily into them, which is probably why I read for plot all the time. I really think you should have no snobbery around whatever books people are reading, whether it's teenage boys into their horror and fantasy or whatever, because any reading is good and it's all a gateway to other reading. Your taste evolves. As I became a more – for lack of a better way to describe it – sophisticated reader, I was more willing to tackle books that were more challenging, not just pulp fiction kind of stuff. Like you, I have fairly eclectic taste. Realistically, though, I probably read a disproportionate amount of stuff written by people like me – that is, middle-aged white women.

🅐 When I was in high school, I felt like I couldn't really tell the difference between great writing and bad writing. I probably had to get my flyer miles up before I started really picking the difference, and that was a really quite exhilarating moment. I went on a Frank Moorhouse jag in probably late high school. And that's the first time I ever thought, 'Oh, this guy is actually a really good writer and it's different from just being a story or whatever.' I think that's kind of an important evolution; getting the confidence to assess and evaluate writing, and having the confidence to know the stuff that you like and not be apologetic about it.

My kingdom for a dunny with a lock

a In in my late 20s through to probably late 30s, because I was full-time covering politics, I didn't read much fiction. Mostly I felt that I always should be trying to accumulate more knowledge and expertise in my job, so I'd have this stack of biographies or critical analyses or current affairs books. If I were reading a novel I was somehow cheating; it was indulgent. **I think heaps of women stop reading so much because they feel like they're spending time on it that they could be spending on their jobs or looking after their families.**

The way I overcame that was that being asked to be a judge for the Stella Prize for Australian women's writing. I think the judging panel comprised four people with really impressive literary qualifications and a fifth judge with a high public profile who was a sort of well-meaning tit. Anyway, I was the well-meaning idiot and they said, 'You've got three months to read all the books.' And I said, 'How many books are we talking about?' and I think they said about 60. And that year there were like 160. That actually got me over the hump because it felt like, 'Right, this is my job. I have to do this. So this is not being indulgent.' That helped me remember how great novels are and also how important they are for giving ideas and inspiration for what you do in your professional life. I'd kind of lost that a little bit, or forgotten.

L I agree that they totally give you ideas and inspiration. I think they also slow down your mind, particularly in this era, when our minds are often very, very busy.

I'm also often struck reading a novel that really speaks to me of this feeling of, 'Oh my god, I'm not the only person who feels like this.' That the author has put into words how I feel about something I couldn't articulate myself. And so it connects you, I think, to humanity and to all the shared experiences we have. This might sound counterintuitive too, but when you're really busy and particularly with a young family, you feel like, 'I just don't have time to read.' You think it's going to take energy you don't have, but it actually gives energy and puts gas in your tank, even if it's just five or 10 minutes, because it's five or 10 minutes that you've got for yourself. I think the thing that is so vital to me about reading is that I feel like for the time investment I give it, it gives me back so much more.

I would add also that we're living through such a tumultuous time at the moment, with such an oversupply of shouty voices telling us what we should do and it's really easy to get overwhelmed by noise. Just the task of mentally organising what to register and what not to is a real challenge. That's particularly the case when a lot of the most intriguing and provoking debates of the day are about things like identity and story and narrative and history and so on.

Over the past few years I've read a lot more Indigenous writers and non-Anglo writers, who have been massively illuminating in a quiet way and made me think a lot about what I assume is a story, how a story is told, what I think about time, what I think about history. Writers like Bruce Pascoe or Alexis Wright. Alexis writes fiction in the most extraordinary, sophisticated way that makes you think differently about how stories are structured. I feel like that has allowed me to reflect more about stuff that's often getting shouted about a lot. That's the incredible gift that literature can give you – the chance to be alone with a series of thoughts, whether you're in a forest clearing or just stealing five minutes in the dunny, which is seriously where I do a heap of my reading. Like, seriously, I find a toilet with a door that will lock.

is this your Nancy Drew?

L Somebody sent me a tweet from Brisbane that said,

'Excuse me, is this your book?'

and it was a photograph of the title page of a Nancy Drew book, *The Sky Phantom*. And in green pen, in the florid handwriting only a 10-year-old or an 11-year-old can have, was written 'Leigh Sales' with the 'i' dotted with a circle. I kid you not. It was my Nancy Drew that she had found in a second-hand bookshop in Brisbane and then posted it to me. I said she could keep it because it was for her daughter and then it arrived at work with a lovely little card. It was the nicest – I thought it was just absolutely fantastic. It just completely made my day that, 30 years after I read that book, it was floating around in a bookstore in Brisbane and someone took the time to let me know about it.

well hello

chat 10's top 10s

Salesy's top 10: fiction

10. *Disgrace* – J. M. Coetzee

David Lurie, a professor in Cape Town, loses his job and his reputation after a predatory sexual relationship with a student. He moves to a remote farm belonging to his daughter, Lucy. It's hard to explain this novel beyond that. It's both a tale of personal ruin and redemption, as well as political commentary on South Africa. It's written with Coetzee's astonishing combination of austerity and lyricism. Gutting. Brilliant.

9. *The God of Small Things* – Arundhati Roy

Describing *The God of Small Things* as a family drama doesn't do it justice but that's basically what it is. It's rich and lavish and so fully realised that it's hard to believe it is Roy's debut novel.

8. *The Children Act* – Ian McEwan

I could not compile this list without including a book by Ian McEwan and it was extremely difficult to pick which one. *The Children Act* is a great example of what he excels at – finding a story that seems simple on the surface and then diving deep to explore relationships and human truths. This is the tale of a family court judge who must rule on whether a Jehovah's Witness boy should be given a life-saving blood transfusion against his wishes and those of his parents. Crabb is also a McEwan fan – we are both great admirers of his mastery of narrative and style. My guess is that the McEwan book on Crabb's list will be *The Child in Time*.

7. *Olive Kitteridge* – Elizabeth Strout

I have loved everything by Elizabeth Strout and this was the first of her books that I read. It can best be described as a series of short stories, with no joining narrative but connected by one character, Olive Kitteridge. Even just writing this paragraph makes me want to abandon this list and go and start reading this book again instead.

6. *The Stone Diaries* – Carol Shields

After reading this novel, I greedily devoured everything else Carol Shields had written. For most of my 20s and 30s it was my favourite novel. What I liked was that it left me with a sense of how even the most outwardly ordinary life is still extraordinary and precious. The only reason it was eventually superseded by other books is just that my taste evolved – it's still a fantastic book.

5. *The Spare Room* – Helen Garner

As with Ian McEwan, there is no way I could write this list and not include a book by Helen Garner. *The Spare Room* reminds me a lot of *The Children Act* in that it has a deceptively simple premise – a very sick woman goes to stay with a friend and tries some alternate therapies for her cancer – but creates something complex from it. When I finished it I thought it was the perfect novel and showcased Garner at the pinnacle of her considerable powers.

4. *Lolita* – Vladimir Nabokov

The book that no politician would ever pick to include on a list of their favourite books for fear of controversy. Yes, it is icky. Yes, it is troublesome. Yes, it is uncomfortable. But it is a phenomenal piece of writing.

3. *The Lady with the Little Dog* – Anton Chekhov

This is cheating a bit because it's a short story, not a novel. A man sees a woman with a little white dog on a boardwalk and they begin an affair. Over time, the affair unravels but then they meet again. This story packs a brutally hard emotional punch and includes many lines and paragraphs that stop me in my tracks.

2. *The Corrections* – Jonathan Franzen

This book is about a dysfunctional family, but dysfunctional in an entirely recognisable and non-remarkable way. Enid Lambert wants her three grown-up children to join her and their father, Alfred, for Christmas. It was published in 2001 and it seemed to capture something fundamental about the time. I find it both profound and funny, and have read it several times.

1. *A Fraction of the Whole* – Steve Toltz

I vividly remember reading this novel for the first time. It had been selected by my book club and wasn't something I would have otherwise chosen, although it had been shortlisted for the 2008 Booker Prize. Two things put me off: one, it was really fat and two, people had compared it to *Infinite Jest* by David Foster Wallace, which didn't grab me. I started reading it on holiday in Tasmania and, about 25 pages in, I turned to my then husband and said, 'I think this is going to be one of my favourite books of all time.' It's almost impossible to explain what this sprawling novel is about, other than to say it's the tale of two Australian brothers, Martin and Terry Dean, one of whom becomes the nation's hero and the other its pariah. The book is overwritten but it is so hilarious and imaginative that I completely forgive that. It reminds me why I love reading and of the power of the human imagination. I've read it at least three times, to the degree that it's almost a comfort read if I'm having a hard time or in a reading slump.

Salesy's top 10: non-fiction

10. *The Tall Man* – Chloe Hooper

Chloe Hooper is one of the Australian writers I most admire. I think she's the best narrative non-fiction writer in Australia after Helen Garner. This book – the story of the death in custody of Indigenous man Cameron Doomadgee on Palm Island – is haunting, evocative and stays with you long after you finish it.

9. *The Good Soldiers* – David Finkel

David Finkel embedded with a battalion of American soldiers deployed on the 2007 'surge' in Iraq. He also spent time with their families, who were left to fend for themselves at home in the US while their loved ones were on active service. It's such a rounded view of the experience of military service, and I felt it gave an account of the Iraq War that nobody else provided. An absolutely brilliant book and first-rate journalism.

8. *First in His Class* – David Maraniss

This biography of Bill Clinton covers his life until he announces in 1991 that he will run for US president. It is riveting and does a good job of explaining his character and some of the qualities we saw on display during his presidency. I'm a bit of a Clinton obsessive and of the many books I've read about Bill and Hillary, this is my favourite by a long way.

7. *Open* – Andre Agassi

This is a stunning memoir and I loved it so much that I sought out other works by the ghostwriter, J. R. Moehringer (he won the Pulitzer Prize in 2000 for newspaper feature writing, and his own memoir, *The Tender Bar*, is fantastic). The opening chapter, in which tennis veteran Agassi describes how much pain he's in every day when he gets out of bed, and what it took at the height of his playing career to

well hello

get his body into shape to get onto the court, is gobsmacking. The other bit that sticks with me is how, when his then girlfriend Brooke Shields was guest-starring on *Friends* he was so immersed in his own tennis world that when she took him to visit the set, he didn't recognise the cast.

6. *Far From the Tree* – Andrew Solomon

This is a long book, and it is so richly packed with insight that it will take any reader a long time to get through it – but it's worth it. The title is taken from the saying, 'The apple doesn't fall far from the tree.' However, Solomon writes about cases in which that is *not* true – when children differ drastically from their parents. The opening chapter is about deaf children of hearing parents, and other chapters include autistic offspring, criminals, prodigies and transgender kids. It's a book I will return to again and again, and I definitely feel it's made me a better parent.

5. *Midnight in the Garden of Good and Evil* – John Berendt

I have a particular soft spot for this one, as I visited Savannah, Georgia, when I was the US correspondent for the ABC to make a radio documentary about how life there had changed in the wake of this book's publication. It was on the *New York Times* bestseller list for more than four years. It's the true story of an antiques dealer on trial for murder, and the unusual characters who populate Savannah.

4. *Red Carpets and Other Banana Skins* – Rupert Everett

Actor Rupert Everett has the most wonderfully languid voice and such a knack for storytelling. He also has the kind of indiscretion I love in a memoirist. Rarely has a book made me laugh aloud this much. Honourable mention to *My Booky Wook* and *Booky Wook 2* by comedian Russell Brand, which are also side-splitting.

3. *Joe Cinque's Consolation* – Helen Garner

Another impossible Garner choice, really. I'm not quite sure why I settled on this one, other than I think it has such a narrative drive and it's such a puzzling case. It has all the hallmarks that make Garner great: the spare prose, the unflinching self-examination, the empathy, the eye for detail. It covers the death of Australian uni student Joe Cinque and two trials relating to it.

2. *Personal History* – Katharine Graham

A Pulitzer Prize-winning memoir by the former publisher of the *Washington Post*. Graham ran the newspaper during a remarkable period in Washington, including reportage on the Pentagon Papers and Watergate. But the reason it's such a memorable book is her unflinching account of her marriage and of the mental illness of her husband, Phil Graham. It has everything you want: a fascinating life, a lot of frank disclosure and wonderful writing.

1. *In Cold Blood* – Truman Capote

This book is regularly cited as the first real non-fiction novel and it's truly incredible. It details the 1959 murders of the Clutter family at their Kansas farm. Two men were arrested six weeks after the killings and Capote follows the case through to the perpetrators' eventual executions. I love it because it's a gripping and unputdownable book but also because I aspire to write that kind of narrative non-fiction and this is the granddaddy of that genre.

Crabb's top 10: fiction

But first: a whinge from Annabel

At the outset, can I please just make clear that the 'Top 10' thing was Leigh Sales's idea. She sent ALL her lists through pretty much the day after having the idea, too. I get the feeling she walks around all day just waiting to be asked to list things so she can bust out her spreadsheet. I am extremely hesitant about such assignments. It's so subjective! Who cares what my favourite things are? And of course I am horrified at the thought of revealing my favourite books and films because it will become clear what a dilettante I am. One thing I cannot do, however, is order one through 10. That would take me another 15 million hours.

One thing I've noticed from these lists is that I immediately found myself over-subscribed on the non-fiction list. I think it's true that I re-read non-fiction more; fiction I consume rapidly and rarely go back for another go. You can see that I've done some sneaky things, like pretending *A Room of One's Own* is fiction. I regret nothing.

Anyway, so here are my top fiction books. I've listed them in the order by which I encountered them.

- ### *The Edith Trilogy* – Frank Moorhouse
  Frank Moorhouse was the writer whose work taught me what good writing was. His short stories set in Australian country towns electrified me as a reader. Prior to reading him, I'd read more or less indiscriminately. Edith Campbell Berry – the central character of this trilogy (*Grand Days, Dark Palace, Cold Light*) – is a heroine for whom I fell completely. You can read my fawning letter to Frank elsewhere in this chapter.

- ### *London Fields* – Martin Amis
  I must have read this book about 50 times. I still think in expressions from it. Amis is so cool and twisty and clever that even now I forgive his narrative crimes against women. My main love for Martin Amis centres around his essays (*The Moronic Inferno* is a collection I've read many times) but *London Fields*, with its elegant plot and its shocking cast of London characters, is THE novel with which I was obsessed in my first year of university.

- ### *A Room of One's Own* – Virginia Woolf

  Yes, I know it's not a novel, don't write in. But Woolf's talent is to bring a novelist's sweep to any prose, so I'm counting it here in order to free up space in my non-fiction queue. It is one of my very favourite books. In her examination of women writers, she draws an eloquent connection between high art and the prosaic realities of life. If a woman does not write a great novel, is it because she is intellectually inferior? Or is it related to the fact that she does not have a quiet place to write, and the intellectual freedom enjoyed only by those who don't have to do the laundry? This book totally changed my life. It certainly planted the seed of a book I wrote many, many years after reading it: *The Wife Drought*. Fun fact: Virginia did have a 'wife': Leonard, her husband, who cooked, did the laundry and managed her business affairs. A great man.

- ### *Lolita* – Vladimir Nabokov

  Nabokov had a great wife too – the wonderful Vera. Martin Amis interviewed her in his book of essays *Visiting Mrs Nabokov*; he describes her as 'intellectually vigilant' and recounts a moment at which she cracks her teacup back into its saucer and glares at him when he makes some lazily undergraduate observation or other. It's superb. Anyway: *Lolita*. I first tried to read it when I was about 15 and was surprised and possibly a tiny bit disappointed by how non-filthy it was. Could it be published now? Probably not. It's an account written from the narrative perspective of a sadistic, sociopathic rapist and paedophile. But the very distance between the implacability of Humbert's depraved acts and the virtuosic intricacy of the prose is the significant element; it's a brutal lesson in how human artifice can be deployed to mask evil.

- ### *White Noise* – Don DeLillo

  I've re-read this book a bunch of times. It's about an academic and his wife, who suffers a crippling fear of death. It's an extremely funny satire on academia, consumerism, mass panic and contains something very unusual in a work of fiction: fully developed child characters.

- ***Beloved* – Toni Morrison**

    I remember reading this book and feeling entirely captured by it; it's one of the first I think of if I'm ever asked about books that changed my life. *Beloved* is the story of Sethe, a former slave who lives with her children in a house haunted by the ghost of her eldest daughter. Beloved is a mysterious girl who appears at the house one day, and Sethe's growing obsession with her reveals a terrifying story of dehumanisation, the legacy of slavery and the spectre of intergenerational pain. It's an absolutely staggering work of art.

- ***The Child in Time* – Ian McEwan**

    I've read this book many times but had to stop re-reading it when I had children, for reasons that are apparent from the plot. It's about a children's book author, the disappearance of whose little girl wrecks his marriage and casts him into a pit of grief and introspection. His friend, a minister in the British government, is meanwhile captured by a mysterious affliction, the revelation of which is a memorable moment, even by McEwan's famously inventive standards. It's about childhood, innocence, grief, bureaucracy, reconciliation. I think it's his best novel.

- ***The Swan Book* – Alexis Wright**

    The Swan Book is about a hidden woman – a girl who literally hides in a hollow tree while the world disintegrates around her. But nothing else about *The Swan Book* is literal; of all the things I learned from this book, the most profound was a new (for me) way of reading, the value of simply sitting still and listening to a raucous, cacophonic, elliptical display of rage and beauty. With jokes. Reading this is like sitting through the most extraordinary electrical storm. For a while, you fight against your powerlessness in the face of it. And after a bit, it dawns on you that that's the point. As you can see from my chronology, the books that moved me in earlier years were largely by white writers, though I never noticed this at the time, thanks to the luxury of never having to question my own membership of the mainstream. Alexis Wright is the writer who finally made me realise, properly, that form is political too. She changed the way I read.

> You can see that I've done some sneaky things, like pretending *A Room of One's Own* is fiction. I regret nothing.

- **The Outline Trilogy** – **Rachel Cusk**

  Look at me, sneaking in another trilogy. My friend Seb put me on to Rachel Cusk and *Outline*, the first book in the trilogy, was the first book of hers I'd read. It is written from the perspective of Faye, a writer and mother who, in the opening scene, is aboard a plane, travelling to a literary conference. The plot is extremely loose, so the first impression is of unstructuredness; much of the text consists of Faye's conversations with people she meets, which are conveyed without quotation marks so they give the impression of a partially internal set of observations. But as you go on, the elegance and discipline of the writing becomes powerfully apparent. It's extremely funny, and piercing. Utterly memorable.

- **The Yield** – **Tara June Winch**

  I think I read this in record time; it's the sort of book you take with you everywhere so you can use any spare second to get in a page or two. It's the story of August Gondiwindi, who returns to her childhood community of Massacre Plains to mourn her grandfather and finds that he has written a dictionary of the Wiradjuri language. It's about intergenerational pain and finding beauty in broken things, and in 2020 (a bloody difficult year) it was the book that most captured me.

Crabb's top 10: non-fiction

- ### *Diaries* – Alan Clark

  Three volumes of diaries charting the political career of the late Alan Clark, who was a junior Thatcher-era minister. He's an outrageous popinjay and snob, whose constant plotting and theorising on how he can become leader of the Conservative Party consistently overlooks the otherwise generally understood truth; that he's a minor figure whom nobody takes seriously. As awful as he is, there is a familiarity to the awfulness, and to his asymmetry of aspiration – you see it in politicians all the time. He's an extremely perceptive observer, however, and the volumes fulfil my one requirement for political memoirs – that the author effectively blows themself up.

- ### *The Journalist and the Murderer* – Janet Malcolm

  I love Janet Malcolm's writing, and I've chosen this one partly because it's my own trade to which she's applied her horribly observant eye, and partly because reading *The Journalist and the Murderer* set me off down another path of reading. The journalist of the book's title is Joe McGinniss, whose first book *The Selling of the President* (about Richard Nixon's 1968 TV ad campaign) was already a favourite of mine. McGinniss agreed, in the early 1980s, to write a book about the trial of Jeffrey MacDonald, a Green Beret charged with the murder of his wife and two children. MacDonald believed the book would be exculpatory, but McGinniss decided while writing it that MacDonald was guilty, a conclusion of which the subject learned only on publication. *Fatal Vision* was a bestseller in 1983. MacDonald sued, and Janet Malcolm's book is an account of their dispute. It's uncomfortable reading for any journalist.

- ### *Hoax* – Clifford Irving

  This book absolutely scratches my long-running itch for books examining the lives of people who are utterly shameless. Clifford Irving, a middling writer, hatched a plan with his best mate Dick in the late 1970s to write an absolute sure-fire bestseller: an authorised biography of Howard Hughes, at the time the world's most famous recluse. The two men planned to write the book based on their own research plus some bits they would just make up. Their theory – brilliant, really – was that Hughes would never come out of hiding to denounce the book. He might even admire their chutzpah! Naturally, it turned into a screaming debacle, but Irving's account of the scam – in which they hoover up a giant advance and sell the rights to *Life* magazine – is a deliriously pleasurable read.

- ### *The First Stone* – Helen Garner
  Obviously, there had to be a Garner book in here. Recently, I've inhaled her published diaries and she is one of those writers whose twin superpowers of observation and muscular structure make her brilliant either in fiction or non-fiction. I chose *The First Stone* because of its impact and because of the way I've changed my mind over time about it. I would really recommend reading this in conjunction with Bernadette Brennan's terrific literary biography of Garner, which fills in a few gaps about the writing of the work.

- ### *The Victory* – Pamela Williams
  I've lost count of how many 'insider accounts' of Australian election campaigns I've read. I even had a crack at writing one, years ago. But the absolute gold standard for me will always be Pam Williams's *The Victory*, the account of how John Howard and the Liberal Party won the 1996 election. There's great material too about the rift between Paul Keating and the Labor campaign team. People just tell Pam things. She's a ninja. Anything by her is worth reading.

- ### *The Devil's Candy* – Julie Salamon
  From the fiasco-tourism files, to which I am a regular and self-loathing visitor. This book is about the making of *The Bonfire of the Vanities*, Brian de Palma's 1990 film version of Tom Wolfe's famous novel. Salamon struck a deal with de Palma to obtain full access to the production, which cost a squillion dollars and was hoped to yield many, many Oscars. To de Palma's credit, he never reneged on the deal, even as the project spiralled

into an unthinkably expensive turkey, bloated with stars and egos and overleaping ambition. It's absolutely absorbing and a fascinating insight into the movie industry.

- ## *The Forgotten Rebels of Eureka* – Clare Wright
  A big thick book about the Eureka Stockade? Ugh. Brings back memories of dusty schoolrooms, right? Wrong. Clare Wright's 2014 Stella Prize winner reads like a thriller, tracing the stories of the women who've been left out of the Eureka story. I have so much admiration for Wright, who has since delivered another great work of history in *You Daughters of Freedom*, about Australia's suffragists. Her enthusiasm and curiosity powers every word she writes, unearthing the experiences, typically, of women thought to be of little importance to male historians. She's a gem.

- ## *Dark Emu* – Bruce Pascoe
  This book, more than any other I've read in the past decade, has changed the way I think and read. Its premise is basic: Pascoe challenges the historic depiction of Indigenous Australians as nomadic hunter-gatherers whose alleged lack of development of the Australian landscape was the major argument on which wholesale dispossession was based. Pascoe conducts a massive sweep of primary sources (colonial diaries, letters, public records) to reveal compelling evidence of Indigenous agriculture, aquaculture and settlements.

- ## *Victoria* – Julia Baird
  Like Pascoe, Baird has done the work. Her account of Queen Victoria is redolent of the grunt work she put in over many years to winkle out sparkling new detail and an appreciably novel analysis of the woman, given that Jules – unlike many of the historians who have scaled Mount Victoria before – is a woman. I love historical writing that goes over well-trafficked events from a new perspective. I know from reporting politics that you get as many different accounts of a single event as there were people in the room. History is always evolving, and it's a fiction to pretend otherwise.

- ***One on One*** – **Craig Brown**

  This is one of the most structurally elegant books I've read. It's written by Craig Brown, satirist for *Private Eye* magazine, one of my favourite sketch-writers and generally a man possessed of an intricate and wonderful brain. I found it in a two-dollar bin at a bookshop about five years after it had won a bunch of prizes in Britain, consolidating my personal reputation for a) hearing about great books long after everyone else, and b) always being able to strike gold in a discount book bin. The book consists of 101 true stories of encounters between famous people. It's a daisy chain structure. The first story is about John Scott-Ellis almost (but not quite) killing Adolf Hitler in 1931 by running him over in his Fiat. In the next story, Scott-Ellis meets Rudyard Kipling. In the next story, Kipling meets Mark Twain. And so on. In a pleasing lunacy, each of the 101 encounters is described in exactly 1001 words. So, *One on One* is 101,101 words long. I've given this book to a LOT of people, including Sales, and you can imagine how satisfying she found it.

Thank you, Frank

Here is Annabel's letter to acclaimed Australian author Frank Moorhouse, as she launched *Cold Light*, the eagerly awaited third book in the Edith Trilogy in 2011, in which she describes the profound influence his storytelling has had on her reading, writing and thinking.

Dear Frank,

Thank you for being a constant in my life for 22 years, though I have never met you. When I found an email from Meredith Curnow last month asking if I would launch *Cold Light*, I felt a little dizzy. Like the rest of Edith Campbell Berry's fans, I had been awaiting her return, politely, for a decade. I'm not complaining about that – Edith fans are patient, and resourceful. And I found other things with which to busy myself in the interim, of which more later. But to have an association with the launch – and, more germanely, to have an actual COPY of *Cold Light* in my trembling hands before almost anyone else? I was terribly excited, let's leave it at that.

When I received the book itself, it seemed miraculously consistent with my – I won't lie to you, Frank – incredibly elaborate expectations, grown wild and tangled over these past 10 years. Hefted in the hands, *Cold Light* doesn't disappoint. It's heavy – incontrovertible proof that you haven't been phoning it in.

The first line – *'I'm your brother,' he said, holding his cap in both hands'* – relieved the reader immediately of any of fears that Moorhouse might have gone off the boil – a more relentlessly sticky and absorbing exordium to Edith's last adventure I could not have imagined. The book is an absolute cracker.

But this letter isn't just about Edith, Frank. Not at all. The first book of yours I read was *The Electrical Experience*. I bought it from the University of Adelaide bookshop in January 1990. I was 16, and starting an Arts degree, and the bookshop had a special offer of five novels for $20. The other books – something by Thea Astley, a very forgettable Christopher Hope novel, and I can't remember what else – didn't open anything like the world that *The Electrical Experience* did.

Frank, I'm ashamed to say that in those early years, that parsimonious expenditure was about as close to a decent royalty as you ever got from me. I borrowed everything else I could find of yours from the Munno Para Public Library, Munno Para being the closest the Adelaide train system came to my country town. To a South Australian teenager otherwise clearing an armload of books each week indiscriminately into her library bag, jammed in that unhappy literary stage at which one reads and reads and reads but has no real ear, yet, for what is good and why it is good, you gave an early and reliable intimation.

Of the books I read during that period, as I came to understand why I felt the way I did about some of them, yours stand out.

Thank you for writing about dusty Australian country towns in a way that made my dusty Australian country town at once more familiar and more mysterious to me. It was as though you narrated them for me, these characters – the bustling Rotarians, the occupants of those tottering governance structures that evolve, part human and part statute, anywhere that people settle within a bull's roar of one another. You showed me the private lives of the public misfits, and the compensatory irregularities of the publicly-beyond-reproach.

But above all, Frank, thank you for your gentleness. Who else could write, as a reborn city sophisticate, about the life of such towns while preserving a tenderness that spreads so irresistibly to the reader? To be understanding about Ambrose Westwood's innate urges is one thing. To be understanding about T. George McDowell's pompous eccentricities is quite another, and this is one of your most profound gifts – I felt it was to me, but really it was to us, Frank.

Writing about one's country is like writing about one's family: a hazardous and unreliable business, crisscrossed with deep human reservoirs of love, protectiveness and shame. It is tempting for the voyager in such circumstances to protect himself with mockery or contempt, but you chose a different way, a harder way – one more vulnerable and infinitely more precious. Thank you for doing it with such love and care, Frank.

It's only now, thinking about those early works and how I love them, that I realise what you've taught me about kindness to a subject. In the years since I first read *The Electrical Experience* and all the others – *The Americans, Baby, Tales of Mystery and Romance, The Everlasting Secret Family, Futility and Other Animals* – I've written about politics at local, state, and federal levels.

I love politicians. I love their madnesses and their vulnerabilities, and I know of very few in whom a good light does not burn somewhere.

To write with fondness, rather than contempt, is something I learned from you, and I think it was a valuable lesson.

well hello

You will be relieved to hear that in 1993, earning a respectable $10 an hour as the late-night and early-morning cash register attendant at Ampol Hilton, Burbridge Road, Adelaide, I was sufficiently liquid to purchase *Grand Days* outright, soon after its publication.

By that stage I was a law student, and not a very industrious one. I read *Grand Days* when I should have been studying, or when I should have been restocking chocolate bars or fuses, or feigning – as I regularly did – greater automotive knowledge than I actually had.

Many's the steaming bonnet I've peered beneath in a grubby Ampol shirt, squinting evaluatively before pronouncing, 'Mate, I think it's your alternator.' What is the alternator? I never really understood then, and I still don't now. I just knew it was an endlessly fallible widget that it was above my pay grade to replace, and thus a thoroughly failsafe diagnosis.

Shortly after reading *Grand Days*, in any event, I was off on my own adventure, bunking off from university to work in a fruit and veg shop in Pollokshields, Glasgow, and thence on a backpacking adventure through Poland, the Czech Republic, Hungary and Slovenia.

I had no idea what I was going to do with the rest of my life, although I had a reasonably firm suspicion that I wasn't about to spend it as a lawyer.

When I fronted up to the *Advertiser* for a cadetship interview, it was really an impulse thing. The application was a friend's idea, and I had no real plans to be a journalist. I had *Days of Wine and Rage* in my bag, purchased (sorry, Frank!) for two dollars at the Odd Book Shop, on Portrush Road, Adelaide.

I have it next to me now, as I type this letter, and I think . . . dear god. Is it possible I even *took it out* and enthused about it to the cadet counsellor, Geoff Williams, during the interview?

I made the cut, but Geoff left me in no doubt that I filled the very last spot, and only then because I had scored unprecedented full marks on the spelling and grammar test.

I bought *Dark Palace* at the Electric Shadows bookshop and cinema in Canberra in the year 2000, by which time I was an 18-month veteran of that city, having been posted there by the *Advertiser* and then hired by *The Age*.

Perhaps it's time, then, to talk about Edith, of whom, like so many chicks my age, I feel so incredibly fond.

Why do we love her? She is a turbulent soup of strength and weakness, of honesty and guile. I am aware of the narrow strain of criticism that argues that Edith is an unwieldy character, representing more about you, Frank, than a feasible woman of her time. This misses the point, rather monstrously, I've always felt.

The friends of Edith couldn't give a flying fuck from which crepuscular quadrant of the Moorhouse psyche she hails. We love her, and that's that. Edith is the sort of character with whom anyone would like to have dinner. She is clever, and principled, and foolish, and vain, and decisive, and fierce, and hopeless, and interested in shoes.

Australian literature is not, moreover, so fabulously replete with non-idiotic heroines that we could ever do without someone like Edith, who traces our national history, and our place in the world, with such élan.

Whether she is entirely you, Frank, I cannot say – I don't know you. But she has your eyes – always open. She is quick to love, and slow to judge. She is wrong – often. But she is never closed, and that is her essential charm. She is ever hopeful, Edith Campbell Berry, and reading her in the past few weeks – at a juncture in Australian contemporary politics which seems designed to test all but the most insanely optimistic souls – has been not only a delight, but a good refresher.

well hello

One of the least appealing aspects of federal politics is the dreadful extent to which daily discourse relies on a competitive chorus of disadvantage, where any politician's failure to exhibit sufficient empathy with one individual's costly fuel tank or one company's vaulting profit margin bespeaks a grotesque failure of Australianism. The more bitter we get, the more we encourage politicians in their desperate overtures to us, and the more we despise them for it.

When did we become such whingers? Edith wouldn't whinge – she'd install a cumquat tree, and get on with it.

May she remind us all to approach each other with gentleness and good humour.

May she inspire us all to extract opportunity from frustration, instead of bitterness and gall. May sales of cumquat trees soar.

When I received my early copy of *Cold Light*, I allowed myself one tiny gloating post on Twitter, and was immediately swamped – as I had hoped, I'll admit – with howls of envy and outrage from around the continent.

Thank you for creating Edith, Frank. There are so many of us who love her, and I bet not all of us have written to say so. But in our defence, you haven't always had a reliable postal address, have you? You've been too busy haring about the globe.

Which brings me to another point on which you are owed thanks, after these 20 years of Edith. Thank you for the work, Frank. For the research and the attention and the living-out-of-a-suitcase and the labour you put in to make these novels so deeply pleasurable. The work lights this trilogy with a thrilling confidence from start to finish.

To be able to live in Canberra while it was still being built, to be in the great ballroom on the night the music stopped playing for Chifley, dead in the Kurrajong Hotel, to feel the tension before the 1951 referendum – these are luxuries we are afforded thanks to your efforts.

These three books – Grand Days, Dark Palace, and Cold Light – are, together, an extraordinary piece of Australian cultural infrastructure,

if you'll permit me the ugly expression. They are built from your hard work and your extraordinary natural gift, and the fact that you did not allow the abundance of the latter to excuse you from the rigours of the former.

You are one of our great treasures, Frank. Do we tell you often enough? Probably not. But as you release this book, this labour of love, into the grateful hands of those who have been waiting for it, let me say it one more time, on behalf of all of them:

Thank you, Frank.

Annabel Crabb

well hello

canon fodder

(aka Leigh Sales has read no Dickens and does not intend to do so)

Sales almost broke the Sydney Writers' Festival a few years back when she admitted to a hall full of book buffs that she'd never read any Charles Dickens. Kinda the literary equivalent of going to Summernats and telling the bloke next to you that you can't drive a manual.

🅛 I confessed that because something's got to fall off the boat in your reading life; you can't get to everything before you die. And so I admitted that I thought I'd probably die without reading Dickens – it's just a whole thing – and the room went feral.

🅐 It was an audible ripple of disquiet. You could hear the cigarette lighters as they lit their torches.

Big Dickens weren't letting 'er get away wiv it, neither. The next year someone from the NSW Dickens Society popped up in a festival Q&A, calling on Sales to commit to reading at least one masterwork. Realising that watching *A Muppet Christmas Carol* wasn't going to appease anyone, Leigh and Annabel threw it open to a *Chat 10* live audience for a show of applause to decide: which Dickens should she read?

🅐 *Oliver Twist*. [Awkward silence, then laughter.]
🅛 See? They hate Dickens too.
🅐 *David Copperfield*. [Smattering of applause.] *Great Expectations*. [Slightly more applause.] *A Tale of Two Cities*. [Less applause, but Crabb cheers obnoxiously.] *Nicholas Nickleby*. [Polite smattering.] *Bleak House*. [Whoops and applause.]
🅛 Okay, elimination. We'll do it out of *A Tale of Two Cities* and *Bleak House. A Tale of Two Cities?* [Whoops and applause.] Or *Bleak House*. [Whoops and applause.]
🅐 Oh, too bad. You're reading both of them now.

2021 update: She hasn't done it. Outlook is . . . bleak.

a dog-earing

dirtbag

a [*Leafing through Leigh's library book*] Excuse me ... is it you folding down these pages?

L Yes, it is

a You dirtbag.

L Are you not a page-folder?

a I am in a book that I don't care about. If it's a book that I know I'm going to chuck – which is hardly any books at all – or that's been mine forever and I know I'm not going to pass it on, but I would never fold down the page of a library book. You are a criminal.

L Let me guess, you use a bookmark that you stitched together yourself from fabric scraps.

a Published in 2003. This book's been around for ... I can't add up ... 13 years, and it was fine until it ran into you. That's the level of respect that you're showing for public property there. That's a disgrace.

L Give it back to me. I wanna keep telling my anecdote.

a I know, but I feel like you don't deserve the air space.

a chucker and

a filthy book hanger-onerer

L I am a book chucker. I love chucking. There's actually not that much to chuck because I'm such a religious chucker of stuff. Do you know what's a big issue – do I keep all of my books and move them to my new house, or do I get rid of them? And I'm tempted to get rid of a lot because I'm reading so much stuff electronically these days.

a I can't even look at you.

L I knew you were going to be upset about that.

well hello

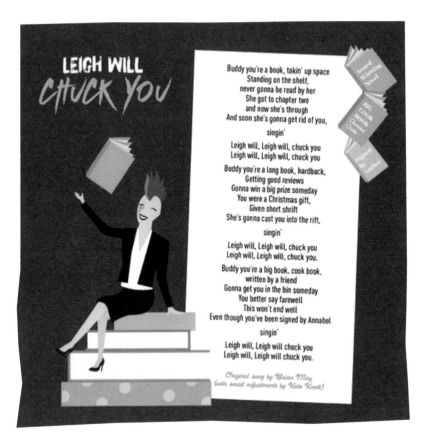

LEIGH WILL CHUCK YOU

Buddy you're a book, takin' up space
Standing on the shelf,
never gonna be read by her
She got to chapter two
and now she's through
And soon she's gonna get rid of you.

singin'

Leigh will, Leigh will, chuck you
Leigh will, Leigh will, chuck you

Buddy you're a long book, hardback,
Getting good reviews
Gonna win a big prize someday
You were a Christmas gift,
Given short shrift
She's gonna cast you into the rift.

singin'

Leigh will, Leigh will, chuck you
Leigh will, Leigh will, chuck you.

Buddy you're a big book, cook book,
written by a friend
Gonna get you in the bin someday
You better say farewell
This won't end well
Even though you've been signed by Annabel

singin'

Leigh will, Leigh will chuck you
Leigh will, Leigh will chuck you.

*Original song by Brian May
(with small adjustments by Kate Knott)*

'Leigh Will Chuck You', an ode by Chatter Kate Knott to Sales's monstrous approach to books she doesn't want any more, sung at a *Chat 10* live show at the Enmore Theatre to the beat of Queen's 'We Will Rock You'.

(a) My house is just absolutely . . . there's just piles. In a couple of years it's going to look like one of those crazy bookshops in Charing Cross where you can't actually get in. Somewhere in the middle of these tottering piles, there's a guy with a beard and a jumper with holes in the elbows, sitting there thinking, 'Why doesn't anyone come into my shop?' 'You stopped being able to get into it about three months ago, dude.'

(L) But he's the sort of bloke that you'd go, 'I'm looking for a copy of the annotated version of Lewis Carroll's *The Hunting of the Snark*. It's by Martin somebody or other. I just can't remember.' And the guy's like, 'Yes,' and he'll just lead you straight to it.

(a) 'Which translation?'

ℒ Leads you straight to it at the bottom of a dusty pile of something completely unrelated to it.

a I love those bookshops, but my house looks like one of them, which is unfortunate. I have these nightmares, particularly when people send you books, I have a nightmare that if I put them in a box outside my house, someone will walk along and see their book in a box outside my house and go, 'Oh, well that's very nice, isn't it.' I know that realistically that would never happen.

ℒ I was looking at my books and thinking, 'What would be the yardstick, the criteria for which book you would keep?' I would keep my original *The Enchanted Wood* by Enid Blyton, and my *The Magic Faraway Tree*, because they're some of the first books I ever read and I've kept them. But, for example, I kept all of my *Anne of Green Gables* books that I read but now I've had two sons, and so I assume they're not going to read *Anne of Green Gables* but I can't really bear to get rid of them. So I don't know. But then, looking at other books that I've really loved, say, Margaret Atwood's *Alias Grace*; do I really need to own a hard copy of that?

a I am a filthy book hanger-onerer. I have an incapability of conceiving that I will ever find a book elsewhere. I work on a system of fear and I know, if I put some book out, I know sure as eggs is eggs that, three to four days from my decision to turf that book, I will be writing a column or something and I'll think, 'Oh, that book.' And the little bits and bobs that I needed from that book I won't be able to find. So, that's my fear. I think of a line that was in that book, I grab the book, I go through it, I kind of enjoy it again by going through it again, and then I find the bit. I do know, thanks to Google, that you can find just about anything in any book that you've read if you can remember a couple of keywords. But trying to flick through and find something in an ebook makes you just want to stab yourself in the eye with a rusty fork.

My books are organised in a really weird way, kind of in the order in which I acquired them. I've got whole bookcases that are books I bought at university. And so that's how I know where they are, because I remember when I got them. But recently my brother-in-law, who's incredibly helpful and kind and as a favour to me when he was house-sitting, tidied up the books and arranged them in order of height – which is great because they look much tidier now than they did. But it's like I lost my memory or something; I just don't know where things are.

ℒ So not even alphabetical.

a You can't even go hey, I need Martin Amis. You've got to remember, is that a 20-centimetre book, or is it a 30-centimetre? You're laughing but now I've done a bit more rearranging and I've gone into sort-of subject areas. I've got British politics and American politics and Australian politics and then American novels and British novels. So I'm approaching a kind of a sensible order.

chapter 4

how to write

conversation

how to write

(aka A sort of staged vomit)

As journalists, Annabel Crabb and Leigh Sales have banged out, oh, bajillions of words over the decades, including 10 books between them. Forgive the shameless plug but for Sales it's been *Detainee 002: The Case of David Hicks*, the essay *On Doubt* and the Walkley-Award-winning bestseller *Any Ordinary Day*. Crabb's cranked out a frankly show-off seven books: *Losing It*, *Rise of the Ruddbot*, Walkley-grabber *Stop at Nothing: The Life and Adventures of Malcolm Turnbull*, the groundbreaking *The Wife Drought* and its subject stablemate *Men at Work*, and the wildly popular cookbooks *Special Delivery* and *Special Guest*, co-written with her bestie Wendy Sharpe.

Yes, yes, very impressive – but could they write fiction? Does Sales really have a decent novel hiding inside her? Should they go on a writers' retreat? Is this whole chapter just a bleedingly obvious attempt to pad out the word count for this book?

Ⓛ Are you somebody who's interested in the process of how other writers write?

ⓐ I'm always interested in how fiction writers write. I've got my head around how I write non-fiction, but fiction is like a foreign country to me. Every time I write something non-fiction, I'm duly aware of the same mistakes I make every single time. I'm better at it now.

Security! A couple of cheapskates ripping off hardworking writers.

Q What mistakes?

a Getting overwhelmed. Losing track. Hating what I'm writing and thinking always of the stuff that I haven't managed to nail down or I didn't get and feeling like what I have written is terrible and useless. I hate most things that I've just written, but I'm also massively weak and fickle and driven by the opinions of others because if an editor then writes back saying, 'Actually, it's fine,' I'm like, 'Actually, yeah, it is.' It's so emotionally immature. I think, actually, self-loathing is part of the process.

Q Yeah, self-loathing is definitely part of the process. Pretty much whenever I finish the first draft of anything I'm working on, I have this fear: 'What if I get run over by a bus tomorrow and someone finds that and thinks it's, like, a proper piece of writing?'

a I totally get that. By why is that so?

Q Because it's so bad.

a It makes you sort of understand Helen Garner burning her diaries and letters and things when she moved out of her parents' house. When she moved to Melbourne, I think. She burned all this stuff in a bin in the backyard because she was worried that someone would find it.

Write the easy stuff first

Q I think the hardest thing with writing is to get something out and onto paper or the screen. That's hard. The temptation sometimes for people is to do a lot of research before they start doing any writing. Some of the best advice somebody ever gave me when I was working on my first book, *Detainee 002*, was don't save all of the writing until you've done all of the research. Starting the writing will help you see where the holes in your research are. It also gives you a sense of momentum, that you're getting somewhere. What that means is that I often write out of order.

a I write the easy stuff first. The stuff that I'm going to enjoy writing. And then I leave the stuff that I'm not going to enjoy writing until the end. It's shocking. It's like eating all the nice chocolates out of the box.

Ⓛ Why is it shocking? I think that's a great technique. You're picking the low-hanging fruit. For me, when I do what I call the initial 'vomit' of trying to get something out, I'll sometimes write a sentence like, 'Crabb was sitting at the table and she looked *right word here* and she cut a slice of cake.' And I let go of trying to find the word I'm seeking if it doesn't come to me straight away. I put a placeholder there so I don't get bogged down. I just want that first, awful draft out as fast as possible. But I find getting the first draft on paper is way harder than fixing that crappy draft up.

Ⓐ When I'm starting something, I tend to absolutely hyper-worry about how it's going to begin. Like, what will the intro be or what will the first chapter be? I think that I've managed to control that over the years because, in my experience, you almost certainly rewrite everything at the start. It doesn't ever end up starting the way you think and sometimes that's because you have to get to the end of it before you know how to start it.

Ⓛ Exactly. Sometimes the act of writing something makes you realise, 'That bit I've put in the middle actually is a really good opener.' Also, I know with *Any Ordinary Day*, my sense of, 'What is this book about and what am I going to make the focus of this book?' – it almost took all of the writing and the research to crystallise in my mind. I think I sent you a polished draft to read. And you said the original opening felt like a bolt-on, that I could do better, that it didn't really fit with what the book was about.

Ⓐ Well, that was supportive of me.

Ⓛ It was helpful! What it did was force me to go back and think more carefully. The problem is, you get an idea and you cling to it because ideas are hard to come by. I had to sit for a long time in silence and just think, 'Does this work? Why doesn't it? At its core, what is this anecdote about? And what's the rest of the book about?' And then once I realised that the anecdote didn't back in the essential premise of the book, I had to be ruthless and say it was going. And I found the true opening hiding in the very next section. My original opening doesn't even appear anywhere in the book. A whole character was gone – it was brutal. But what ended up there was so much better because it's much more sharply focused.

Already padding this thing out

a Don't you feel like in the early part of the process, because you've got these little ideas that you're kind of hanging your hopes on, you don't want to sacrifice one of them early because it seems like there's nothing to replace it? I still can't get past this massive undergraduate concern about just getting to the word limit.

L Hang on, are you adding this diversion about word limits to try to get us to the word limit for this book?

a That's exactly what I'm doing. Let me tell you a long and complicated story about my friend Amy, whom I'm just making up now. It'll be at least another 1200 words. Yeah, as I'm writing, I'm like, 'How many thousand words is that now? Am I nearly at 50,000? How many more days will I need to write like this to have the word limit?' It's so stupid. And then once I've got a substantial enough pile of content, then I feel like I can afford to start chucking stuff overboard.

L One of my favourite parts of the process is tightening up the writing and slashing words and paring it down as much as I possibly can, which means that I might start with 3000 words and it'll be 1800 by the time I'm finished editing.

a Wow. The flourishes are the bits I can't get rid of. If I'm happy with a form of expression, I will fight tooth and nail to keep it just because I'm pleased with it. And that is often a dispute to be had with copy editors.

L When I feel like it's as sharp as I can possibly make it, and I don't see how you can carve any more words out of it, to see a copy editor then just tighten the screws that tiny bit more, I find really exhilarating.

a Oh my god. It's like a red room.

L I love it. One of the most exhilarating experiences I've had – and I just count myself so privileged to have been able to do this – was writing the foreword for the 25th anniversary edition of *The First Stone* . . .

a Really? CLANG! You've not mentioned that. Are you . . . friends with Helen Garner?

L I was so honoured and thrilled to be asked but, because I'm such a huge fan, I felt like, oh my god. I baulked for about 24 hours, thinking, 'I don't know if I can do this.'

a Did you feel like you had to write it in a Garner style?

🖋️ No, I felt more like I was just so horrified at the prospect of having my writing banged up directly alongside Helen Garner's writing.

🅰 That's a reasonable fear.

🖋️ But then, it's such an honour to be asked, how could I not do that? I just needed to put on the big girl undies and do it. I think the piece I wrote is about 2500–3000 words. I would've spent the most time on it of anything of that length that I've ever written because of the pressure I felt for it to be really good. I felt like I'd polished it really well; that there were no unnecessary words. Before it was going to be published, I sent it to Garner for a look. She was awesome because she didn't give me any direction at all about what to write about or what to say or not say – I had total freedom. But there's an anecdote at the start of that essay and Garner asked me, 'Would you mind if I had a go at sharpening that up a bit?'

🅰 Oh my god. That's like Roger Federer saying, 'Do you want to come for a hit?'

🖋️ Oh, 100 per cent. The version that she sent back . . . I mean, I thought mine was really tightly written but I reckon she'd probably taken a third of the words out and it was so much better. The thrill of seeing how brilliantly edited it was, it was almost . . . sexual.

[*Cackling, thigh-slapping, raucous laughter*]

Let's just call it 'Leigh's Book'

🖋️ I love having conversations with editors about 'does this really deserve to be here?' I love the back and forth about that. I remember, again from *Any Ordinary Day* . . . oh, you can tell how much I love this whole process by how much I'm dominating this bloody conversation. I'm not shutting up. Sorry.

🅰 No, that's fine.

🖋️ Ben Ball, my editor for *Any Ordinary Day*, is a really wonderful editor. He gives you the most gentle steers but he doesn't try to dominate your thinking. He just tries to help you find more clarity about what you want to say. For example, the working title was *Ordinary Days*. It was that for quite a long time, right into the final part of the editing process. And then Ben rang one day and said, ‘Do you think the title's right? Because, to me, *Ordinary Days* sounds like a pretty boring string of days all in a row where nothing much happens and that's actually the exact opposite to what your book's about.' So we batted that back and forth for a while. And because you're really fatigued at the end of the process, all you want to do is shout,

> *I don't care, call it "Leigh's Book" if you want, I just don't care!'*

L He said, ‘You're talking about one specific day on which a life changes. You're talking about a day, singular, not days plural. You're talking about *an* ordinary day.' Then we decided, let's call it *An Ordinary Day*. I had liked *Ordinary Days* because I thought it sounded lyrical and I thought *An Ordinary Day* also sounded quite nice and lyrical, so I was happy. And then, at the last possible minute, Ben rang and went, ‘I know we've already had this conversation. But now I don't think *An Ordinary Day* is quite right either, because isn't what you're suggesting is that life can change on *any* given day?' I went away and thought, well, he's absolutely right, it needs to be called *Any Ordinary Day*. I really loved that negotiation; Ben's attention to detail about the perfect word: any. I love having those conversations when you're deep, deep, deep in the editing process. It's my favourite thing.

a You're such a nerd. I see manuscripts come back and I just think, ‘Oh my god.' Because once I've finished writing something, I never, ever want to see it again.

L When you're writing, do you fix it up and sub-edit as you go so that when you finish a chapter, it's pretty well formed? Or do you use my method of the vomit and then the clean up?

a I do a sort of staged vomit, I guess. Once I move on from a chapter I like to be basically happy with the content. Then I'll go back and reorganise and restructure. But I won't send a copy of it to anyone until I'm quite happy with it. I loathe the idea of someone accidentally coming across something that's not quite finished. I remember when I was writing *The Wife Drought*, I sent a chapter to my friend Samantha. It was the first bit of it that I'd shown anyone and she just didn't reply. I became completely convinced that she hated it and had no idea how to break the news to me that it was terrible. I went to bed just absolutely freaking out . . . but really she'd run out of battery on her phone. Now, if somebody sends me a manuscript or something to read, I will often say, 'I've received it. I'm not starting to read it straight away, though!'

🅛 Oh, that's good.

Welcome to Journalism 101!

🅐 I remember how daunting it was learning to write as a cadet journalist. That muscle memory of how to compose an intro, how to structure a news or a feature article or something, hasn't really kicked in yet, so you feel almost agoraphobic about the range of possibilities. 'What do I put in the intro? What do I put next? What's the most important thing?' Sometimes these things are really hard to judge when you're not an expert in the subject matter. When I was a baby journalist, a news story would take me ages to write. But it's like driving. The first time you drive a car, you think, 'How can I possibly not hit every single thing on this road?' But then as your body learns how to do it, it becomes easier and easier. Structuring a piece of writing is like that, I think. It's also hard when you start off as a journalist because nobody returns your calls because they don't know who you are. It's unfair that the more senior you get, the easier your job is, because people will actually talk to you and because you know how to write really fast.

🅛 Also when you're a junior journalist, you actually, I think, get sent on the hardest stories to write because they're assignments that may not quite shape up as stories.

🅐 It's like, 'Go and sit in front of this Estimates Committee for six hours and then write one story out of it.'

🅛 Whereas the senior journos, they're being sent on 9/11 and things that are obviously stories. Juniors get, 'Annabel, go to the Royal Easter Show and find a story.' That's actually a way harder story to write than a disaster.

a Or even to take an assignment where the story isn't obvious or where there's a lot of confusing detail. Sometimes the active journalism isn't really anything to do with the writing. It's about prosecuting and organising the information so the reader doesn't have to do it. One of the most important things you can do as a writer is the work to untangle that stuff and answer the questions for yourself: 'What does this exactly mean? Why is this a problem? Why is this causing an issue?' And start from the beginning, like any reader would be reading your piece, and make sure you explain it to yourself clearly and, in so doing, you explain it to the reader.

L That's hugely important.

Don't read my trash

L Where do you get your article and book ideas from?

a Conversations. Reading things. I'm having a shower and I'm thinking about things I don't quite understand, and then I think, 'It would be interesting to investigate that.' If you've been fortunate enough to have a sustained career in journalism, you can refer back to things you've done or written before – and they provide a base from which to investigate something new.

L Do you have any interest in writing fiction?

a Oh, absolutely. I'd love to. I think I can write well when I've got a subject I know about and I'm writing creatively within those constraints, but the idea of making something up is much, much more intimidating.

L I feel exactly the same about it. I'd love to do it, but have the same fears. Non-fiction imposes a structure because you can only deal with the facts. That imposes some limitations

I do what I call the initial 'vomit' of trying to get something out, I'll sometimes write a sentence like, 'Crabb was sitting at the table and she looked *right word here* and she cut a slice of cake.'

on where you can take things. It's sort of safe because there's boundaries and I feel like I know what I'm doing in that space. Fiction feels way scarier. Any time I have sat down and thought, 'Okay, let's have a stab at this,' I just immediately ... I'll often have a premise and then I just can't do anything beyond that.

ⓐ Because your characters sound weird, or why?

ⓛ The characters seem weird and I don't know what to do with them. I don't know how to make a plot.

ⓐ You always read these acknowledgements at the ends of books that you've enjoyed and it's like, 'I want to thank everybody at the West Bethesda Writing Retreat, they made me feel so at home.' Can you imagine going to a writers' retreat and all sitting around and working on your books?

ⓛ Oh my god. That sounds terrifying. But it's probably what we need.

ⓐ Should we go on a writers' retreat?

ⓛ I would love to, but ...

ⓐ Oh, I'd stab you in the eye within two days or vice versa, probably.

ⓛ I think it'd be pretty full-on.

ⓐ Wouldn't you just sit there and go, 'That person seems to be making excellent process on theirs, they seem to write characters so easily. Why do mine still sound so shit?'

ⓛ Everything we've said about fearing people seeing our half-arsed trash. That's the whole point of a writers' retreat. ==You're inviting people to come look at your half-written trash!==

ⓐ Also, every time I read a great book that's highly original in style I immediately think, 'Maybe I could write something in that style?' If I read anything of Helen Garner's, I'm like, 'How can I make my writing more Garnomic?' I think if you're proceeding in a field that doesn't have the same rules as non-fiction, you'd be at risk all the time of accidentally adopting someone else's style in desperation.

ⓛ Totally. Or I fear what I'll do is end up sliding into non-fiction. I'll see some newspaper article and think, 'Well, that's a good premise for a novel,' and then research it and sit in a court and then thinly veil it as fiction.

ⓐ I look forward to your forthcoming novel. When someone writes a truly

well hello

original, terrific novel, it also worries me that there'll be absolutely scads of copycats that are not quite as good.

(L) That happens in television as well.

(a) Maybe what holds you back from writing that novel is just the knowledge that it would spawn so many dreadful knockoffs.

(L) Everyone trying to replicate my badly disguised non-fiction.

(a) It's just a cross you bear.

Writer's block

(L) Do you ever get writer's block?

(a) I feel agony when I can't quite get the right thing. I find writing super easy once I've got my idea – every columnist is the same, I suppose. But the horrible flapping around that you do when you're not quite there. And then sometimes you just have to file it with bile in your mouth because it's still not quite right.

But I did have really bad writer's block once when I was writing this book called *Losing It*, years ago in London. It was so stupid. I was writing this book on the Australian Labor Party – at night. I'd be working all day and then I'd spend the night on the phone to Craig Emerson or whatever, which was not a way to live, but I couldn't quite … I really struggled writing it. It was the hardest thing I've ever written. And at one point – oh my god – I went to get hypnotised, because I read somewhere that people who have writer's block can find relief through hypnosis.

I'm a bit of a sceptic about all that. I'm not very good at all that mindfulness stuff, because I think maybe I have a short attention span and my brain is like this terrible pack of terriers that you try to take for a walk in a park. I just jump around. I know that there must be things I can do, and I've tried to do mindfulness stuff just to calm everything down.

So I went to see this guy. In my memory, he was on Harley Street, but that doesn't sound right, does it? It can't be. Unless he was a brain surgeon doing hypnosis on the side.

I walk into this place and there's a comfy chair, of course, and this guy is droning on about how he's going to put me under and I'm thinking, 'Sure you are, buddy.' And to be honest, I thought, 'Well, this could be funny. Also, I might get a column out of it.' And I sat back in this comfy chair and he did this counting down and then he did this long and really annoying routine about how you're in a garden and you're walking in the garden and there's flowers everywhere. It's a lovely sunny day and you're following a path that leads through an arch and then round a thing. And then suddenly you're at a staircase and you're climbing the stairs, one foot after the other.

I really wanted this to work because I was interested. But all I could think was just, 'What kind of . . . are they wooden stairs? Is it a stone thing? Where's it going? How many of these were . . .' And then it led up to, inexplicably, a hillside. And then I was climbing the hill. I'm like, 'How am I . . . steps? And then a hillside?' But I'm thinking, 'Well, I can't wait to see what's at the top of this hill.' In the end I had to stand at the top of the hill, and then a CLOUD materialises next to me, and then he instructs me – and this is what made me angry, because I thought, 'This is lazy hypnosis' – he then instructed me to unload all of my worries into the cloud and then just push it away. And that was it.

That cloud cost me 60 quid.

I've been sitting here, working away, and I think: What do I need right now? Oh, I know. I need a pointless anecdote from Leigh Sales – and then you turn up like this. Like absolute magic.

well hello

flora's fancies

In 2015, Leigh was moving house and 'stumbled upon' this absolute pearler: a box of her long-lost youthful writings including *Flora's Fancies* – a dark, unintentionally comic novel she wrote in 1987 at just 13. Twenty overwritten pages long, this melodramatic masterwork features a hand-calligraphed and illuminated title page and enough gothic horror to stun a gargoyle.

Sales introduced *Flora's Fancies* to a delighted Crabb over several podcast episodes that were almost abandoned due to cry-laughing. This introductory passage sets the tone:

The cover page of Sales's classic 1987 novella. Includes bubble 'i's and the prescient application of copyright.

Flora thought about how many toes she'd trodden on to get to the top. It enraged her to think about how many times her own toes had been trodden on. Oh, revenge was sweet. Certainly, two wrongs didn't make a right, but it felt good to get your own back.

Say it again: Sales was in Grade Eight. A horrifying harbinger of her take-no-prisoners adult philosophy. Please enjoy the many trials and scant triumphs of young Flora and her doomed fancies . . .

L I'm going to read you all this. This is a novel that I started writing in 1987 called *Flora's Fancies*. It's so horrendously bad. It was 1987, so I was 13.

a Can we just drop that literary turd into the atmosphere?

L *Part One. Flora's Childhood. 1942 to 1958.* I love the ambition of a 13-year-old.

Chapter One.

I hate you, Aunt Muriel. I hate you. These were the first words Flora could ever recall uttering and the truest. She had hated Aunt Muriel for as long as she could remember. And it wasn't just Aunt Muriel, it was those horrid, horrid cousins too.

a It's always the horrid cousins.

Flora truly hated living with Aunt Muriel, in case we haven't established that. It wasn't by choice on Flora's part. It certainly wasn't on Muriel's either. Muriel Walters was under an obligation to her dead sister.

a Oh my god.

Flora's mother, Muriel's sister, had died giving birth to her child and shortly afterwards, Flora's father had committed suicide.

a Pretty gothic, isn't it? Surprised no one's got the plague in it.
L This is just the tip of the iceberg of the gothic-ness.

As a dying wish, Flora's mother requested that Muriel take Baby Flora. Muriel loved her sister so she heeded her wish but she bitterly hated Flora. Flora had taken her sister's life! Muriel was reminded of the secret agony she felt whenever Flora was around, even when Flora's name was mentioned. Muriel had to punish Flora for the life she had taken.

a Must've made margarine usage very difficult . . . I'm sorry.
L I'm not going to read the whole chapter. I'm just reading to the end of a certain piece of tragedy.

well hello

Muriel had four of her own children so Flora was an unwelcome addition. Muriel encouraged her children to be hateful towards Flora and that they were. One of the children was Flora's age and a more conceited little bitch could never be imagined.

ⓐ Whoa, saucy!

Her name? Megan. Flora was given any clothes Megan didn't want. When Megan didn't want something, she would accidentally tear it, stain it, and present it to Flora with, 'Here, Flora. You're lucky you got this but what a pity you can't have a lovely fashionable dress like my new one.' And Aunt Muriel would add, 'Yes, Flora. Your cousin is very kind to you and I didn't hear a word of thanks. Not a word.'

Flora's other cousins were cruel, but not like Megan. The two boys, Richard and John, liked to play practical jokes on Flora, like put toads in her bed and rip any of Flora's pretty dresses to threads. The only cousin who was the least bit merciful was Percis. Percis had the loveliest nature and—

ⓐ Why Percis? As in the Greek . . . um . . . Perseus?
ⓛ I don't know where I got these names from. You should see some of the names in subsequent chapters.

Percis had the loveliest nature and when Flora came she offered her friendship. But dear Aunt Muriel quickly stepped in and Percis was severely dealt with. Although Percis was lectured, she still managed to give Flora kindly looks and slip her cakes and sweets. But at the tender age of eight, Percis died of pneumonia and Flora lost her only friend in the world.

ⓐ It's kind of like Enid Blyton meets Hanya Yanagihara.

How to Write   119

🅛 I reckon you can tell what I must've been reading at that age, which must've been a big dollop of Danielle Steel with a healthy serve of Jackie Collins on the side.

🅐 A bit of Dickens? Oh, no – that's right. You've never read Dickens so it can't be that.

🅛 Why would I have been bothering Dickens when I had Danielle Steel on tap?

🅐 Well, it's very florid. And quite gripping. I'm already unwillingly hooked now after coming to the death of Percis.

🅛 When I was reading it, I was cacking myself with the layered-on levels. She's got no friends. Now the only friend she's got is going to die of pneumonia. As I said, that's just the tip of the tragedy that I have laid out for this poor girl.

🅐 That is so great.

Sales then decrees they have run out of time and also that the content is 'a bit rich'. But, a couple of podcasts later, young Flora is again dragged out – to Crabb's glee.

🅐 Oh, *Flora's Fancies*!

🅛 Now, I wasn't sure whether I should keep reading this because I was a bit worried that it's like telling someone in detail about your dreams. It's really bad and boring and you think it's interesting, but it's really not. But a lot of people have said to me, 'Oh my god, I just cacked myself at your stupid story.' So, I thought, 'Oh, well . . .'

🅐 Do you think this is one of those moments that politicians have when they've screwed up really badly, like: 'I've been heartened by, just absolutely swamped with messages and support.' Then you realise it's, like, four people and their mum. So I'm accurately, I think, surmising that some drunk has rolled down their taxi window and yelled '*Flora's Fancies*!' at you.

🅛 No, but look – if you are a regular listener, let me know if you do want to hear more of *Flora's Fancies*. There's only another—

🅐 There's just so much.

🅛 —it's about 20 pages altogether and we're up to page five.

🅐 It's all that roundy-roundy girl-like stuff. Did you ever do that 'do your "i" dots as circles' phase?

well hello

Ⓛ Of course I went through that phase.

Previously on *Flora's Fancies*: Flora is an orphaned child whose mother died in childbirth, whose father subsequently suicided, and has just been taken in by her cruel aunt.

Ⓐ She blames Flora for the death of her big sister. And she subsequently offed the only one of her children that Flora liked, correct? Although, wasn't it like she died of pleurisy?

Ⓛ Percis, I believe you're referring to, died of pneumonia.

After Percis's death, Flora became very reclusive.
She couldn't even try to be friendly with Aunt Muriel and her cousins.
Aunt Muriel's two butlers, Harrison and Reginald—

Ⓐ You said Harrison and . . .?

Ⓛ Reginald.

Ⓐ Reginald.

—were nice to Flora, but, well, they weren't any fun, and Flora
couldn't really feel comfortable with them. Christina, the maid, was fine,
and Flora liked her, but she couldn't adore her the way she did Percis.
Aunt Muriel's house on 13 Black Street suddenly lived up to its name.
A black and more dismal house couldn't be imagined,
especially during the cold English winter.

Ⓐ Keep in mind, this was written in Queensland.

Ⓛ I know!

No light ever entered the house, it seemed to Flora. The house
named Walter Manor was extremely big and foreboding.
Its windows were eyes and the door was an ugly mouth.
All in all, the house was like a great monster,
ready to eat you after your first step across the threshold.

> *Megan said the house was elegant, but Flora knew it was just an evil dwelling full of evil people. Once Flora said to Christina, 'When I grow up, I mean to have a lovely little house with a light in every window and flowers growing in abundance.' Christina replied—*

It's written exactly like this.

ⓐ What I really like about you is that your derision and enjoyment is 100 per cent sincere. Even though this is you that you're laughing at.

ⓛ If you can't laugh at your old self, who can you laugh at?

And Christina replied – I've got tears fully running down my face –
'Aye, you have too many—'

ⓐ Oh my god, really?

ⓛ It's the accent.

ⓐ You've now lapsed into Thomas Hardy just for a couple of paragraphs.

> *'Aye, you have too many of these fancies*
> *about how your life's going to turn out.'*
> *'But Christina, life's meant to be "fancied about", as you put it.*
> *Dreams are the essence of life, after all!'*
> *'Aye, little one . . .'*

ⓐ Christina is being played by Hagrid in this performance.

> *'. . . but you live in a world of fancy. It's not good for a little girl,' said Christina. Flora just sighed and began daydreaming again. That's how Flora was: distinctly creative with a flowing imagination.*

ⓐ Flaming red hair, and a Highland dance outfit.

ⓛ Get this:

> *Every now and then, Flora would get an urge to write a story. Not a short story, but a great novel. After a while, Flora would lose the urge and her stories would remain incomplete.*

well hello

ℒ Remind you of anybody?

Once Christina found a story of Flora's, and although it was certainly no masterpiece, here and there were touches of genius.

ⓐ Ah.

*Christina realised that Flora had talent and that she would accomplish great success because of it one day.
How true Christina's predictions were.*

I think I'm going to have to leave it there because the end of *Flora's Fancies* – I'm sorry to say for anyone who was looking forward to it – actually becomes doggerel. It becomes really, really bad.

ⓐ Doggerel means 'rhyming', though. That's not the right word. You just mean crap.

ℒ I think the word I'm looking for actually is 'dribble'. It was too much repeating of the same stuff about her being mistreated. I can pretty much just tell you what happened before I ran out of puff. There was a shameless bit of plagiarism of, I believe, a scene in *Anne of Green Gables* where Flora is accused of stealing Aunt Muriel's ring. And then she didn't, and it's revealed that that little bitch of a cousin did it.

ⓐ Nothing to me will ever bring as much joy as the use of the term 'bitch' in *Flora's Fancies*. I just love it.

ℒ And then Flora gets shipped off to Ms Finselback's boarding school. And it just ends sort of mid-sentence, something to do with, *Ms Finselback was a disciplinarian and*
Not even an ellipsis, it's just 'and'.

> Flora is accused of stealing Aunt Muriel's ring. And then she didn't, and it's revealed that that little bitch of a cousin did it.

Pretty gothic,
isn't it?
Surprised
no one's got the
plague in it.

@ Wow.

@ So I thought, it's not really worth reading.

@ You're like Truman Capote's unfinished work.

@ I think I should take it to a Helen Garner masterclass or something and say, 'Garner, could you . . .?'

@ Oh yeah. 'What can I do with it?'

@ I don't reckon that, having now read that aloud, I'm ever going to be allowed on this podcast ever again to go: 'Yes, I just knocked over such-and-such. It was a bit mediocre, I thought.'

@ It's no *Flora's Fancies*.

@ It is no *Flora's Fancies*.

shit on my dreams

At a show in Canberra, Annabel betrays . . . reservations at the prospect of Leigh writing a novel.

a You know when people you admire write a novel and you think, 'Well this could go either way.' So if YOU wrote a novel I'd be like, 'Really? Okaaaay.' Now, obviously you're the most bankable author in Australia right now, so obviously you can write books . . .

L It's what I love about you – that I feel like when I share my dreams with you, you just . . . you enable me to fly.

a I'm just pre-trampling you a tiny bit, so that when you ask me to read your draft of your novel—

L Can I just say, ladies and gentlemen, the thing that's just profoundly upsetting about this is that Annabel Crabb knows good and well that I have an idea for a novel in my head.

a Don't say that, because now all these publishers will ring you up.

L And she's chosen in front of an audience of 1000 people to shit on my dreams.

a Working title is *Fifty Shades of Sales*. It's full of sex, basically.

icons of chat 10:
Helen Garner

Ⓛ If we went back through this podcast for the past five years, why do you think Helen Garner would be the number-one-most-talked-about writer?

Ⓐ I always feel confident when a Garner book goes to a dark place, because she does a lot of the processing. It's like adult birds who are feeding their kids pre-masticated food. She never shies away from really painful stuff – she processes it in a way that makes it meaningful to the reader.

Ⓛ She brings that labour to both the external events that she's looking at and reporting on, but also to herself, at her own internal thought processes. She often judges her own reaction to things quite harshly. I feel like when she examines an issue, it's as if she has a shell that she's turned around and looked inside and outside and at every groove and examined it in every possible way. I'm not saying anything particularly insightful here, because eight million people have said it before me. But her powers of observation about everyday life are one of the things I really love about her writing. She notices things. She's described it herself as her 'third eye'. She notices things to a great degree of detail that would bypass most people.

Ⓐ I remember hearing her talk about what happened when *Monkey Grip* was published. It was fabulously popular and sold very well, but she was always a bit wounded, I think, by reviews saying, well, you know, 'It's just sort of . . .'

Ⓛ 'Non-fiction dressed up.'

Ⓐ Right. 'It's just the banal details of this uninteresting group of people.' I think the strongest element of her writing, that's always been there from the beginning, is an egalitarian interest in observation, without any preconceived ideas of where to look for observation that is 'relevant' or 'important'. I think that that's a very feminist instinct, because she writes about how people feel in domestic situations. That has never really been, in the years before she became well known, a super fruitful area for great literature.

Ⓛ Yeah. That's the stuff I like, because I do sometimes think that a lot about life comes from those microdetails. That's what she's an absolute expert at getting to.

On that 'micro' thing as well, the other thing I love about her work is the utter precision about the choice of word, and the way the writing is so sparse.

a When you go back and read *Yellow Notebook*, so much of her record keeping about the writing that she's doing – apart from being soaked in self-loathing, which I find massively reassuring – is that she's going back and back and back to a scene that she's writing in a novel or whatever. She's absolutely curry-combing it for excess syllables, for excess words, for excess adverbs. She's scraping it back to its purest form.

L Do you have a favourite of her books?

a I find that quite hard to answer. To be honest, it's usually the last one that I've read. I read *Yellow Notebook* in a really tough time. My sister-in-law had just been diagnosed with cancer. My concentration span was poor and I felt this sense of despair. The only book that felt like it helped was *Yellow Notebook*.

L I think you're right, that whatever you've read most recently you tend to like. I do have a soft spot for *The First Stone*, because it was the first of her books that I read. *Joe Cinque's Consolation* I found riveting, too. But equally, I love the collections of essays and observations because you can dip into them really easily. There's no one I would want less to write a profile of me than Helen Garner. Don't you think? There's no way would I agree.

a Let's make that your 50th birthday present. A 1000-word personal profile. Maybe 10,000 words.

L I feel absolutely ill at the thought.

a My anxiety about Helen Garner getting older is that I'm genuinely fearful of when she dies.

L I was just thinking that before. I could feel my eyes tearing up.

a I grew up on a farm so I'm quite reconciled to the cycle of life. But if there was one person in Australia that I could make go on forever, it would be her.

L What was upsetting me when I was thinking about it before was thinking that when she dies, there will never be any new Helen Garner to read.

a Let the record show, there are tears now in Sales's eyes. Oh my god. You're pathetic.

chapter 5

I don't care

I just don't really care:

The Leigh Sales philosophy

When I was a child, if ever I asked what somebody thought of something I'd done, my grandmother would archly reply, 'It's none of your business what anybody thinks of you.'

Forty years later, thanks to social media, it's hard for us to avoid hearing what other people think of us. We're on there in our spare time, and many jobs require the use of social media, too, so it's fairly common to hear from a total stranger about what a massive git you apparently are. If you have a job with a public element, you may find yourself subject to regular abuse and bullying. If you make a big mistake that goes viral, or you have an opinion that goes against whichever way the wind is blowing, you might find your entire life destroyed by a puritanical online mob. (Crabb and I have talked extensively on the podcast about Jon Ronson's book *So You've Been Publicly Shamed*, and it's a great read, should you ever be unfortunate enough to find yourself burning at that particular stake.) I've seen friends who are normally pretty robust become rattled by the vehemence of social media abuse and how personal it becomes, particularly when directed at women. In my job as an ABC journalist, it's a rare day where somebody isn't berating me for what they perceive as my personal and professional failings, ranging from being a fat slut to a barracker for one side of politics or the other.

Pretty much every time I make a speech anywhere, I will be asked in the question-and-answer session how I cope with that kind of abuse.

The simple answer is: I just don't really care.

well hello

If you asked my former husband, he would tell you I've always been somewhat oblivious to the opinions of other people and that one of my defining qualities is how little I take into account what anyone thinks of me. My thought process goes something like this: 'I like the music of Herman's Hermits. Other people may perceive that as being not cool. What do I prefer: other people thinking I'm cool and never hearing Herman's Hermits again, or listening to Herman's Hermits and not giving a shit?' The answer is most definitely keep listening to Herman's Hermits. Perhaps it's the early family training as well; it just seems somewhat uncouth to seek to know what other people think of me.

When it comes to social media, I'm really not at all sure why I should care what some anonymous person thinks about my hair, my figure, my interviewing technique or the quality of my journalism. Actually, I sometimes find the idiocy of such people amusing. My favourite ever criticism on social media came from some bloke calling himself @gumtreewanker, accusing me of being 'unAustralian'. I thought, 'Mate, it's pretty rich to be called unAustralian by somebody who apparently goes around wanking gum trees.'

When it comes from people I loosely know or voices who aren't anonymous, I'm afraid I still just don't care that much. I stick to a few good mental health practices on social media and I'll share them, for what they're worth (and they're not really worth that much, I hasten to add, it's just what I do).

1. My bar for blocking people is insanely low. On a day when I'm particularly punitive, I might block somebody because they think the Rolling Stones are better than the Beatles. I mostly block ideologues who bore me with the monotony of their political views – both left and right, it's all equally tedious to me. In real life, if I'm walking down the street and somebody attempts to stop me to speak to me, I'm under no obligation to listen to them. (Though if it's a Chatter, it's most likely a delight!) Same on social media, as far as I'm concerned. If I think you seem like a bit of an annoying dickhead, or the kind of person I'd try to get away from at a party by pretending I need to go to the toilet, I may well just block you to keep you out of my face.

2. I rarely look at comments on my posts and I certainly don't check my mentions on Twitter that much. I prefer to spend my free time thinking about more interesting and useful subjects, such as whether the extra beat in the chorus of 'Straight Lines' by Silverchair is any good.

3. I have allocated myself specific times during the day where I look at my mentions. I almost never do that after work and definitely never when I'm getting ready to go to sleep.

4. I don't get into fights with strangers – or anyone – online no matter how much what they've said has annoyed me or how stupid they may appear. That way madness lies.

5. Ridicule and humour are the most potent weapons out there so, if you must, I reckon it's always best to poke a bit of harmless fun at someone rather than berate them. One of my favourite comebacks of recent times was when I tweeted that I was interviewing a Liberal cabinet minister, and some fool tweeted, 'Dinner after?' and I replied something like, 'No thanks, but good on you buddy for having the guts to ask me out!'

There's one other rule that I constantly drill into colleagues and friends who pay too much attention to social media.

It's that the positive feedback is equally as worthless as the negative.

If you seek out praise and attention, and you get a sense of validation from what strangers say about you, then naturally your brain is going to think equal weight must be given to criticism and negative feedback. All of it is worthless. I put as little stock in people telling me I'm awesome and amazing as I do in people telling me I'm useless. None of it matters. What matters is what I hear from people close to me in real life. As my nana would say, the rest is none of my business.

well hello

conversation

I don't care

aka Get off my lawn

a So I read your essay 'I Just Don't Really Care'.

L Can I interrupt you here to say, 'It's really none of my business what you think about my essay.'

a It mainly made me laugh and laugh and want to meet your nana, and my first thought was, 'You are going to make the most hilarious, nuts old lady.' And you're halfway there.

L I can't wait to be a nuts old lady. 'Get off my lawn, you little punks!'

a Do you worry about getting older? Is this something that plagues you?

L It doesn't plague me. I do worry about it, because I think by the time you hit your mid-40s, you're old enough to have a sense of the passage of time and that this is how your life's turned out, but not old enough to really not care too much about that yet.

a Right. Okay. So you think, 'Well, this is the shape that my life has taken and I'm really unlikely to massively change the shape of it.'

L Yeah, I think so.

a I think it's rare where I haven't thought on any given year, 'Oh, I'm glad I'm this age and not younger.'

L That is definitely true. I wouldn't trade being 47 to be 27 again.

a No. The thought makes me feel so tired. There are heaps of 20s things that I don't want to have to do again, even though they were fun at the time.

L I've written in that essay that I've never really cared that much about what other people think but people usually say that's the case as they get older.

a I've read a bit about this phenomenon of as you get older you find you have more time and fewer things to worry about. That's certainly not my experience in my 40s. I feel like I've got a million more things to worry about that persecute my every living minute, but I'm hoping that lays up.

Connie Britton's perfect, perfect hair

a One thing, though – I don't have that sense of worry about ageing in that sort of magazine-y sense that women are supposed to worry about. Like, I don't really care about looking older. I never ever think, 'Oh! I might pop off and have some botox.' That idea makes me panicky. Imagine if you were at the point where you were trying to hold back the visible signs of age and then you went for more and more crazy botox and surgery, and then you end up looking like the Bride of Wildenstein, but there's no way you can jump off that moving train. I feel very sorry for people who get caught up in that, because I think it just ends in complete horror and ridicule. That said, I think your nose job's great.

L How about the boobs?

a Yeah. Loud and proud.

L I hate looking in the mirror and seeing myself get older.

a Really?

L I wouldn't do anything about it, but I don't love it. But what's the alternative? Not looking in the mirror and seeing yourself getting older.

a Or looking in the mirror and sort of seeing some weird, stretched-out simulacrum of a younger person.

L I think people look more attractive when they just go with nature. When I look at, say, Emma Thompson, I think she looks the most beautiful she's ever looked. And as I get older, actually, I do find older faces more interesting and attractive.

a You were telling me about this article that you read about Connie Britton, one of our joint pin-up ladies, who was talking about the experience of being a woman who hadn't had lots of cosmetic surgery work.

L Unusual in Hollywood.

a Yeah. And then kind of finding herself being offered more interesting roles because she actually has a face that's capable of expression.

L But she said she had had to stop looking at herself in the mirror. Like, she'd had a period in her house where she didn't look in the mirror.

a Wow. `If I were Connie Britton I'd be glued to a mirror.` I'd be carrying a mirror around.

L I'd be brushing my hair all the time.

a Just tossing it every now and again.

I'm picturing you as an 80-year-old

L Why did my essay make you think about ageing?

a Because `my first thought was how funny you're going to be when you're 80.`

L I'm sort of hoping that I'll be like my friend Michael Fullilove's mother, Patricia. I just absolutely love her – well, firstly, because she and Michael's late father had the best meeting story I've ever heard. They met on the set of *Skippy*.

a I love it already.

L Michael's father, Eric Fullilove, was the director of *Skippy* and his mother was Sonny's tutor. That is the best backstory ever, right? Michael should be the prime minister because of that Australian backstory. So, Mrs Fullilove – she's just really warm and encouraging all the time.

a See, that's not what I'm picturing you like as an 80-year-old. I mean, I wouldn't be visiting for the cookies. Put it that way.

L You'd be visiting for the acerbic commentary.

a And the extreme tidying. Because by that stage, of course, I'll be living in like a crazy old . . . oh my god, what was the name of the house in . . . you know . . . the house next door in the book that I've never read with Scout and Atticus.

L Boo Radley's house.

a Boo Radley's house!

L Readers, the book to which she's referring is *To Kill a Mockingbird* by Harper Lee. So, if, for example, in the course of reading THIS book, Annabel

Is this the face of a child who cares a jot that she's dressed as an extra from *Brigadoon*? No! It's wee Leigh Sales, who developed her tough hide by being a redhead in Queensland, a keen Highland dancer and a budding organist.

Crabb gives you some instructions about how to have a better reading life, you need to keep in mind that here is a person who has not deigned to read *To Kill a Mockingbird*.

Ⓐ One of the things that I've learned over my reading life, Sales, is to not give a shit what people think I should have read. I will be the smug person that gets to sit down and read that book when I'm 80, while you're busy tidying and yelling at your grandchildren. Which gets me back to your essay – it did enhance my admiration for one aspect of your character. And I'm not really quite there yet myself, but I think I've picked up a lot from you about whose opinion to care about and whose to not. It's really unusual for a kid or a teenage girl in particular to be so sure about that or to be confident enough to disregard the opinions of people who should not matter.

Ⓛ Well, if you want to learn Highland dancing or how to play the organ, it becomes essential.

Ⓐ How about that picture of you with the Highland dance outfit on and the most beatific smile on your face, absolutely thrilled with yourself and having no sense of how deeply ridiculous you look? It's actually one of the most exhilaratingly enchanting photographs of all time. It's just like someone going, 'I am amazing!'

Maybe I am a fluffhead

Ⓐ I remember I wrote down in my book of funny things that my kids say, the time I was walking to school with my youngest daughter, Kate, and her brother, Elliott. Kate had tucked her school jumper into her pants, so it was all incredibly lumpy. And I said, 'Hey, you don't have to tuck the jumper into those pants, you know, it makes you look like a bit of a wally.' And she turned around and said,

L   At our kids' school presentation day last year, this young boy got up and sang a song. I forget what the song was now, but he was in love with doing it. It was really daggy, but he was totally loving it and he was loving himself sick. And I just thought, 'Wow, I hope that no one ever beats you down and makes you lose that quality.' But, unfortunately, I think life does do that to people. Because of the nature of my job at *7.30*, and your job as well, we get a tonne of abuse on social media. My boss will sometimes raise it with me, and my colleagues do too, and they're like, 'Are you sure you're okay? My god, the volume of stuff you get.' And I think they sometimes don't believe me when I say I just don't really care very much.

a   **I believe you NOW. Ten years ago I was like, 'Is she for real?'**

L   I know you handle it okay now, but how did that kind of relentless negative feedback and abuse on social media affect you at first?

a   It made me feel constantly uneasy. I would post something, an article or whatever, online, and then feel this sick sensation that I was bracing myself for the comments. And I guess lots of people at the time would have said to me, 'Don't read the comments,' but I did because I was new to working on an entirely online platform. I think in my time, I've never blocked anyone. I always like to actually see what's there, but I have become much better at disregarding it. In a funny way, when you get so much of it and for such a sustained amount of time, you think, 'Well, it's not actually a human option to take all of this stuff seriously. So the only evolutionary response is to stop caring about it.'

L   Did you ever feel when you were reading it, **'Maybe I am a fluffhead?'**

a   All the time, because I am full of doubts about myself and my own abilities and I think I'm probably wrong about lots of things. And when you write opinion, I guess you take a stance and you try to back it in. The thing I get more than anything else is, 'You're a lightweight who has a cooking show, so bugger off with your views about politics.' My way of dealing with that is knowing that, really, there's lots of people in the world who are interested in cooking. It doesn't mean they can't have reasonable opinions on other things. Also, it's a real double standard because I think male journalists who write about other things apart from politics are never given a hard time about how they're also interested in motor racing.

L I remember when we started doing *Chat 10 Looks 3*, a really respected senior journalist said to me, 'Look, I don't know why you'd be messing around in those shallow waters, because you've got such an amazing journalistic reputation and I don't see why you would risk your credibility like that.' At the time Barrie Cassidy, the host of the political show *Insiders*, also hosted a sports show called *Offsiders*. And I said to my friend, 'I just wonder, have you had this conversation with Barrie about the sports show that he hosts and how that's undermining his credibility for his politics show?' It's such a double standard that something like cooking or reading or music undermines your cred in a way that sport doesn't.

a There's plenty of political journalists – blokes – who bang on about Bob Dylan or whatever and it doesn't seem to have the same deleterious effect. I've got a joke with myself now where if somebody says, 'Get back into the kitchen,' I'm like, 'Drink! You're the 75th person to say that today. Thank you.' Also, I have to say sneakily: I get to do the stuff that I'm interested in, plus make a show that involves something that is one of my recreational pursuits. So suck on it, dudes.

How to genuinely not care

L I think something else people find hard to deal with on social media is that when there's a huge pile-on directed at you, it can feel like everyone in the world thinks exactly that of you.

a Yeah. And particularly if it's aimed at a weak point. As a journalist and as a columnist, you will screw up sometimes and write something that's incautious and that you regret, or that you've got the tone slightly wrong on. And when a pile-on happens around that, you can apologise but it doesn't really do much. Public shaming is an incredibly ancient phenomenon, but it's the facility with which a group of people can now just casually jump all over another

well hello

person and then move on to the next thing without really, I guess, having any culpability or responsibility for what it does to that person that's quite a modern phenomenon.

The only way to genuinely not care is to be wary of the amount of weight you place on feedback, good or bad. What I thought was really interesting about your essay was where you made the point that if you invest heavily in receiving praise or positive feedback through social media, then it makes your sense of devastation when the majority of that feedback is negative so much more difficult to survive. I think that's a really, really good point.

Ⓛ Whether it's praise or negative feedback, it's all caring about what other people think of you. And I think that, that's not really the key to living . . . ugh, I was about to say, 'the key to living a happy or authentic life' and then I just was like, what the fuck is this, a self-help book?

ⓐ What does it mean for 'wellness'?

Ⓛ What does it mean for your 'journey'?

ⓐ What does it mean for your gut?

More help than head lice

ⓐ Don't you ever think, though, that you're in danger of one day realising that you're Howard Hughes and that you've told everybody to get knotted?

Ⓛ Yes. One of the fundamental components of human interaction is that you do have to be reading what the other person might be thinking and adjust your behaviour accordingly. What I'm describing there about 'not caring', if you took that to the nth degree, you'd have no friends because you'd be constantly saying to people, 'Yeah, I've had enough of talking to you, now I want to leave.' And not putting any social niceties around your interactions. You can't do that. But caring about what *strangers* think of you is way less important. Caring about what your friends think and feel and considering how you act towards them and how you build closer relationships – that's important stuff. It's also where empathy comes from for people you don't know – thinking about how things look to somebody else or how they might be feeling and what they might need in a particular moment of their life. Every minute that you spend worrying about what idiots on social media are doing or saying, or replying to them, is time that you are robbing away from your actual friends and family.

🄰 One of the things I've learned from you a little bit – loath as I am to remark that I've picked up anything from you apart from head lice over the years – is how to triage the people you do worry about and the people you don't. I think you do have to remain open to criticism, but be able to recognise people whose line of attack on you is more about their own agenda, or sometimes their own insecurities, than anything else. Realising the difference between a deep and underlying cause for concern and something that is a passing fetish attack is really valuable. But it's a hard thing to do because the only thing that can teach you that is experience and repeated exposure to trauma.

🄻 Yeah, that's right. I don't mind criticism from people I trust and who, at their core, have my back. So, if I send you a piece of writing and say, 'Hey, can you tell me what you think of this?' I don't want you to come back and go, 'Salesy, you're a brilliant writer. It's fantastic.' I want you to come back and go, 'Well, that structure doesn't work and it's a little bit overwritten here and I think you should do X, Y, Z.' Because I know when it comes from you, it comes from a place where you want me to put my best public face forward because you're trying to insulate me from the criticism of all of the other idiots out there and to stop me from putting my foot in things. Or there are friends who give me advice, not about professional things, but in my personal life – 'You're acting like a bit of an ass' or 'You should give that person another go' or whatever – and I trust their judgement. I like my 3 am worry slot to not be full of the opinions of anonymous idiots that I don't even know.

🄰 I'd say my 3 am worry slot is entirely peopled with people that I've let down in real life, or people that I haven't paid enough attention to or haven't been able to get to.

🄻 True. The other 3 am it was like, 'Oh my god, Murph's sister had brain surgery last week and I haven't asked her about it for three days. Oh god, I am the worst friend ever.'

🄰 I'm sure that Murph would have been lying awake worried about something tangentially associated with slighting us. You can probably relax on that front.

well hello

In your face, Punky Brewster

a You pretend to not care what people think, but I know that the thing you really, really enjoy is receiving unsolicited advice on social media and helpful tips about how to interview.

L Oh, I DO. I sometimes will scan those things, looking for ones that I can make a funny comeback to, just because I get great entertainment out of it. And I love doing it when people insult you too.

a You wrote some poetry recently about some dude. That was pretty funny.

L I can see sometimes that someone might've been so unfair to you and you're trying to be polite. But I think, 'Ooh, I can weigh in on this.' What I usually try to do is to find a way to sort of just gently ridicule the person, but also make you laugh and to diffuse the annoyance. The one that still makes me laugh is the person who tried to insult you by claiming that you looked like Punky Brewster.

Leigh

L Every time somebody mansplains to me on Twitter how to do my job (and that's literally daily), I hear the Hall & Oates song 'Maneater' in my head but the key lyric is 'Whoa, here he comes, he's a mansplainer!'

Any sting that was in it has been thoroughly destroyed by how much fun you and I have had with it.

Beware the Leigh Sales Strategic Silence

a What I wanted to ask you about, too, is your scientific development of the Leigh Sales Strategic Silence.

L Now, let me tell you, silence is a very hard weapon to deploy, 'cos when you're angry your natural instinct is that you want to defend yourself or strike back straight away. But silence is so powerful, because if somebody says something or sends you a nasty email or makes a nasty public remark about you and you don't respond, it really messes with their head. A lot of people have a big ego and they imagine that you care what they think and so they want you to respond – and they find it puzzling if you don't. But they're also left wondering, 'Did she actually hear what I said?' or 'Did she get my email?'

Let me tell you an anecdote. I was at a party at a friend's place; there were 70 or 80 people there. And this woman I had never seen before said to me, 'Oh, Leigh Sales, I just finished reading your book. I've never liked you on television, I think you're really harsh. But your book made me feel differently about you and now I quite like you.' I just looked at her and it did rattle me because here I was, at a party having a lovely time, and then that. At the time she interrupted, I was having a really pleasant conversation with someone I don't get to speak to that often. Anyway, I told a friend and he, dead seriously, was like, 'I am going to find that person and I'm going to tell them what I think of what she just did.' And his wife said, 'No, let's not do that. Leigh, let's just get you a champagne and let go of that and move on.' Which we did.

But then several days later, the person obviously had dwelled on it and felt incredibly bad. And she emailed me, saying,

'I have been thinking about what I said to you at that party. I got your email from our mutual friend so I could apologise profusely and I just feel so horrible about it.'

And it went on. She was wanting me to absolve her and say, 'It's okay. Don't worry about it.'

ⓐ I would have broken my fingers hurriedly replying and saying, 'Please don't give it a second thought, thank you so much for taking the trouble of emailing.'

ⓛ I just thought, 'No, I'm not under any obligation to tell you that it was okay that you were really rude to me. And perhaps next time you might think about being rude to somebody like that. You've already occupied some of my mental load by flattening me at that party. And I'm not giving you any more of my time or my mental load by replying to your email, whether to absolve you or rip into you.' And so I just deployed the Leigh Sales Strategic Silence. I've never heard from her again and I don't know what effect that had on her, but I don't really care because beyond telling you this anecdote, I've never given her another second's thought.

ⓐ This is like the most chilling horror movie I've ever seen. You are thrilling and horrifying me at the same time. This is why I sit at your knees and say …

ⓛ `'. . . teach me all you know, O Wise One.'`

Silence is also an incredibly useful tool in interviews, because people feel the need to fill the silence. I don't have the luxury to do it very often on *7.30*, but in an interview, or in real life, particularly if you can hold the eye contact and not break it, very few people can resist filling the silence if you're being silent yourself and looking at them expectantly. When you give people more time, they say more revealing things. But it is very, very hard to do.

ⓐ It's expensive on television, right? Silence is an absolute indulgence.

ⓛ Sometimes political interviewees use it well, too. The normal expectation for a political interviewer is that the politician will waffle but every now and again, you'll ask something and the politician will go, 'No, I don't.' And then stop speaking and just look at you and you're all discombobulated and like, 'Argh, what's my next question?' So it can work both ways.

ⓐ I was interviewing somebody on the phone the other day and I do shorthand, right? That's how I like to take notes when I'm interviewing somebody, I can't be bothered with long recordings that I've then got to plough through. She said something really good and I was letting my shorthand catch up. I was absolutely consumed with my own thoughts and making sure that I got all this down accurately. I didn't realise she thought that I was deploying a strategic silence. Then she said, 'Are you still there?' I said, 'Oh yeah, I'm just letting my shorthand catch up. Sorry.' And she said, `'I thought you were doing that thing where you were being silent so that I would say something reckless.'`

ⓛ See? Some people are very clued in to how this works.

law & order: SWU

a *I guess when you do half an hour* of demanding live TV every day, you tend to become conscious of the clock. In my opinion, Leigh Sales has gone significantly further – essentially, she IS a clock now. At least, part clock. Let's say 80 per cent high-performance human, and 20 per cent timepiece. Think Arnold Schwarzenegger crossbred with one of those Casio digital watches that Sales almost certainly sported as a kid.

She has a special sensitivity for two minutes before the hour. Because in her day job 7.58 pm is the point at which shit gets real and she starts to run out of time, you will find that if you're ever in a social situation with her or indeed any interaction that has lasted 28 minutes, the antsiness will set in.

She'll start inserting summaries. 'Yeah, mate, it certainly sounds like you've had a crummy week.' 'Well, that's bundt-making, I guess. There's always an element of risk.' 'We'll probably never know.'

One begins to realise that one is being wound up like the end of a show. This is especially likely to happen if one is, say, recording a podcast with her, which is at least explicable in the sense that it's something like a half-hour broadcast. Less explicable if it's a cup of coffee you're having, or a phone conversation.

But the SWU – the Sales Wind-Up – is horrifyingly evident in other contexts.

If you're a dinner guest chez Sales, she will think nothing of letting you know, come top of the hour at 9 pm, that it's time for you to ship out because she wants to go to bed.

I wasn't there on this particular night, but there is a legendary New Year's

Eve when Sales and Phil were entertaining guests for dinner and Sales encouraged the guests to pop out at 9 and undertake a short walk to witness the early fireworks over Circular Quay, a mission from which they were strongly encouraged not to return.

The SWU is not just a ninja move applied to others, however. It's just as regularly self-applied. I have seen that lady ghost a lot of functions. And if you're Leigh Sales, ghosting a function isn't as simple as just nicking off without saying goodbye. If you're one who feels awkward about leaving a dinner early, or a charity fundraiser, imagine the added degree of difficulty if you're the KEYNOTE SPEAKER, and the very act of standing up from your seat ignites a secondary wave of people popping over to tell you a brilliant idea they had for what you should have asked the prime minister on your show last Wednesday.

Annabel

Peak of our New Year's Eve: Outlasting the Leigh Sales 9 pm cut-off.

Nevertheless, I've seen her do it.

Back in early podcast days, I remember an event from which Sales was keen to make an early exit due to the extremely valid reason of being pregnant, and I decided to be her accomplice. We made coordinated visits to the bathroom. I raced round and grabbed her wrap from the back of her chair (so much easier to ghost if you leave an item hanging on your chair, because people foolishly reckon it means you'll be back. I imagine Sales has lost a shitload of pashminas that way). We dive-rolled into a taxi and no one was the wiser. There was a real Steve McQueen vibe about it, or at least as Steve McQueen as you can feel when you're a six-foot pregnant ginger. Recently, a friend of mine was housesitting for Sales over the Christmas holidays. Leigh was in Queensland, so we had a tiny little tasteful New Year's Eve party at her house. I took great delight in posing next to her giant kitchen clock as 9 pm came and went, with her fancy crystal held carelessly in my inebriated paw. It may be the only chance I ever get to evade the SWU.

> It's true that I am an unapologetic ghoster and this is difficult when you are prominent in the room.

a rejoinder from Leigh 'Last Word' Sales

L May I add two points:

1. I did indeed own a Casio digital watch. I would have really liked one of those colourful Swatch watches but they were too expensive.

2. It's true that I am an unapologetic ghoster and, as Crabb correctly points out, this is difficult when you are prominent in the room. I remember once having to launch a book at a pub. (A quick aside: when I arrived, I realised I couldn't read my speech. 'The lighting's too dim in here,' I grumbled to the book's publicist, who scurried off to try to get it fixed. Murph, who was with me, said, 'Mate, have you considered this might be a glasses issue?' 'It's not a glasses issue,' I sniffed, 'my eyesight is 20/20.' 'Look, you're hitting that age where your eyes go, why don't you try mine, just in case,' Murph said. I put them on; the speech text was crystal clear. I was crushed.) After the speeches, I began sidling towards an exit. Even a tap on the arm from a very handsome bloke who wanted a chat wasn't enough to derail the mission. 'I was just on my way to the bathroom,' I said to him, heading towards a fire door only five or so metres away. Here are some tips for a clean escape: don't make eye contact with anybody, move purposefully as if you're on your way to do something urgent, and go for the exit with the fewest people near it. You can also ask a friend to be bad cop so when people stop you to chat, the friend adopts a sour expression and you say, 'Look, I'm sorry, Murph wants me to get going, I'd love to stay and chat, but *(gesture apologetically at sour friend)* you know, Murph's a bit . . .'

On this occasion, Murph was actually Having Fun so I was on my own at the exit. I slipped out and found myself in a dark alley in the backblocks of Sydney's inner west. I pulled out my phone to find my location on Google maps and triumphantly texted Murph that I was already outta there. I was home in my PJs binge-watching *The Americans* by 7.46 pm. If that's not winning at life, I don't know what is.

Annabel, hogging the last word

a Not to hog the last word, but point one is the least surprising confirmation of a suspicion in my long career of being right about things.

> Point one is the least surprising confirmation of a suspicion in my long career of being right about things.

the frump nightie

Ⓛ So Annabel texts me. 'I've dropped a bag of stuff out the front of your place and a frump nightie,' it says. I'm thinking . . . she drops me off a frump nightie. Anyway, so I've put it on. It certainly is frumpy, it's gigantic. It's black and it's neck-to-knee coverage. No – neck-to-ankle coverage, actually.

Ⓐ I've got one in grey marle and I love it. I love it uncontrollably.

Ⓛ How did you get into these things?

Ⓐ I bought them from a website. It's not a good website, it's one of those ones that seems suspiciously cheap and I don't really shop there very often, but for a neck-to-knee coverall situation . . .

Ⓛ Are you wanting me to never have sex with anyone ever again?

Ⓐ I will come and live with you here and we will just be entirely chaste but also covered from neck to knee.

Ⓛ I think any men who walked in here would not only be turned off, they might actually even be scared.

ouch

Ⓛ I had to go to an appointment with my son this morning. And the lady who was taking us said, 'Sometimes I see you on TV and I think, "I need some of those hair and make-up people" because I see you every Monday morning and then I see you on Monday night . . .'

Ⓐ And you look like a real dirtbag.

well hello

get out of the way,
you nobody!

Ⓛ Something I hate and dodge as much as possible is if we have to go to the Logies and they want you to walk on the red carpet and get your photo taken.

Ⓐ I did that once. It was the most upsetting moment of my life because I was a nominee so they were like, 'Go down the bit where people take photos,' and I'm like, 'I feel like the greatest nong ever.' So I'm mincing along and making eye contact with nobody because nobody knew who I was. And I got to the point where I walked along and all these photographers were just going, 'Nah, it's all right.' It was cameras down, like you're waiting for Hugh Sheridan or someone instead.

Ⓛ My friend Lisa Millar once had to go to the Logies and she was shouted at by a photographer who said: 'Get out of the way, you nobody!'

just the idiot
in the '50s dress

Ⓛ Do you pay attention to contemporary fashion?

Ⓐ It's hard for me to demonstrate any commitment that I have to contemporary fashion because the fashion I admire doesn't tend to really change that much. I very rarely go into a shop, but sometimes I buy things online that I know will fit me . . . and they're kind of unchanging, I must say, which makes me a loser, I know. But at least I'm just the idiot wearing a '50s dress all the time. And when I look back in 20 years' time, I'm still kind of doing that. I just think, 'Hey, I looked great. I continue to look great.'

Ⓛ Also, that look really suits you and you do look great. So why tamper with that?

Ⓐ I did some photo shoot where I got put into something and I looked at it and just went, 'I can see that this is a great outfit. It's very fashion forward, but I'm just going to look at that picture and think, "Dear god, I look like a lunatic."'

what if we were more

beautiful?

a Really, who can be bothered?

L No offence, love, but we haven't started out as great beauties. So I don't think that we probably put a lot of currency in our appearance.

a That is the most insulting compliment I've ever received, just unpacking it.

L If we were more beautiful, don't you think that if that was our primary currency, we would be more likely to try to protect that currency?

a Whereas your currency is being irritating.

L And I am world class at that. Having said that, I still find it sometimes confronting to see myself on TV or whatever and think, 'Is that what I look like now?'

a Well, yeah, I guess you have a sort of internal idea of what you look like and then you're confronted by the mirror.

L Internally I look like Angelina Jolie and then I see myself and go, 'Nope, I look like Tilda Swinton.'

a I find it hardest to listen to myself. I have the stupidest sounding voice. I can't bear it. I really can't hack it.

L And yet you talk so much.

a I do. I never shut up.

frock up

or cop out?

L Crabb, do you ever put make-up on? Like in your everyday life?

a Yeah, I do if I'm going to speak somewhere. I always do my hair and put make-up on. Because I feel like there's something weird that happens once you do a bit of television. People expect you to look the way that you look when you're on television. And then when you turn up looking like you normally look,

well hello

which is like a robber's dog, then people get weird. I've had, I don't know, like, some people will get offended if I'm not wearing a dress.

🅛 If you're not wearing a frocky type?

🅐 Right, it's so weird.

🅛 It freaks me out when you're wearing jeans.

🅐 And I feel so strange. One day I'll understand the psychiatry of this, but I feel as though if I don't make an effort to try to form some sort of approximation of what I looked like once on TV, then I'm insulting these people by not having made an effort, right? Isn't that so strange? And I think, 'Annabel, you're a bloody idiot.'

🅛 Somebody in the street once said to me that I was much better looking on television. Which is true. I mean, it'd be nice if you didn't tell me that, given I'm only on television for half an hour a day, and I'm off television for the other 23 and a half.

🅐 I turned up to do someone's book event once. I was having the worst week, and my children were like, 'Where are you going?' and I cried a little bit on the way there. Anyway, I turned up and this woman looked me up and down and said, 'Oh, you're quite slender in real life, aren't you?' I just thought, 'I feel now I'd like to punch your face.' I didn't – I said, 'How ... how *kind* of you to say so.' Anyway, we recovered from there, it was fine, but it's funny – there is a thing where once you're on television, people can think that everything about you is up for generalised comment.

behold:
the Diabolical Mum Bag

If any fashion accessory screamed 'I don't care' more than Sales's much-maligned and yet somehow much-loved Diabolical Mum Bag, we'd like to meet it and shout it a cheap feed.

Leigh arrived to record a podcast episode hauling two holdalls: one that carried the Medieval Contraceptive Device and the other a massive green, orange, red and yellow striped canvas bag that contained *everything* else, including 'gym gear and, like, actual crockery', according to an appalled Crabb.

'It's a lovely bag, lovely,' an indignant Sales retorted. 'I bought it at a Thai restaurant. The waitress was selling bags out of her boot out the back.'

Annabel: 'Yes, of course you did. *[Rummaging through DMB]* I'm sure there's another piano in here. You throw out books but you kept *this*?'

Stung by the criticism, Leigh appealed to the Chatters for some boosterism, posting a photo of her questionable sack on the *Chat 10 Looks 3* Facebook group with the caption, 'Annabel Crabb accuses me of carrying a "diabolical mum bag" around the ABC. This is it. Nothing wrong with it!'

Some Chatters tut-tutted her tote.

'It's the bag you want when you can't choose your favourite colour,' joked one wag in the comments.

'Or you want it to camouflage with your couch,' replied another.

'Or with a hotel curtain.' (Another.)

'Or a 1992 motel bedspread.' (Yes, very good everyone.)

Sales was trolled by her own mother, the redoubtable Ann Sales, who remarked that it 'would go well with my red bandana, black tie-dyed shirt and yellow bell-bottom pants'.

But then: a groundswell of solidarity! Chatters Put Out Their Mum Bags, posting pictures of their bulky carriers and messages of praise for a portly portmanteau.

'Everyone gives me stick about my mum bag,' reported one comrade. 'That is, until they need tissues/chewing gum/roll-up shopping bags/sunscreen/ear plugs/sanitary items/a Korg tuner/notepaper/pens/hand cream/wipes/throat lozenges/random confiscated Lego pieces . . .'

Then this: 'I found two umbrellas in my handbag; I thought I had lost the first, so I bought another one. Not sure if I should be proud or ashamed of that.'

And this piece of nicely done diplomacy: 'Well, it's . . . capacious. What I am *loving* though, is how super-accomplished Salesy is AND she's totally unapologetic about her bag. Clearly. Does. Not. Give. A. Rats. I personally wouldn't be here if it was all Birkin bags and $1000 shoes. Have whatever bag you want, Salesy – you're awesome.'

Chatter Megan Mundy went so far as to set up a 'Group fund for a new bag for Salesy', which unbelievably raised $100 before a bemused Leigh gratefully redirected the cash to Story Factory, a creative writing centre for young people.

Leigh

In the latest podcast Annabel Crabb accuses me of carrying a 'diabolical mum bag' around the ABC. This is it. Nothing wrong with it!

Top marks, though, to the cheeky TV visionary who wrote: 'In Annabel Crabb's new series *The Bag*, she will be exploring the never-before-seen side of Sales's bag, including the subterranean levels, rituals and the characters that make it so special.'

Sadly, that show was never made. But we can report that, after literally years of lugging Leigh's crap around, the Diabolical Mum Bag has been retired to live on a lovely farm for old handbags.

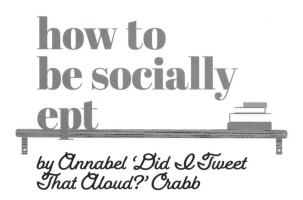

how to be socially ept

by Annabel 'Did I Tweet That Aloud?' Crabb

Social media is a thing I would struggle to explain to my 13-year-old self, and yet my 13-year-old daughter has never known a world in which it didn't exist. It's an astonishing generational gap to bridge, and it's not necessarily a negative one, either. In a remarkably short time, social media has provided a solution to geographical isolation, allowed long-distance friends and family to stay in touch, and ensured that no one with a phone ever has to be 'the only gay in the village' again. But the perennial question for every young person – how to be in the world? – has morphed into an ancillary one: how to be on social media? Here are the five questions I ask myself before I post something.

1. **Am I giving or am I taking?**

This is a fairly easy one to answer. Is whatever you're planning to post providing something – an image, a link, a thought – or is it seeking to devalue or take down something that someone else has posted? If it's the second kind, it doesn't mean you shouldn't do it, but if you look at the kind of posts you typically make and the second kind outweighs the first, you might want to ask yourself why. And then ask yourself Question Two:

2. **Is this useful?**

The big question. Usefulness doesn't have to be as boring as it sounds. Being useful might be as simple as bringing a tiny, harmless moment of delight to someone. And that's more than fine. I remember back in

well hello

the early days of Twitter hearing endless denunciations from people who didn't see the point of it, declaring that they 'didn't want to know what strangers were having for lunch'. And yet, I also recall at that time reading a tweet by a total stranger that said, 'This sandwich is exactly as disappointing as I feared it would be.' And it made me laugh and laugh, because I too am the person who goes into a sandwich shop and looks at the sandwiches and leaves empty-handed because I fear sandwich disappointment. Was that tweet world-changing? Would anyone else remember it? No. But I've always remembered it because it said something small and funny and true. And the 'small, funny, true' things are the engine room of these vast information exchanges.

There are more important forms of usefulness, of course, but the general principle is to try to tick one box or other. Am I sharing something powerful, thought-provoking, beautiful, exhilarating, or in some way useful for another person to see?

3. Am I hurting someone? And if so, is it worth it?

A social media post can absolutely still be useful even if it hurts someone. Hard things have to be said in every format of communication. But the big question is: is it worth it? By which I mean, with reference to Question One, is the harm or hurt caused by what you're about to post outweighed by its usefulness? If you're exposing a wrong, or speaking up for someone vulnerable, or indeed if you are that vulnerable person, then yes, of course it's worth it. If you're joining in on something you are not practically enhancing or developing further by your presence, then I direct you to Question Two.

These questions are important even if you are – and you most assuredly are – only a teeny tiny speck in a vast ocean of communication. If you dislike the negativity of social media, then consider deeply whether you are a part of the problem or a part of the solution. You might be a speck, but you're responsible for your speckdom.

4. Is this really about me?

The way social media works is that it brings to your attention things that people are saying about you. As you scroll through your replies or mentions or responses to something you've posted on Facebook, it's almost as if the universe recalibrates with you at the centre of it. It makes it seem like the whole world is talking about you (or shouting at you, on a bad day). It also makes your own contribution seem more weighty and necessary than it actually is. Essentially, it exaggerates the self. Before you join a pile-on or call someone out or pick a fight, ask yourself: am I doing this because it will help change a bad situation or right a wrong? Or am I doing it to change someone's perception of me?

Needless to say, if you're posting a selfie, do pause to ask yourself whether the world really needs another one.

5. Will I regret this later?

This question is not about posting boozy shots that your future boss might later see and draw CONCLUSIONS from. I think most of us have had that hammered into us by now. What I'm talking about here is the importance of remembering the role that time plays, even in an instantaneous communication platform. Just because you *can* make an immediate riposte on social media about something that exercises/outrages/upsets you, doesn't mean you necessarily *should*. Time holds extraordinary properties on social media. For one thing, it marches things on pretty quickly, and while the argument with which you are preoccupied at this very second might seem large and all-consuming in the moment, by tomorrow it will have assumed a different shape and perspective. This is especially true in cases where *you* are the target of others' contempt or abuse. Striking back in such circumstances can be overwhelmingly tempting. But take a moment to ask yourself, slowly, Questions One and Two. Time is on your side.

Also, personally, before I post a tweet I like to read it in my head, in senator Eric Abetz's voice. This might not work for everyone.

well hello

sure-fire way to a nervous breakdown

ⓐ I've got my children on school holidays and so I sit before you really on the verge of a total nervous breakdown. I cried a bit on my way in to work today. The last few weeks I've been about to lose my 'nana. It's full-on. Budget and election times are freaky anyway, but I've got a *Quarterly Essay* due in July

and then a book due in August. And then I've signed up for a bunch of things in the Sydney Writers' Festival. And I think, actually, as this podcast has got a bit more widely listened to, I've been fielding the most hilarious range of different requests – all of which are so much fun, and interesting, but they all kind of mount up, as well. So, I've actually had this situation in the last few weeks where I've done a very, very, very serious thing – and I'm not sure if, when I tell you, you will change the way you think about me.

ⓛ Well, two things come to my mind. One is: really interested to hear this; and two is: I'd better not tell you about an email I received this morning from somebody asking us to do something.

ⓐ Oh, good. So . . . I have read a self-help book. [*Laughs hysterically.*] Your face. We should just take a picture of it. This is Sales's face.

Sales's face on hearing that Crabb has read a self-help book.

𝓛 Not a genre generally of which I approve, no.

ⓐ I just thought, I'm really bad at saying no. I've probably been a busy person for, like, 20 years. And during moments in that time, I felt overwhelmed by juggling stuff and, you know, feeling guilty about not paying enough attention to everybody, or doing all the jobs that I have well enough, and all that sort of bullshit that we all lie awake worrying about from time to time. And people have periodically said to me, 'You need to learn how to say no,' and I've sort of got cross with them when they've said that sometimes, because I think, 'You're a person that's asking me, do you want me to say no to everybody else and say yes to you?' That's a bit of a problem, because when you get to that stage where you feel a bit overwhelmed, then what happens is sometimes you get snappy with people who you love as well. You're like, 'Oh god, don't ring me for a lovely chat right now, I can't bear it.'

𝓛 I refer to you Exhibit A, when I was cranky last year that people dared to ring me on my birthday.

ⓐ That was a dark time. 'Don't even be nice to me, because I haven't got enough time to thank you for being nice.' Honestly, it's actually really messed up. I had this problem in budget week – and this is how I came to get onto this – I had a really sore jaw. And I thought, 'This is where my failure to go to the dentist for about five years is going to catch up with me, because I've now got an abscess. And if I go into budget lock-up and my tooth blows out – they don't care.' They won't let you out.

𝓛 Luckily for you, before I was posted as a foreign correspondent I had to do disaster survival training, and one of the things I was given was a home dental kit and a few basic lessons in the event that I found myself in a disaster zone and somebody had an abscessed tooth or something like that that needed immediate removal.

ⓐ You could have extracted my tooth *in* budget lock-up. Imagine that! Like, you know, Scott Morrison's wandering around, and Josh Frydenberg, and you're like, 'Excuse me, I'm just extracting Crabb's third molar.'

𝓛 'Don't stand too close, it's gonna blow!'

ⓐ I went to my dentist, who said, 'There is nothing wrong with your teeth. You are clenching your jaw.' And I've been seeing a physio who's been doing

well hello

all these insane things to my neck. And she's like, 'You need to get a bit less stressed.' No shit, Sherlock. So, I thought, why am I stressed? I feel guilty because there's all these people who have asked me to do things I haven't responded to, and I've ignored them for so long that I feel like I've got to say yes. **Hang on a minute. Let's unpack all of this.**

So I asked my busy friend. I texted her at five past five, loading it into her emotional carry-bag when she's trying to get her kids organised. But she gave me a few pieces of advice. One was a really good set of rigorous rules around saying no, and the other one was that she recommended that I listen to Oprah Winfrey talking about this on the first podcast of the Goop series with Gwyneth Paltrow.

Ⓛ You are excelling today. Self-help books. Goop with Gwyneth Paltrow.

ⓐ I'm wearing a Yoni egg right now. I was hesitant about listening to a Goop podcast. But it made me realise why Oprah is so incredibly popular. She said something that really made me start thinking about why I'm bad at saying no. So she's done stuff for this guy a couple of times, and he's come back again. And she was kind of like, 'Why are you asking me, dude, I've just done something for you. Why are you asking me again? I'm getting kind of enraged.' And then she thought, 'Well, hang on a minute. Why wouldn't you ask me again? Because every time you ask me, I say yes. And I make out like it's not really a big deal for me, because I'm trying to make you happy. And that is on me; I'm engineering this situation.' And *I* thought, yeah, actually, if someone is asking you to do something, it's not in itself a stressful thing.

Ⓛ Is this really a long-winded way of you telling me that you—?

ⓐ I can't come to your birthday party. **Who am I kidding?! You're not having a birthday party.**

Ⓛ Just for any of my friends: I'm not actually having a birthday party. We're just being horses' arses.

ⓐ When someone asks me to do something, my default position is yes. And then I sort of sometimes feel relieved if there's a reason I can't go. And most of the things I get asked to do are actually awesome things. I know I would enjoy doing that thing. No, don't titter . . .

Ⓛ I'm tittering, because I'm thinking of my next line: 'ABC Fat Cat Moans About Being Invited to Opening Nights and Lovely Parties.'

ⓐ The only problem is, of course, that I've got to go on the day . . . and explain to the kids why I'm nicking off. So I've changed my settings now. And my main thing is, I will assume that I won't do things unless there's a compelling reason why it can work. I found a book on how to say no, and it's called *How to Say No Without Feeling Guilty*.

ⓛ My issue is I assign problems to Future Leigh so that Present Leigh can feel good. I'll say, 'I'm really busy at the moment, but you know, I could do it next month.' And so then it comes the next month, Future Leigh turns into Present Leigh, who wants to kill Past Leigh for having locked her into it.

ⓐ That Past Leigh is a real jerk.

ⓛ I've talked to a friend about this exact thing. And he was saying there's a great Oprah Winfrey quote where she says, 'You have to remember "No" is a complete sentence.' You can just say no, and not then, 'No, because I've had to blah, blah, blah.' Just: 'I'm really sorry. Hope you have a great event,' or whatever. He also told me a friend of his who edited a literary journal sent out a request to a whole lot of writers to say, would you consider writing X, Y, Z for me? Somebody replied, 'Dear So-and So, no, I don't want to.' How good would that be, to just say that? So good.

ⓐ Oh, what a bunch of whining gits we are.

ⓛ What whining sooks.

well hello

strobe cream

Crabb and Sales are in Leigh's hotel room in Canberra, getting ready for the Federal Parliamentary Press Gallery's Midwinter Ball. In an earlier episode, Sales has already given Crabb a tutorial on how to cunningly angle one's face near a window to provide flawless selfie lighting. Now they bunglingly attempt to self-educate about how to apply a highlighting cosmetic called Strobe Cream.

Backstage at a show in Sydney, as evidenced by the bottle of wine and the baked goods. Strobe Cream has been deftly deployed by Sales for a subtly intense dewiness.

Ⓛ I've just been googling Strobe Cream and how to use it and what it even is. Neither of us know what it is.

Ⓐ You just put some on your face.

Ⓛ Well, they said put a little bit on your index finger, in the apples of your cheeks, down your nose, and dot in your Cupid's bow – or, as you referred to it a moment ago, your moustache.

Ⓐ All right. I still look old and crazy. It's not working.

Ⓛ If anything, even crazier.

Ⓐ What about the forehead? Is that allowed or not?

Ⓛ I don't know. There were two instructions on the website. One said for 'subtle dewy effect' and one said for 'intense dewy effect'. Isn't that contradictory? How can you have intense dewiness? Like 'knowing innocence' or something.

Ⓐ 'Nymphomaniac virginity.'

Ⓛ Do you reckon that Tony Jones and Kerry O'Brien are in a hotel room doing their make-up together somewhere?

Ⓐ Almost certainly. You do look quite dewy.

Ⓛ Intensely dewy, or subtly dewy?

I Don't Care

Leigh's wardrobe spreadsheet is a real thing

Despite their – how shall we put this? – distinctly different personal styles, Annabel Crabb and Leigh Sales have on occasion turned up at events in almost the same outfits, either by blunder or by design. There was the live show in clashing geometric frocks, the one where they both turned up in polka dots, the one where they wore near-identical black dresses and the one that went all Dorothy when they both donned red shoes.

Any accidental outfit awkwardness is made all the more baffling by the stunning revelation in one podcast episode that Sales maintains a wardrobe planning document – henceforth known as Leigh's Wardrobe Spreadsheet – that *plots the outfits she wears on 7.30 each night literally weeks in advance.*

As Crabb scooped her mandible off the floor at this news, Sales defended her galactic level of organisation as reducing her mental load by 'saving a lot of time and hassle when I'd rather spend my time thinking about how to interview the prime minister'. She just consults the spreadsheet and – voila! – this evening's clothing choice was already made back in July.

Here it is, folks: Leigh's outfit planner for *7.30*, aka the Wardrobe Spreadsheet, nutted out weeks in advance with the advice of her friend and make-up artist, Christopher Sall. **(Crabb notes: Ummm, why is she wearing a wetsuit on air in Week Seven?)** (Sales has the last word, as usual: The wetsuit is a nickname Chris and I gave to a particularly figure-hugging navy-blue suit.)

well hello

To be fair, a lady who fronts a national current affairs program can't just rock up in the same clobber every evening, Karl Stefanovic-style. Much like the Queen, one must keep track of which natty jacket one wore with which blouse, with which skirt, with which tiara and when.

However, Annabel – whose modus operandi is 'consulting my floordrobe every morning and working out whether that grubby top's got one more day's wear in it' – accuses Leigh of self-insufficiency. 'Because you've done a spreadsheet for what you wear every day, you are *deskilled*; you are no good at something really basic that the rest of us have to deal with every single day, which is: what am I gonna wear today?'

The sort of nonsense that happens when one of you doesn't have an Official Leigh Sales Wardrobe Spreadsheet™.

Right of reply, as usual, goes to Sales. 'Are you really going to pretend that you don't meticulously pre-plan the outfits you wear on your TV programs? Spare me. You'd spend more time on eBay buying clothes and hanging out in your bedroom trialling various looks than I spend studying *Hamilton* lyrics.'

Leigh

Giving everyone a migraine at a Perth live show.

chapter 6

friendship

conversation

how to friend

(aka 'Listen, lady, you're not even in my Top Three')

a Now, I've been looking forward to having this conversation with you, Leigh, about friendship with a capital F.

L You've called me Leigh. It makes me feel a little bit nervous.

a I've noticed that whenever we're asked about friendship – sometimes people have interviewed us and kicked off with, 'Well, I'm here with Leigh Sales and her BFF, Annabel Crabb'– you quickly jump in every time to say, 'She's not my best friend. I mean, she's my friend, but I have many other friends who are better and older friends.' And I'm like, 'Okay, well actually I feel the same way.' But it always sounds really defensive when I say it. Now, what's going on here?

L Look, the reason I do that is not because you're not one of my best friends – because you are – it's just I have this anxiety about other friends of mine feeling hurt that you publicly get portrayed as my best friend when I feel like, say, my oldest childhood friend, Mandy, or—

a Childhood Friend Mandy, my nemesis.

L Or my friends Cath or Lisa, or any number of people. It's completely irrational, of course, because none of them are the kind of people to sit around going, 'This is an outrage! I am rightfully Sales's Best Friend!' But I don't want anyone to feel hurt. Do you know what I mean?

a I do know what you mean, but still – Mandy, I'm coming for you on a BMX.

L I assume you feel the same about your friend Wendy Sharpe, with whom you write your cookbooks.

a Yes, of course. She's my oldest friend. It's a funny thing, but friendship over a long period of time can turn into something like a relationship, like a romantic relationship, although ideally without the incessant sexual contact.

In some ways, our friendship is quite bizarre. People would listen to the podcast and assume we're constantly braiding each other's hair and living in each other's pockets and squeezing each other's zits.

Ⓛ I'm curious to see where you're taking this.

ⓐ What I mean is this notion of exclusivity or this sense that there is someone with whom you have a closer bond than anybody else. It's a prejudice around friendship, I suppose. And it's about the way others see you, and who is the closest to that person then? Is it *you* or is it *you*? I think it can get quite fraught.

Ⓛ I guess it depends on how both parties view the relationship and how central and important it is to both people. If one person feels that we should be speaking every day but the other person doesn't want that, then it can become tricky. Or if I had a friend to whom I was speaking every day and then they got usurped by you because I started talking to you every day instead, then I think that can sometimes get antsy.

ⓐ In some ways, our friendship is quite a bizarre friendship. People would listen to the podcast and assume that we're constantly braiding each other's hair and living in each other's pockets and squeezing each other's zits. I actually said this once to somebody who was saying, 'You must have so much fun.' And I'm like, 'Well, we do have a lot of fun but you hear about 95 per cent of it if you listen to the podcast.'

Ⓛ Totally.

ⓐ This friendship is incredibly focused and fulfilling because we do set aside time just to have a conversation, which is actually something that I do with hardly any of my other friends. I mean, hardly any of my other better, closer and more charming friends.

Ⓛ That is true. But the result of that is we almost never have a conversation about anything personal or deeply meaningful because we are always recording and broadcasting them. We don't go into a deep personal level, which is what is required to be truly close friends.

ⓐ You are my conversational sex worker.

Save it for the podcast!

𝓛 I also think there's an element of performance in our conversation because it's being recorded. I notice that even more when we do a live show and we've got an audience. We had dinner at a pub the other week and I was sitting next to you. And I can't even remember what we were talking about, but I was struck later by the thought, 'Jeez, I really enjoyed that conversation with Crabb.' And it was partly because it was just a normal conversation with no need for me to be actively listening in a performance sense and thinking, 'Right, where are we going to take this? How are we going to segue into the next thing? How much time is available, blah, blah, blah.' It was just really pleasant.

a Welcome to the world of the normal person. Also, I wish I had a buck for every time we've had a conversation and one of us has said, 'Quick, stop talking about this, save it for the podcast!' Which is so weird, right?

Childhood friend Mandy

𝓛 One of the other things I often think about regarding friends is the different types of friends that you have. For example, Childhood Friend Mandy: we speak fairly infrequently, but because we've been friends for nearly 40 years, and we grew up together, there's some kind of muscle memory around that friendship. She's like my sister because we used to just ride our bikes around every single day for years and years. Whenever I see her, it literally does pick up exactly where it left off and we just never stop yapping. It's nonstop the entire time.

a Do you talk about things that happen when you grew up, or do you talk about your lives now?

𝓛 You know what? I find it really hard to even tell you what we talk about. I can tell you we never talk about our jobs. We just fill the space talking and we're always laughing our arses off. On paper we have absolutely nothing in common. I probably wouldn't meet Mandy today. She did accounting at uni, she works at a university now and she lives in a semi-rural area on the outskirts of Brisbane.

And I live in inner-city Sydney and work as a journalist. Our paths would never cross. She has two daughters. I have two sons. Her kids are more than a decade older than mine.

a She loves fairy-wrens.

L Yes, she's an avid birdwatcher. It's such a divergence of experience since childhood. But we talk so easily and I'm often struck by those childhood bonds and how tight they are.

a There's only a handful of people in the world with whom you can share a common awareness of all of your early life experiences, I suppose. There's siblings and other close friends if you have them, but there's not many of them, particularly if you've moved around a bit, like you have. So that's a vanishingly small commodity, somebody to whom you can say one word and they know exactly all the funny stories that are connected to that word.

L If you're talking to somebody about Two Wells, which is where *you* grew up – I've never been there so I don't have any shorthand for when you say 'Two Wells'. Whereas if you mentioned it to Wendy, there's this whole rich history and background that her brain can immediately fill in. I remember when you did Julia Zemiro's show *Home Delivery* and I saw the property where your parents live and where you grew up. It was nothing like what I'd imagined.

a Really?

L No. With my old friends from school, if I mention my mother or my brother or something about Bald Hills, where we grew up, I don't need to background any of that. When you meet new people, though, they're at the level of 'So is your brother older or younger?' and you think, 'God, there is a helluva lot to explain.'

Childhood Friend Mandy, Leigh's oldest friend from primary school, who performed the role of Annabel Crabb until Annabel Crabb came along – notably, being dragged into mad schemes like inventing new choreography for the school production of *Grease* (pictured) and being badgered into taking organ lessons. She did withstand the bullying about starting Highland dancing, which is possibly why one of this duo managed to have a boyfriend in high school.

Childhood Friend Wendy, in a hand-crocheted jumper she now wishes she had kept.

a I've got a whole vocabulary of stuff with Wendy where we both know what each other means, but the original meaning of the phrase or the reference is so bizarrely random. For example, when she was a teenager, she went to high school in Adelaide and she used to live with her grandmother, a fantastic woman who ingrained a lot of Wendy's cooking habits. Her name was Gwen, and she was widowed. So she was pleased to have Wendy around and I used to go and stay at Wendy's grandma's too.

There was this friend called ... I think his name was Doug. He had been a friend of Wendy's grandfather. And he used to pop around every now and again, just to check that everything was all right and whatever. Wendy's grandmother had a dog and you'd know if Doug had visited because he would give it a bit of meat. Wendy would say, 'Dog's chewing a piece of meat. Doug must be here.' And now the expression 'Dog's chewing a piece of meat' for us means 'odds-on this is happening'. So we might say, 'Dog's chewing a piece of meat, Australia will win the World Cup' or something like that. It's part of our unique language.

L Then you have your people who, I guess, circumstantially become your friends because you're mixing together every day through work or school or whatever. Sometimes those friendships transcend the shared experience and they go on to become long and old friends, but sometimes they only last for that period of time.

The test of time

L One thing I've learned is not to feel any sense of pressure to extend a friendship beyond its point of utility, or sadness if it was only for a season. When I was younger, I used to feel like, 'I'm not speaking to so-and-so as much as I used to now that we've finished university' and I'd try to push it to last.

well hello

But sometimes whatever the thing was that you had in common, once that's gone, the friendship is just not as close. It's better to view the friendship in a way that says, 'Well, that was a wonderful friendship for that time and now it's not so intense and that's okay.'

ⓐ So as a whole entity, rather than something that you've allowed to decay and disappear. That's a really healthy way of looking at it. And then particularly, I mean, you've moved around, you've been a correspondent, it really throws you from intense situation into intense situation and you develop friendships to deal with those circumstances . . . why are you sniggering there?

ⓛ Oh, just because it's reminding me, when you said I was a correspondent, something I once said to Lisa Millar that she still raises. So Lisa and I met . . . it would have been in the mid '90s. She was a journalist in Canberra for the ABC, and I'd only just recently started in the ABC in Brisbane. We had some mutual friends and we'd both been invited to this dinner. I got to the restaurant two minutes early and she'd already been there for 10 minutes and we introduced ourselves. I said, 'No matter how much I try to be fashionably late, I'm still always on time. I just tried to arrive five minutes late and I'm still two minutes early.' And Lisa said, 'Me too! I'm always 10 minutes early for everything!' And, as I've learned over more than 20 years of friendship, she really is. Anyway, we became great friends. Then we ended up living in Washington and being correspondents at the same time. At the end of her posting, I said, 'Well, I guess now we'll see if we're as close friends as we think.' And she said, 'What do you mean?' I said, 'Now that we won't be working together every day, we'll have to see if we remain as close and if the friendship survives the test of time.' She had no doubt we'd stay friends and she was appalled at how blunt I was. Today, fifteen years later, occasionally she'll do something lovely for me and I'll say, 'Thank you so much, you're an incredible friend. I don't know how I would survive without you.' And she'll go sarcastically,

'But, Salesy, have I stood the test of time yet?'

ⓐ Honestly, how has she tolerated you?

Hanging on the telephone

L You always have friends you talk to every day about all the minutiae of your life. At the moment, the person I talk to most is my *7.30* colleague Justin Stevens. We have to discuss work a lot so we talk or text a dozen times a day; we have a constant series of running jokes as well. But then I have a few little WhatsApp groups that are pretty much a constant running conversation. There's one that you're in, another one called the London Gang. I get a lot of pleasure out of them because the beauty of those is that if you've got something to say, you can contribute, but also you can just read and enjoy it if you're busy or you don't have anything to add, and you still feel connected to your friends and to the group.

a Do you ring friends for a chat or do you default into keeping in touch over, like, those WhatsApp platforms?

L I've definitely become more reliant on texting and keeping in touch on those kinds of platforms. But I do still like to ring. I have certain friends I ring multiple times a week, like Lisa and my great friends Cath Sullivan or Pam Williams. I try to speak to my mother once a week, although I don't always. What about you?

a That's good. I think it's really, really hodgepodge, to be honest. I hardly ever talk to Wendy. We keep in touch now mainly via WhatsApp, but I mean, that's got to do with different time zones. We tend to have bursts of exchanges and then nothing for a month.

I think one of my flaws is that I'm slightly shambolic and it means that I spend time feeling guilty about not keeping in touch more with people. Whereas if I were more organised, like you, I would probably do it in a more structured fashion.

I don't think I'm a super great friend, really, to be honest. I mean, I will come in bursts of helpfulness of dropping around soup or something. But I'll realise that two months have gone by and I haven't checked in on somebody and then you feel like shit. I avoid some platforms. I avoid Facebook because I find it so full-on. I can't keep up with the traffic and the interactions.

well hello

I'll keep your details on file

'You seem really lovely and I've enjoyed meeting you, but I don't have any openings for new friends at the moment. I'll be in touch if I do.'

L How do you handle it when you feel like a friendship has run its course, particularly if the other party is still like, 'Hey, we should catch up,' or if it's somebody you only know a little bit and they're wanting to be a closer friend but you know that you don't really want to be?

a The problem is I really like people. I enjoy meeting new people, I enjoy talking to new people, and I love hearing about other people's lives. My favourite thing is to meet someone, for example, at a dinner party who's got a tremendously strange job. I really find that thrilling. I'll sit next to someone at an event and be genuinely fascinated by that person. But I wonder sometimes if I'm behaving like, 'let's be friends forever'. There's a limit to how many people you can be close friends with and I guess when you get to our age, you're like, not recruiting. I've got enough friends that I *already* neglect.

L 'You seem really lovely and I've enjoyed meeting you, but I don't have any openings for new friends at the moment. I'll be in touch if I do.'

a 'I've enjoyed your presentation and I'll certainly keep your details on file.'

L 'I'm happy to give you a great reference to Annabel Crabb, she's got a position going for a friend at the moment.'

a The thing that I feel guiltiest about in my life, like the thing that wakes me up in the middle of the night is always, 'Have I paid enough attention to this person? Am I looking after that person? Or am I a terrible friend?'

L I feel guilty as well about not giving my good friends enough of my time. When I have a free night, I prefer to see my good friends, not meet new people. In Sydney I've got probably a dozen people that I would consider my inner circle. And so if I'm free on a Saturday night I'll think, 'Right, I haven't seen George and Derek, I haven't seen Melanie and Knut, I haven't seen AJ.' My small group of people are the same people I would prefer to see more of.

ⓐ I was thinking about old friendships recently because, in a tragic, awful circumstance, a friend of mine from years ago – decades, really – took her own life. It was terrible, unthinkable. But one thing that was incredibly moving to me was realising how that person had reached out to other old friends at the end of her life, asking for help. Some of them she'd kept in close touch with, some of them she'd not seen for many years. And they'd readily helped her. She'd asked for support and they'd given it so generously. I wasn't one of them, but it was a very affecting experience and, in a way, a comfort to know that she didn't need to feel alone. It made me think, you can reach back. Those friendships are like bank deposits, I suppose, that sit there for ages. Maybe they don't get as whittled away by federal government fees and charges as you might imagine.

ⓛ I'm often amazed at how fully formed our personalities are from a young age, and people I really liked when I was 12 or 13 or 21 or 22 I can see today as 47-year-olds, and there's still something about them that I really like.

Who's doing the bloody dishes then

ⓐ As I get older, I get so much more uncomplicated pleasure out of friendships, particularly from my female friendships. I guess maybe in the early part of your life, you're more preoccupied with romance, the exciting stage of being in love, that sort of thing. And then once that's not really a dominant motivator, you start really enjoying your non-romantic friendships as a real bonus to life.

When I think about the friendship that *we* have, it's all upside because we plan a time to have a conversation, which we absolutely enjoy. We both come away – or, at least, I do – with ideas of things to read and watch and think about. I feel like I have an opportunity to borrow your brain and scrounge some things from it and then I'm never going to have an argument with you about doing the dishes. It's like an intimate relationship without the inevitable bickering over things. And that's an amazing thing to have.

well hello

Ⓛ Totally. A lot of my female friends say they have a sense that our close female friendships are the defining relationships of our life, not our relationships with men. My romantic relationships seem to come and go, but my female friendships are constant.

Ⓐ I really enjoyed the book *The Weekend,* by Charlotte Wood, because I'm probably just old enough to be thinking about long-term female friendships. That book is this incredible portrait of these four women who are massively different and who are spending a weekend together. Well, no – three of them are. One of them is dead and the other three are clearing out her house. They've had fallings-out over the years and rapprochements, and it made me think about how much bullshit you put up with from your friends, how you ignore things to preserve the friendship, how you get around and survive fallings-out. I thought it was really interesting because I don't habitually have massive fallings-out with my friends.

Ⓛ Me neither.

Ⓐ And it made me wonder, do people put up with more bullshit from their friends than they would from their romantic partners, for instance?

Ⓛ I think with your romantic partner, it's more in your face because you're usually around them a lot. Whereas with your friends, you can get away from them. Guaranteed if we moved in together, we'd have more fights than we do now.

Ⓐ You'd last two days with my personal mess lying around and you'd be like, get me the hell out of here.

Dirty pool

Ⓛ We got off track! If there's somebody who wants more from friendship than you're prepared to give, how do you put limits around that?

Ⓐ Well, I hide and then I emigrate somewhere. No, I mean, it's hard. I feel very bad about it, but I also think that in the end you can only do what you've got room for in your life.

Ⓛ I guess people get the message.

Ⓐ That's what the human experience is like. You can't look after every person's expectations. I'm certainly the last to judge or feel resentful if I'm not invited somewhere. I don't ever hold that against someone because I just think life is so busy and weird that, in the average case, you're doing well if you're out of bed with your pants on.

🅛 I feel like one of the signs to me that a friendship is not great is if I start having any creeping sense of obligation. Like, I haven't spoken to that person and I owe them a call, or they're going to be cross at me because I haven't invited them to dinner or they've just sent a second email asking if I've seen their first. They've emailed me three times asking for coffee. Once I'm feeling a bit nagged—

🅐 Is that when you have your lawyers send them a letter?

🅛 You just hope that the laws of nature kick in. Like, if someone asks you for a coffee and you say, 'I'm not free, I'll get back to you when I am,' and then you never do . . . I feel like normal people let go lightly and think, 'Well, I guess she's busy or she's a single mother with two small boys or whatever, I get it.' And they don't hold it against me. Occasionally I'll get somebody where I feel like, 'Why do you keep hassling me so much?' Sometimes I say yes to somebody who wants something just to stop them from pestering me and then I really hate myself.

I'm not talking about good friends here. I'm talking about people on the periphery of my life. The reason I feel cross at myself is because I feel as if the two hours that I'm giving this person is two hours I've taken away from a genuinely close friend to whom I'd like to give more of my time. Or even just two hours where I could get some rest.

I've got better at it, actually, at just refusing to buckle. I think the reason for that was that there was a period where I looked in my diary and every social thing for a two-week period was something that I didn't really want to do. I was exhausted. And my diary had ended up with too many things that were sparked by conversations such as, 'You must come around for dinner, give us any date that you're free.'

🅐 That's dirty pool.

🅛 My good friend Cath called me on it and said, 'Why do you give your time to people who drain you instead of your actual friends? You need to learn to put some barriers up.' So now I am better at saying, 'I'm really busy. Sorry. I'm not putting anything in my diary at the moment. I'm trying to get some rest and spend more time with my boys.' You need time in your life to do nothing.

well hello

To give, and receive, a kindness

a I often think I would be happy to do something quite complicated for someone I've never met if they're deserving or in all sorts of strife. I'd be more likely to do that than go and have a cup of coffee with someone I don't care for.

L Totally. I try very hard when I do things for people – acts of kindness, I'm talking about – to ensure they feel they have to offer me absolutely nothing in return, not even for me to come in for a cup of tea. For example, if I'm dropping somebody off a meal because they've been unwell or they've had a baby or whatever, I will often drop it at the door and then text to say 'This is at your door' because I think any sense that you're doing an act of kindness and something is expected in return negates the act of kindness. Sometimes if people say to me, 'I don't know how to thank you for this,' I will say, 'You know what you could do for me that would be the best and most useful thing to return the favour? Please just never mention it ever again.'

a I think accepting kindness is a really important and huge thing to learn. Often people develop it in the course of trauma, like when something bad happens to them and they need so much help, they have this crash course in learning to accept help and not keep track and feel like they've got to repay. And, understanding that for somebody who does a kind thing, it is its own reward in many ways.

I've spent years looking at the *Chat 10 Looks 3* Facebook group and being regularly absolutely overwhelmed at the degree of effort that people will go to to do a conscious thing for somebody else or make somebody else's life a bit easier. It's been a really instructive lesson in understanding what the return is to the individual for being part of a group that is doing kind things for people or just doing something that makes somebody else's life easier.

There's a huge amount of research about the mental health benefits of doing something helpful for somebody else, because it lessens your own feelings of self-loathing because you think, 'Well actually, I can't be that much of a jerk, because I did that nice thing for that person.' It also helps give you a sense of control, that you have the power to make another person's life a bit easier.

L Exactly. It alleviates your sense of guilt and helplessness, because when something terrible happens to somebody, particularly somebody you're close to, you often feel so bad and you wish you could do something. The act of giving them some money, making a meal, taking their kids for a day or whatever – yes, they get the benefit of it, but it relieves your own bad feelings as well.

ⓐ There's nothing worse than feeling powerless and helpless. I have talked to a lot of people who have found your book *Any Ordinary Day* really useful – not just as an interesting read about how you'd respond if something terribly traumatic suddenly happened to you, but as a handbook on how to be around other people who have just had something absolutely, inexpressibly bad happen to them.

I'm just going to show up

ⓐ There are lots of bits of your book that I think about regularly. One that comes back to me again and again is Walter Mikac, whose family was killed in the Port Arthur massacre, talking about how he would see friends cross the road rather than speak to him because they just felt they couldn't deal with the scope and depth of the tragedy that had befallen him. They didn't know what to say or how to treat him. And I thought, 'That's strikingly unfair that someone to whom the worst has just happened then has these aftershocks of losing other friends because they don't know how to talk to that person.'

Weirdly enough, just after I had read the proofs of your book, your dad, Dale, suddenly died, and you called Murph and me and we went over to your place, to just help you get sorted as you went to the airport.

And on the way we were both remarking that, having just read your book, we felt much more capable of just being there with you, in the knowledge that there wasn't much we could do except be there and try to act normal.

ⓛ And you guys did an amazing job with that. It's not easy. Even when you're armed with that knowledge it's still hard to front up and be with people who are in pain. I remember it distinctly because it was a truly terrible period of my life. My son had had a big operation the week before and I was like, 'Oh my god, are you joking? This, and now Dad's died, how much more can I take?' And you guys came around and you were sympathetic, obviously, but you also acted normal – we were having a laugh. The next day, you went around to bring in washing I'd left on the line. You texted, **'We need to have a serious talk about your underwear because I'm sure all this stuff was fantastic when you got it at Pound Savers back in 1983, but it is in need of an upgrade.'**

When you're dealing with the funeral director and picking out the clothes for your father to be cremated in, those little bursts of normal life or stuff that makes you laugh really helps. Gwen at the time was on a holiday in the UK and she and her husband, Stephen, every day would send me funny little messages and check in.

Walter, who you mentioned, also said that later people would say to him, 'I avoided you because I felt like I didn't know what to say and I didn't want to make it worse.' And he was like, 'My wife, my six-year-old, my three-year-old had just been murdered. What do people imagine they could say that could make that worse?'

And there was a priest as well who I interviewed in the book who said, 'Anything that you think where it's like, I'm worried I'll say the wrong thing – you're making it about yourself instead of about the other person.' It's best to think, **you know what, I'm going to show up.** It's a sign to that person that I'm available if they need.

I read this wonderful story that Trent Dalton wrote for the *Weekend Australian Magazine* about a women's netball team called the Bayswater Boilers. Did you play netball when you were a kid?

ⓐ No, I could never ever get my head around the not-stepping-with-the-ball thing. I mean, it's really the only thing you have to remember with netball and I just couldn't do it. So no, I played hockey.

ⓛ Ah. You might not know, then, that there's a common little thing that you say on the netball court when you're open—

ⓐ 'Here if you need.'

ⓛ Yes, here if you need. Anyway, this group of women met in the 1980s when they played netball together, and that's become not only what they said on the court but also their saying in life. It means, basically: I'm not going to pry into your life and be a pain, but just so you know, I am here if you need me. I thought it was great shorthand for what women's friendships are like.

ⓐ In hockey it was more like, 'Stand back, bitch, because I'm going to knock your teeth out.' Also useful.

regretfully yours

The section in which our loveable bunglers write letters to each other, explaining why their friendship is over. Featuring passive-aggressive baking, fairy-wrens and show tunes (of course). Thanks to the Sydney Writers' Festival and Michaela McGuire and Marieke Hardy, whose idea this was in the first place for their 2015 People of Letters show 'A Letter to My Other Half', and who let Sales smuggle in a recording device not-quite-in-her-undies so it could all be turned into a podcast.

Leigh *to Annabel*

Dear Crabb,

Recently I've begun receiving a lot of correspondence addressed to both of us. Invitations, complaints, tweets decrying our hairstyles, even television viewing suggestions. 'You should watch *The Katering Show* on YouTube,' emailed my friend Ben the other day. 'You and Crabb will love it.' Even an Easter picnic invitation arrived with the disclaimer that 'perhaps your friend Annabel might like to come, too'. It's as if we've morphed into a double act. Admittedly, more Laverne and Shirley than Thelma and Louise, but a dynamic duo nonetheless.

All of this makes what I'm about to say that little bit more awkward. I'm afraid it's time to tell you that we can no longer be friends. I know that may seem harsh. It may even be surprising or leave you with the same sort of bewildering numbness that all Australians felt when Michael Kroger cut adrift Peter Costello, but in much the same way that back in 2005 Paris Hilton and Nicole Richie parted ways, it's time for me also to share your private sex tape with a group of friends. Oh, I mean, sorry – explain why we can no longer hang out.

Here's why my Number Two and Number Three best friends now have the opportunity to fight it out for the top spot. First, you are so funny that it's simply a matter of time until you cause me to pee my pants in public, possibly even on national television. I don't mind when you're funny in print. Like the time when all of our ABC salaries were leaked and you wrote in your column that the whole excruciating episode had an upside: offering indisputable assistance on some nagging workplace etiquette issues, such as 'when sharing a coffee with Quentin Dempster, who should pick up the bill?'. That was a close-run thing, but at least I was in the privacy of my own home.

The problem is, you selfishly keep causing me to burst into hysterics in places of considerably less convenience. Cinema lobbies, for example, such as the time we saw *Fifty Shades of Grey*. Or in crowded restaurants, such as the time recently when we were seemingly stood up for lunch by one of our great literary heroes.

No, I'm afraid that, as a woman of advancing years and receding pelvic floor control, I can no longer risk your company.

Second, this little passive-aggressive competitive baking thing that we have going on has to stop. You show up at my place with a lemon curd meringue cake, and I show up at yours with a mixed berry hazelnut cake with toffee-dipped blueberries. You pop by with a banana caramel layer cake, forcing me to retaliate with chocolate plum and almond Paris-Brest. Breaking point came when I swung by your place one morning recently with a pistachio and rosewater cream cake and you airily plopped down a plate of store-bought jam fancies and Tim Tams and declared, 'I've not had any time for baking this week. I've been too busy sewing Easter bonnets for the children.'

I see exactly where this is going, Crabb. And if you think we're going into some sort of Halloween sew-off where your three kids look exactly like Harry, Hermione and Ron, and your dog wears some contraption that makes her convincingly look like she has three heads, you've got another think coming.

This final reason may be a little paranoid, but I have a niggling suspicion that you don't actually like it when I break into musical numbers and show tunes. When you were once moaning about having three columns to write and I burst into, *'In every job that must be done there is an element of fun/ You find the fun and SNAP the job's a game'*, there was an old tightness to your smile. Another time when it was the 50th anniversary of *The Sound of Music*, I thought it would be lovely if we did a road trip together so you could hear me sing the entire soundtrack. It did strike me as odd that you asked me to pull over somewhere just outside Katoomba because you were busting for a wee and then you never came back. I assumed that you were so moved by my performance that you decided to do your own version of 'Climb Ev'ry Mountain', but it did give me a moment's pause.

Actually, no, I think I really am being paranoid about the show tunes thing. Forget I mentioned it. There are only TWO reasons, after all, that we can no longer be friends.

With fond, yet hopefully more distant, regards,
Sales

Annabel to **Leigh**

Dear Salesy,

We've had a good run, old bean. We've had a nice time, we've eaten some quality cake, and we have proved that there is a moderate listening audience for two forty-something women who squeeze themselves into an ABC utilities cupboard, piss themselves laughing for 35 minutes, including several actual snorts, and record it on their phone. If nothing else, we have established a new floor for media content and that's . . . well, it's an achievement of sorts. But – and this is going to be a hard letter to write – I'm not sure we can still be friends.

In explaining why, I'm going to start with the hardest reason. It's the hardest one because I'm absolutely certain that you are sweetly unaware of the extent to which I really am not that into show tunes.

You see, when I told you I liked show tunes, I meant I liked show tunes in an ironic way. I meant that I liked *Cabaret*, and some of the catchier numbers in *A Chorus Line*. When you said you liked show tunes, how was I to know that what you meant was 'I am the actual reincarnation of Ethel Merman. I not only know every show tune ever written, but also I can accompany myself on the piano and – given any excuse – I will. I can relate any contemporary event, breaking news story, emotional conundrum or indeed menial household task back to some piece of musical theatre, and if you turn your back for a second, I'll have shimmied into a pair of legwarmers faster than you can say *Sunday in the Park with George*.'

Sales, how could I possibly have foreseen your vast and unquenchable need for performance opportunities? I'm haggardly familiar with the signs now. You'll remind me that someone's written a new biography of Liza Minnelli, or did I know *Chitty Chitty Bang Bang* was first performed in Budapest on this exact date 30 years ago. You'll casually mention that the only free room you could find at the ABC to record our podcast was the Eugene Goossens Hall, and when I get there, you're already seated at the grand piano, your eyes shining. You're like one of those dogs who's always got the leash in its mouth, pleading for walkies. For god's sake, your three-year-old son can sing 'All That Jazz', including twinkle fingers.

But I can't go on playing Rex Harrison to your Audrey Hepburn. I adore you, but I sense that, at any given time, you are a heartbeat away from suggesting we co-write a high-kicking political musical, and I just can't live with that kind of fear. If we stay friends, I know with deadly certainty that on retirement I will be required to join the Glebe Community Players with you and be involved in their production of *Oh! What a Lovely War*. I can't do it, love. I'm out.

While we're having this tough conversation, I might as well say that another reason we're going to have to stop being friends is your relentless political bias. I mean, you're always nice enough to me, but something happens to you when you sit in that *7.30* chair. You get all, I don't know, womany. Kind of shrieky and interrupty and shrill and mean. And the worst thing is, you're not even consistent. I've seen you be mean to everyone from Tony Abbott to that dear little chap who is now the leader of the Greens. That's quite a typical female trait, you know. Indecisiveness. You wouldn't have ever got that with Kerry. I'm just saying this stuff because I'm being honest. Okay? We could keep being friends if you were just a little more . . . you know. Forensic.

Why else do we need to stop being friends? Well, for another thing, I don't think I can put up with your personal organisational skills anymore. Week after week, you email me at podcast time with a crisp list of all the fascinating, erudite things you've read this week, while I vaguely cast about for something I've perused that isn't a LEGO instruction book. I know for a fact that you wrote your letter for this thing a full month ago, while I am hurriedly writing it now because the event is this afternoon and I was going to devote more time to it and make it funnier but now it's the last minute and so it'll just have to do because I am VERY TIRED. I cannot be around your super-competence any more.

The last reason is pretty straightforward. You have a family of fairy-wrens living out the back of your place and you don't care. Seriously. What kind of psychopath is unmoved by fairy-wrens? They are the most adorable bird on the planet. So, yeah: it's over, lady.

As a final gesture, I enclose your birthday present. Your birthday was weeks ago. I did get the present on time, and I was going to give it to you at the budget, but then I couldn't find any wrapping paper and – oh, you know. Here it is. Thanks for all the memories.

Regretfully yours,

Crabb

well hello

candle Melanie

(aka *It seems to be . . . a candle in the bin*)

Episode 149 contained confronting material for anyone who's ever given Leigh a scented candle, after she excoriatingly dismissed them as **'the gift that says "I don't know who you are"... god, I hate scented candles'.** Episode 150 demonstrated yet again that people Crabb and Sales know and love actually listen to their deranged ramblings and thus Leigh received some personal blowback for being an ungrateful wretch. Crabb, naturally, enjoyed Sales's discomfort.

L Can I give you an update relating to the last podcast.

a My mind is already luxuriating in the thought of the humiliation that's about to befall you.

L You might remember last podcast I was somewhat dismissive of the gift of a candle.

a Oh, yeah. I remember that. **So do the good people at Overpriced Candles 'R' Us. Have you heard from a hundred people who gave you a candle?**

L So, my friend Melanie's texted me.

a By the way, the loveliest, most thoughtful, perceptive person in the world. I hope you feel bad about making her feel bad because she is the nicest person alive.

L Melanie's texted, 'Oh my god, I feel so bad 'cos *I've* given you a candle,' and I replied, 'No you haven't, because you give the best gifts in the world.' Melanie's an amazing cook, she's always showing up with, like, passionfruit curd, and honey from her dad's farm, and bowls of beautifully made rocky road . . .

a . . . and that candle that you forgot about. Because you instantly binned it! That's the thing. You've never registered anyone giving you a candle. So you think, 'No problem. I'm all clear.'

Candle Melanie's original photo, triumphantly dug out of her phone files and posted on the *Chat 10* Facebook group. *Picture: Melanie Andersen*

Ⓛ Melanie has texted me a photo of a candle she's given me *sitting on my dressing table* because at some point, I think, to say, 'Thank you, Melanie, for the candle,' I actually took her candle upstairs and lit it a bit before—

Ⓐ And then straight to the bin.

Ⓛ Can I just point out for all of you, Melanie supposedly being 'a lovely human'... what sort of a psychopath keeps a photo, years on, so they can prove to you that they gave you a candle?

Ⓐ YOU'RE the crazy person! You're the crazy person – you don't keep anything! The rest of us keep things sometimes.

Ⓛ Well, it really paid off for Mel but I told her I was going to tell the story in the podcast, and in the same way that people are now known as Hot Callum and other nicknames from the pod she would forever now be known as Candle Melanie. So – suck it, Mel.

A word from Melanie:

🅕 'Exhibit A: the photo of the candle I gave Sales, incriminatingly placed on her dressing table next to her favourite things. On the latest pod, Sales called me a psychopath for being able to produce this photo. Nice. Real nice. Look, Sales, it's not like I slept with the photo above my bed or anything! When you CLAIMED never to have received a candle from me, I thought, 'I'm sure I gave you one. I think you even sent me a photo of it in your room.' I then scrolled back through the photos in our text history and there it was, glinting away at me – gotcha! It's true I had to scroll for a while, but it was worth the RSI to catch Sales in a LIE! A TANGLED WEB OF DECEIT, I TELL YOU! Let's think about this for a moment, shall we? I give Sales a lovely, high-end scented candle from a place of love, kindness, and generosity. She takes this candle to her room, lights it, STAGES a photo, sends it to me (in lieu of sincere thanks), then throws it in the bin and forgets it ever existed. Who's the real psychopath?!'

oh, so you disagree?

Annabel analyses a few of the key disagreements between herself and Sales

margarine

a On most cooking-related matters, I think Leigh and I both (despite our public banter) know, deep down, that I am right. And on no topic am I more brutally and conspicuously correct than the matter of Butter v. Margarine. So why does she not capitulate? It's INFURIATING. I recall the very moment when (and I was well into my friendship with Leigh, so I suppose in some ways I blame myself for not having spotted it earlier) I was at her house, and I first witnessed her making sandwiches for her children. Out popped the tub of marge. Would I like one?

Reader, I would not. Noting the colour draining from my face (she is a trained observer), Sales observed blithely that she finds margarine more convenient. Plus, she pointed out, it's got pictures of olives on the tub so it's mainly olive oil, possibly originating from some sort of Tuscan hillside. It's amazing, really, that someone so otherwise smart can have such a yawning credibility gap on spreadables. Look at the label, lady. If it says 'soy lecithin', surely there are questions.

Sales making a sandwich in a deliberately provocative manner.

Now, I'm not a butter snob. Honestly, I'm not. I'm down with supermarket-brand butter; I don't need butter that's hand-dusted with flaky salt crystals and rolled lovingly into a wax-papered log (which is not to say I don't want it furiously). I just think, given the low differential in price point (about $4 for a 500 g tub of hydrogenated Frankenspread, about $5 for the same weight of butter) why would you deprive yourself?

🅛 [*Yet again seeking the final say*] Look, she's right – we basically agree on this matter. I would never use margarine in cooking; I always use unsalted butter. I just hate spreading butter on bread (and yes, yes, I know about leaving it out of the fridge, put your writing paper and your quills away, would-be correspondents).

interfering with recipes

🅐 Anyone who's ever written a cookbook knows that it's very hard to copyright recipes. You change an ingredient or a proportion, add some sumac, make it with gluten-free flour and suddenly it's a different recipe. Now, to most cookbook fans, this fact is nothing more than a vaguely interesting piece of trivia. To Leigh Sales, it's a personal challenge. I do not believe there is a single recipe of mine with which she has not personally meddled. 'Mmm, yes, I made that salad of yours the other night. Not bad. I added [pine nuts/pecorino/chopped mint/monkey testicles] which really improved things, I found. Maybe you should try it?'

I don't mind the idea of messing about with recipes a bit. But to report it directly to the author? That takes a special brand of shamelessness.

🅛 Your Honour, I plead guilty. Please see page 298 for some of my best work.

podcast has to be 30 minutes

🅐 We turn now to one of the most ancient and cellular disagreements between us: time itself. As you may have noticed, our podcast generally lasts about half an hour. Not because of any natural constraints; not because we run out of things to say at the 30-minute mark, but because Leigh Sales is pretty much unable to function after the minute hand ticks past the 12. If you listen, the entire character of her conversation changes according to where we are in the half hour. For the first 10 minutes, she is witty and expansive. She is prepared to squirt away entire minutes laughing, or doing her weird songs. For the middle 10 minutes, she likes to chew on some fibrous question or content, and then the final 10 she devotes more or less entirely to wrapping me up. Even if I'm being incredibly interesting. In fact, ESPECIALLY then. As I write this, I have fielded Sales's suggestion that for this book we include an article about the one cultural creation that's most influenced us in the years we've done the podcast. I know without even having to ask her that it will be Christian Marclay's *The Clock*. She went to see it about five times when she was in London. Why? Because it was, essentially, created entirely for her: an artwork that allows you to sit in a darkened room, obliged to talk to no one, whilst being reminded EVERY SINGLE SECOND what time it is.

L I hate to be predictable but please see page 277 for my essay on *The Clock*.

capers

a I don't know why I have included this. It's so minor. But Sales hates capers. And I love to sneak them into things so that she will be annoyed. That's about the size of it. But now that we're talking, I do think it's worth reflecting that the caper itself has a spectacularly romantic and brutal history. It's famous for growing up the walls of Rome. It responds to the baking sun. The flowers of the caper plant are impossibly beautiful – full of frilly filaments, a bit like a passionfruit flower. But if you're operating your caper bush competently, you shouldn't actually ever see a flower, because the caper is the bud, which is pinched off before it opens to be salted and made into a delicious addition to your pasta or fish or salad. It is, literally, nipped in the bud. But if you do let things go and your buds open, you just stick around and wait because once the flower dies back, in its place will grow a caper berry, and all sorts of things can be done with those.

My mum planted caper bushes a few years back and I had a go at processing the things. It's scandalously easy. You get a jar, and put a layer of coarse salt at the bottom. Then a layer of caper buds. Then a layer of salt. And so on until the jar is full. Cover with cheesecloth or tea towel and secure with a rubber band. The salt draws out a bitter liquid from the buds. It's amazing how much foul liquid comes off them, and you just pour it off every day, and after about a week you'll have salted capers, which, after you rinse off the salt, aren't bitter at all, but full of that salty, almost fruity taste that everyone except Sales really enjoys. My caper tip? Pat them dry and fry with butter, pine nuts and breadcrumbs with a hint of garlic. If you toss that through some pasta, only one person alive will complain.

L As this riveting exploration of capers illustrates, Crabb has never used five minutes to tell a story when 15 minutes will do. I recently read Helen Garner describe her mother as a woman who would open an anecdote 'days, months or even years before its proper starting point'. Let's just say, it was a sentence that stuck with me.

"*As difficult as it is to believe, love, there'd be people who meet you and they'd find you very disappointing in reality*"

"**What a blunder. You really suck at this**"

"**YOU LOOK LIKE A ROBBER'S DOG**"

"You're such a smug bundt!"

"**YOU CLOTH-EARED BINT!**"

"**Bite me** you little punk!"

"...you are, at your core, ridiculous"

"**TUNE IN, TOKYO! OH MY GOD, YOU'RE SO DENSE**"

"I can tell that you probably wouldn't be a *Generous Lover*"

"*Monster!*"

"*You look so crazed. And you've got about 50 different plaids on. It's headache-inducing*"

"YOU WRETCH"

"**Slag Face!**"

"*Why are you so ill-tempered today?*"

*"I'm happiest when correcting your grammar,
you're happiest when persecuting me with live performance"*

"YOU'RE VERY ATTRACTIVE, IN YOUR OWN WAY"

*"She's not as **GREAT** as you all think she is!"*

"I JUST WANT TO SPRAY YOU WITH GLEN 20"

"Stick it in your bundt hole!"

"YOU GREAT BUFFOON!"

"Who even are you?"

"Why do I have to put up with this fluff-head?"

"Fat Cat!"

"I love a short film"

"You're just bloody lazy, that's why"

"CAN YOU STOP SALESPLAINING"

"How do you even exist in the world?"

"You indolent wench"

"I will come for you in your sleep, you raggedy-haired moll!"

"SOMEONE JUST NEEDS TO COME AND TAP YOU ON THE HEAD WITH A BLUNT IMPLEMENT"

chapter 7

the art of conversation

conversation

the art of the chinwag

a Leigh Sales, let me open this conversation with a question: what are the elements of a good conversation?

L Oh god, I feel like I'm at some sort of speech and drama exam.

a And sit up with your spine straight while you answer.

L I'm going to be judged not only on the content of my answer, but also on my deportment.

a Yes, exactly.

L The elements of a good conversation are that it is a proper back and forth, where each party is listening to what the other person is saying, and nobody's trying to hog the limelight. It also depends on each person's ability to be interesting and to tell stories that interest their conversation partner. What do you reckon?

a I think suppleness is the key to a good conversation. That's suppleness, S-U-P-P-L-E-N-E-S-S, for the benefit of our robot transcriber.

L I thought you were spelling it out because as well as securing points in this eisteddfod for your answer and your deportment, you want some sort of spelling points as well.

a I'd smash you on spelling. The only reason I got a cadetship at the *Advertiser* was because I got full marks for the spelling test, which was an unprecedented feat, apparently. The editor explained this when he hired me. I was the number eight hire of eight cadets, and he said, 'Your general knowledge was ratshit but spelling – full marks. You might make a good sub.'

L I bet you these days, though, he dines out on that. 'Well, I was the one who hired Annabel Crabb and spotted her brilliance.'

a I don't know about that, but I *can* spell. Anyway, we're already off the track, which is actually the sign, I think, of a very good conversation. A conversation that bounds all over the place like an exuberant puppy is a good conversation, in my view.

Leigh

Little treat for you, Chatters – Annabel Crabb back when she was a baby journo at the Adelaide *Advertiser*.

🖋 I completely agree, which is weird, isn't it? Because you'd think in some ways that's maybe the mark of a *bad* conversation, but what it shows is that the conversation's flowing naturally.

🅐 And that you have good chemistry with the person with whom you're conversing. The sign of a bad conversation is when you make a conversational gambit and you have that slightly sweaty feeling that it's your last idea for what to say to this person. And you end up kind of really chasing that pathetic idea, which is often weather-related. As you get to the end of the potential of that conversational topic, you are horrifyingly aware that there isn't another option. That's the worst kind of conversation.

The best kind is when you are so replete with options that you gallop off down another conversational pathway, knowing full well that you're abandoning another equally fruitful line of discussion, but it doesn't matter because there are so many opportunities to have an interesting conversation that you wish that it lasted forever. That's a good conversation.

🖋 That feeling of, 'What am I going to say next, or what am I going to ask next,' is a really horrible feeling. I remember a couple of years ago I was in a relationship and one night I was on my way home and he texted me and said, 'Whenever you leave, no matter how long we've had together, I always feel like we haven't had enough time, that it's always cut short.' And I thought that was a great compliment and felt the same. It's a sign that you have good chemistry with somebody.

But another time, I was seated next to a senior New South Wales police officer at a function. Fairly quickly I ran out of stuff to talk about or ask about. And then I started feeling a little bit resentful because I'd been working hard to drive the conversation and it wasn't going anywhere and he wasn't holding up his end. I felt like, 'Why should I carry all of the load to try to make this social interaction work?' So I stopped trying.

But interestingly – and I suspect he was maybe a more introverted person – once there was some space in the conversation and a bit of silence, he started talking about some fascinating things and the conversation sparked up in a more natural way.

It was a lesson to me that if you're driving the conversation all the time, you're putting that person into territory that maybe isn't ideal. I think, for him, a bit of silence and a slower pace enabled him to feel more comfortable.

a Isn't that fascinating? I guess you project your own needs or ideas about what constitutes a functional level of communication or quality of communication. And then you get a bit shirty when that person doesn't hold up their end of the bargain. But I guess, as with all relationships, temporary or longstanding, you've got to develop an awareness of where the other person is at.

I went to the US in 2011 on an Eisenhower fellowship to research the rise of digital media and its impact on politics. I was with about 20 other delegates from different countries. There was a guy from China who probably had the least functional English of anyone in the group, and I spent all this time worrying about him – that he was being excluded, that people weren't talking to him enough – and I did lots of sitting next to him and yabbering at him. Then part of the exercise was these psychological tests, and I'd never done one before.

ℒ Like a Myers–Briggs thing?

a Yeah. It was called the FIRO-B test. You fill out hundreds of repetitive questions about how you feel about certain circumstances – things like, 'There's an office party and you're not invited. Are you: A, devastated; B, slightly devastated . . .'

ℒ 'C, absolutely thrilled.'

a And what it measures is your need to control others, your need to be controlled by others, your need to be included, your need to include others, your need to be loved, your need to love others. And it spits out at the end a ranking, a number. I was sitting next to this guy when we got our numbers. I just burst into laughter because they were completely the opposite to mine. His need to be included was zero. His need to include others was zero. I was quite high on both of those things. And I said to him, 'I just realised that I'm constantly coming up to

well hello

you and trying to talk to you and trying to include you in conversations when you don't really care,' and he just smiled and went, 'Absolutely.'

🍷 I read this thing about extroverts and introverts at a dinner party, and it really resonated with me because I'm also one of those people who worries someone's being left out. I'll try to include them and go, 'Bob, I'd be really curious to know what you think about that.' And this thing said that if you're introverted, you hate people like me because you don't want to have the spotlight and have everyone at the table looking at you.

It changed my thinking. Now I go, 'Well, people are responsible for their own contribution.' I have a friend who definitely does better one-on-one than in a group, but even then she leaves a lot of space. You have to relax and assume that when you're with her, there's going to be a fair bit of silence. Once you accept that, it's quite restful.

Numerous times I've had her at dinners at my house and other people who were there will ring me the next day with, 'I was really worried about your friend. She seemed to be not having a very good time.' But then my friend will ring to say, 'I had such a great time last night.' She's having a good time just watching and observing and listening to the conversation and not having to contribute necessarily. Other people fear that because she's not an extrovert, she must be having a terrible time.

🅐 If somebody got murdered Cluedo-style at that dinner party, she'd be the first person I'd go to.

🍷 Thinking that she did it?

🅐 No, no – just the observer.

After you . . . no, I insist, after you

🅐 A conversation is essentially a series of compromises and demonstrative offers and acceptances, right? When you start a conversation you're making an offer and then the other person takes it up. And if you are a courteous person or a generous person, you try to think of something that you imagine would appeal to them. You start off by asking something about themselves or whatever.

It's such an interesting and culturally complex little dance – it's an exchange. And I get annoyed if I make an effort to ask a lot about their lives and what they're doing and I don't get anything back.

Ⓛ Exactly. Or you go, 'What did you think of the play?' And they go, 'Blah, blah, blah, blah, blah.' And then don't ask what you thought of the play.

Ⓐ The worst conversationalists I encounter are those who think the best thing that could possibly happen to me is to get the full benefit of everything they think about everything. And to be honest, I do notice quite a gender difference in this circumstance, and I don't mention that to be unfair to all blokes, because some of the best conversationalists I know are men. But also, I speak at a lot of functions and things, and I'm always really, really interested to note the interactions that I have with people afterwards.

There's one kind of person who will come up afterwards to ask you something and seek your view on something, and then there's another kind of person who will come up to tell you something they think you've missed or that you haven't quite understood properly. And I've got to say, the gender divide there is pretty clear.

Ⓛ I think the best conversationalist I know is probably my friend George. He's really delightful company and pretty much I can plonk him anywhere and people will always go, 'He's great. He's really fun.'

Ⓐ That's a really good friend to have.

Ⓛ And I've often thought, 'What is it about him that makes his conversation so sparkly?' Firstly, his job for most of his life has been a comedy writer. So he's very, very witty, but because he's a writer he's not like a razzle-dazzle, performing, 'look at me' kind of person. Also he's got an absolutely fantastic knack for finding funny anecdotes in just everyday stuff that's happened to him.

It's often quite gentle conversation, where he'll be asking you about yourself, but he has a way of filling spaces with interesting stuff that keeps the conversation going. And not only is he interested in you, but also he's interested in the world around, so he often brings little tidbits to the table, like, 'I read this interesting thing' or 'I went to this thing' or 'I made this recipe'. You always leave a conversation and an interaction with him feeling happy.

Ⓐ Do you feel like if you were having a dinner party and you sat somebody who didn't know George next to George, that that person was about to get a real treat?

𝓛 I'd also feel like I'd put them in a safe pair of hands.

𝕒 My friend Wendy has a really good memory. She's super smart, and she's a science-y smart person, but also a human-smart person. And she is really attentive to people – she listens and can get quite deep into a conversation quite quickly and is very, very funny. So when she hits it off with somebody . . . she can wind up talking to the most overlooked person in the room and then forge a really great exchange with that person. **I often think if I see her talking to someone, 'Oh, that lucky person,'** because she's so attentive in that way.

My sister-in-law Margot is also somebody who you could drop from space into anywhere.

𝓛 Margot's very easy to talk to.

𝕒 She has spent a lot of her life teaching English as a second language. So she has absolutely no qualms about . . . you know how sometimes people are awkward about speaking to somebody whose language skills aren't the same as yours? I feel anxious about that sometimes, because I think I'm about to commit some sort of terrible blunder or make someone feel overwhelmed, but she's got this incredible knack for putting people at ease. I often think if there's a tricky situation, 'Oh, thank god, Margot's here,' and just throw her at it and it'll be easy.

ConFidler in me

𝕒 You know how Richard Fidler's *Conversations* podcast is a runaway success?

𝓛 Yeah.

𝕒 What I really enjoy about his conversations and his way of interviewing is that he's clearly got a great research team behind him and he goes into each conversation immaculately prepared, but I never hear him ask a question whose purpose is to show the extent of his preparation.

𝓛 One hundred per cent agree, hard agree.

𝕒 It makes the interview wonderful because you know from listening to him, that if he's done all this prep on Subject A and the interviewee digresses into a promising new, but unprepared-for Area B, Fidler will not hesitate to just ditch everything he's prepared and go off in this new direction. That's an important and hard thing as an interviewer because when you spend all this effort accruing knowledge and preparedness on one issue, it can be frustrating to then bin that and go somewhere else.

In conversations that's important as well, because if you leave behind this need to perform the work that you've done or the expertise that you have or your own personal brilliance, then the conversation will be by definition much better.

L Following where the other person wants to go often opens up a rich vein. Speaking of Fidler reminds me – a trap for journalists in conversations is that you fall into interviewing instead of having a conversation, and I do that sometimes. I find myself hammering people with questions all the time, because that's what I'm used to doing. And I think it can be draining for people to feel like they're being interrogated over lunch.

Dance, Stephen Fry!

L Probably my least favourite sort of person at a dinner party other than the kind of bloviator you mentioned before is the life-of-the-party person, the loud party girl or party boy who comes over and wraps their arm around you and says, 'Come and dance, Annabel!' I hate that sort of personality.

a I guess there are people who feel like they're obliged to liven a place up, maybe because they have their own really elevated standards of what constitutes a good night, and for them if it's subdued, then that's not a good night. I had this dinner once with Stephen Fry – CLANG! Well, when I say I had dinner with Stephen Fry, it wasn't him saying, 'Annabel it's been years since we caught up.' It was organised by his touring squad, and there were 15 of us there. It was brilliant, of course, and he was amazing, but it was clear that this happens to him all the time where a group of people are brought together for the pleasure of having dinner with Stephen Fry and everybody does a bit of chitchat. And then when the mains arrive, Stephen has to hold court and everybody listens.

L God, how exhausting.

a He was so incredibly gracious about it. And of course intuited that we were all there to hear Stephen Fry. Because his performances are essentially him just wandering around the stage, perambulating about and holding forth upon this, that or the other. What we were in essence getting was a semi-private lap dance from this guy, which was fabulous, really fabulous. But there are so many expectations on that person, and I thought afterwards about how he talks and has written a lot about his struggles with mental health. Surely, that crushing expectation wherever you go that you will turn it on and you will entertain everybody endlessly must be a huge part of that.

L The expectation that you'll be funny when actually, well, certainly with a lot of comedians I know, the comedy comes from them being extremely sharp observers. That means in a party kind of setting, they're not the life-of-the-party people, they're the fairly quiet people because they're just looking around and taking stuff in.

Because everyone wants to hear him holding forth all the time, would Stephen Fry be able to turn that off in his private life when he's just having dinner with friends?

a I assume so. Lots of comedians, as you say, are actually quite internally focused.

L I wonder if Magda Szubanski or Andrew Denton find leaving the house really tiring, just because strangers want to be dazzled by them.

a Or they want them to say something funny. Andrew Denton is an unbelievably great conversationalist. But not really in a gag-cracking way, he's just a really thoughtful and insightful person. He also reads widely and is curious about things, which I think is the key to great conversation rather than being funny or being erudite.

I was having a chat with him a few months ago about podcasts we were listening to. And he asked me a question that I thought about a lot afterwards, because I was unable to answer it. We were talking about *Chat 10* and I was saying to him, 'The best thing about our podcast is that it's really good fun, and we both enjoy it. And it's not that much work, but it produces all of this content that other people can then enjoy. So it feels like a perfect deal because it's fun to do and it's also productive.'

And then he said, ‘What is it you do for no reason apart from the fact that it gives you pleasure?’ And I couldn’t think of one thing. It was so bad. It was terrible because I was thinking, ‘I really love cooking, but I love cooking because I enjoy doing it and it produces something that is really useful. I can take it to friends or I can feed my children or I can whatever.’ And I think one of the reasons I allow myself to read so much for pleasure these days is because I know that there’s a purpose and that it will end up making content, right?

🅛 So that means it’s not straight pleasure.

🅐 I know. I felt terrible after that – not that he had made me feel terrible, but that he had asked a really, really perceptive question and I couldn’t answer it. Two days later I bunked off work and I went to see a movie in the middle of the day, and I texted him and I’m like, ‘I’m in a movie. No one knows I’m here. I was supposed to be at work. I’m having the best time.’

🅛 That’s funny. See, I feel like I could say ‘music’ for that question.

🅐 Yeah, that’s true – but then you can also spin it into *Chat 10 Looks 3* content.

🅛 It’s not like every time I play the piano, I turn it into a song to be on *Chat 10*. Not *every* time.

Alpacas: useless

🅛 But listen, this is interesting: when we started this conversation we said, ‘Let’s have a conversation about the art of conversation.’ Then we were like, ‘Okay, but what are we going to talk about?’ And we had no idea. Now here we are and it’s ranged across a lot of areas and it’s almost moved away from the art of conversation. As you said before – that’s the hallmark of a good conversation.

Still, if somebody now said to me, ‘How do I have a conversation like that?’ I don’t feel like I could give them any tips about how we just did what we did. To me, it feels like magic and just some sort of chemistry or something that it just happens.

🅐 Could you train yourself to be a better conversationalist? I guess you could, if you had little pieces of paper saying, ‘Keep an eye out for this, listen properly.’ For example, you ask somebody, ‘What are you doing today?’ and their response is, 'It's pretty wet. I'm stuck at home with my alpaca and I'm just waiting for it to stop raining so that I can pick the kids up from school.'

Ⓛ If somebody threw out that line, what would you say next?

Ⓐ 'Back up the truck – you have an alpaca?'

Ⓛ That's exactly what I would say.

Ⓐ Right. So maybe the conventional rejoinder to that would be, 'Oh yes, it's been very rainy where we are too. How many children do you have?' or whatever. The eye for an (in this case, screamingly obvious) opportunity to digress and go down a different conversational borough is the art of great conversation. It's following a little trail of clues, following these little sparkly possibilities and seeing where they lead. If somebody has a truly fascinating job, that can be wonderful.

Ⓛ I get tired of people asking me about my job. My friends never give a shit. They rarely ask anything about what I'm doing at work. But when I meet new people, they often ask about my job. And I think that makes complete sense because it's a point of interest to people. Also, I've met a few people over the years, if they were in that alpaca conversation, whose blowhard follow-up would be 'Oh, alpacas – alpacas are useless. What you need is goats. Goats are wonderful.'

Wrap like a pro

Ⓐ Is there a question you get asked that you just wish you could change the universe so that nobody ever asks that question again? Like the most boring question you can possibly be asked?

Ⓛ I get a bit tired of, 'How do you juggle everything?' which I get asked a lot.

Ⓐ I don't really mind that because I think it's a sensible question.

Ⓛ It is. Also, I get asked more than you might imagine, 'Do you write your own questions?'

Ⓐ Really?

Ⓛ Yeah.

🅐 Well, who do they think writes them?

🅛 I've no idea, and how did they think that you actually do an interview? You're listening to what the person's saying, you're not always just going off a list of questions. I think it's because people watch too many movies where there's a producer in the ear of a reporter telling them what to ask. But I just think, how dumb do I seem that I need someone to write my questions? What about you? Have you got one?

🅐 You seem like an idiot, Leigh Sales.

🅛 Have you got one?

🅐 Yep. 'Who's your favourite politician?'

🅛 Oh, yeah. I've heard you get asked that a lot.

🅐 Or, 'Who was your favourite from *Kitchen Cabinet*?' And I think I should have just prepared an answer, but I don't really have one because it's not really relevant. I do often get a bit of, 'In your dream dinner party, who would you invite and what would you cook?'

🅛 At this point of our conversation, I'm reminded of another thing to do with conversations, which is: when a conversation has been going well, like, say you're at a party and you've been chatting to someone and it's going well, but it's hitting a point where you're feeling like it's time to move on to somebody else or 'I've just had enough, I want to go' or whatever – how do you wrap it up? I ask because I'm ready to wrap this up with you.

🅐 I think the original and the best is, 'I'm going to pop off and get myself a drink.' Brilliant. Or, 'I've got to pop to the loo. It's been lovely talking to you.' And you've got to do that. I mean, so many times I've let it go on past the point where it's all good. Because, really, the time to nip a conversation is when it's still fun, right? You've got to leave the audience wanting more, you've got to leave thinking, 'That was great. I'd love to see that person again.'

🅛 On that note, I'm just going to go and get myself a cup of tea. It's been lovely chatting.

well hello

typical interruptions to an episode of chat 10

- phone calls
- text messages
- text message from Helen Garner (CLANG!)
- fumbling with audio equipment
- aircraft noise
- jackhammer noise
- cafe noise
- dog barking
- puppy attacking cable
- kids coming in
- cry-laughing
- coughing
- chewing
- tea sipping
- food arriving
- make-up being applied
- hairspray being sprayed
- stopping to chat with a Chatter

Brenda 1.0

One woman's futile quest for anonymity

In 2016 Cathy Beale was living a relatively peaceful life. She had a great job as a research librarian at the ABC in Sydney, and she loved hanging out with her family, reading books, seeing pub bands and mixing mean gin cocktails. Then her colleague and friend Leigh Sales asked if she'd fancy a little side gig succeeding 'Brendan' as *Chat 10 Looks 3* podcast producer ... and her secret life as 'Brenda' began.

It's true, Cathy loves a knotty challenge, and giving herself a crash course in audio engineering and RSS feeds (whatever they may be) was the easy bit.

Will the real Brenda please stand up? The Facebook group ran hot with theories on the person behind the Brenda Chats pseudonym, prompting this fine fashion line whipped up by *Chat 10* merchandise queen Gwen Blake.

She dragged Crabb and Sales's luddite butts to complicated new recording equipment. She dealt patiently with the consistently chaotic material they delivered and even saved the entire *Chat 10* back catalogue from falling off Leigh's iTunes account once when Sales forgot to update her credit card details.

Cathy also inherited compiling the show notes, which are helpful links for listeners to find everything talked about in the podcast. Our gun librarian could often be found ferreting around in microfiche from 1974 or some such to dig out something casually referenced by Crabb or Sales. And she drew on her rock chick background to liaise with techie/soundie/front-of-housie logistics at *Chat 10* live shows, including at her local, Sydney's Enmore Theatre.

Beale set up the official *Chat 10 Looks 3* Community Facebook group in 2017 but eventually passed its mammoth moderating duties on to dedicated social media manager Bec Francis and the podcast producer role to *Betoota Advocate* chap Antony Stockdale. On her 'retirement' from official *Chat 10* duties Crabb and Sales said,

'On behalf of everybody, Cathy, that you have ever looked after so beautifully online, or in real life: you are the most kind and gentle and brilliant, insightful, funny, witty, kooky, gin-and-tonic-cake-making woman; you are the greatest.'

You can still spot Brenda 1.0 in the wild, helping herd cats at *Chat 10* shows.

I wanna keep telling my anecdote.

I know, but I feel like you don't deserve the air space.

5 questions for...
Cathy Beale

1. What made you decide you wanted to dip a toe in the water and take over as 'Brenda' when 'Brendan' moved on?

I had been helping Leigh with some research for her book *Any Ordinary Day* and had also been involved with research on Annabel's ABC show *Kitchen Cabinet*. I thought it might be fun to try my hand at helping out with *Chat 10 Looks 3*, since they both knew me, and I knew them. (I also secretly hoped I could eventually do something about the godawful audio quality!) The rest, as they say, is history.

2. On a scale of Donald Trump to Hillary Clinton, just how shambolic are Crabb and Sales to attempt to wrangle?

I couldn't possibly comment.

3. Over time, your identity became known and you were outed as Brenda. How did that come about and how did you feel about it?

I remember the first time I outed myself to anyone as Brenda. It was quite early on, well before the Facebook community was set up. I was in Perth for the first time meeting my partner's cousin, Sam. She kept mentioning a lot of the books and podcasts that had been recently discussed on *Chat 10 Looks 3*. I casually asked her if she listened to Sales and Crabb's podcast and she exclaimed that she 'LOVED *Chat 10 Looks 3*!' I then very quietly admitted to her that I was Brenda. I was expecting I would need to explain what the hell a 'Brenda' was but I recall she LOUDLY SQUEALED!

Fast forward: I retained the pseudonym and my anonymity for the *Chat 10 Looks 3* Facebook group when that was initially set up. Unfortunately, Facebook's transparency rules finally caught up with me. I was unable to continue with the pseudonym and I had to come

well hello

clean. It was a terrifying moment for a shy introvert to 'out' herself to tens of thousands of strangers. I would have preferred to have remained anonymous forever!

4. What is the thing you've most enjoyed about being part of the *Chat 10 Looks 3* community?
- Witnessing the incredible kindness of strangers.
- Thousands of instant virtual best friends, leading to a few 'real life' friendships.
- Unexpectedly learning a range of surprisingly useful life hacks!
- Having access to the most nuanced research tool: a question to the Chatter brains trust is often better than an internet search.

5. Your day job is a librarian. This is a podcast that has its origins in the love of books. Tell us anything at all you'd like to say about libraries, their importance, their future and what they mean to you.

I won't write you a thesis on this huge topic, as someone would then have to catalogue it in a library. One thing's for sure, those ladies are big readers! They've introduced me to a lot of terrific books. What I love is that they don't necessarily have the same taste as each other – they can disagree on a book, plus they can admit when they are in a bit of a reading slump. It keeps it all real. The thing about books is that everyone has different needs, everyone has different tastes.

To me, *that* is what reading is all about: finding what is right at a specific time or when you are in a particular mood. I obsessively need to be prepared with options, to make sure I am ready with the right book, just in case. That is where libraries fit in. They provide endless choice. You can look up recommendations or randomly pick something off the shelf. A world of possibilities. Who doesn't love that!

just one important question for Antony Stockdale

Chat 10 went fully professional when it engaged Antony Stockdale of Diamantina Media — otherwise known as our erstwhile country chums the *Betoota Advocate* — to manage podcast production and handle advertising. Somehow Antony managed to achieve what his predecessors could not — wrangling Crabb and Sales to actually record in a studio. There's really only one question that needs to be asked here.

Q. Who's better: *Betoota* or *Chat 10*? Think carefully before answering.
The *Betoota Advocate* is arguably better than *Chat 10*, but only when it comes to the turnaround of their content. As our friends from the Diamantina Shire have told us on many occasions, the only thing that matters is output. Forget quality — these days, all that matters is quantity. This explains why their newspaper has succeeded where the other major Australian mastheads have failed. The *Betoota Advocate* is also much better at swearing.

> *This conversation needs a good edit.*
> *Can you imagine an editor going*
> *through this and just going,*
> *'I'm sorry, I couldn't salvage*
> *anything. It's all ridiculous.'*

> **It's uneditable.**

well hello

odd places to pod

(aka The professional podcaster's guide to appropriate places to podcast)

As soon as I got your text, 'Come to the room with a piano in it' ... ugh.

- someone's kitchen table
- Sales's bedroom
- a bathroom
- an electrical cupboard
- backstage at various writers' festivals
- in the piano room at the ABC

    Ⓛ Hello Annabel. I guess you're wondering why I'm sitting at a piano?

    Ⓐ Oh, I'm not wondering. As soon as I got your text, 'Come to the room with a piano in it' ... ugh.

- in a designated breastfeeding room at the ABC

    Ⓐ 'Privacy Room – not in use.' Okay, let's go! Convention would now dictate that I breastfeed you.

    Ⓛ I hope not.

- in a hotel room, while getting ready for a ball

    Ⓐ Every time I walk into a room and you're there, you're there with microphones now. And you're like, 'Hey, we're in the same room alone. It's reasonably quiet. Let's start recording.' So now we're here, applying make-up. I mean, there's a limit to how much interesting material can be extracted from this arrangement, right?

- in make-up chairs with exceedingly tolerant makeup
  professional Belinda

(a) We're about to do to Belinda possibly the worst thing you
can ever do to a make-up artist, which is, 'Do you mind if we just
knock over a podcast while you're simultaneously trying to paint
the face of one of the people talking?'

- in the priest hole

(a) So we're in the priest hole. And it's just like, it's just like
a crazy person's office or home. It looks like a hoarder's paradise,
there's pairs of shoes everywhere and piles of books and . . .

(L) I keep expecting a cat to – meow! – up on my shoulder.

(a) It's a lot like that. And yeah, it's a debacle because we've
got no microphones and now Sales is just holding her phone
up to my mouth.

- in the foyer at the movies, insensible with giggling when
  going to see *Fifty Shades Of Grey* and *Cats*

(a) Hi, can we have two tickets to *Fifty Shades of Grey*, please?
I'll get this, Salesy.

(L) Oh good. So it'll be on your credit card. There's no evidence
I was around.

(a) Do you want anything? Popcorn? Full-face mask?

(L) Bag to cover my head, large hat and sunglasses.

- at the Art Gallery of New South Wales cafe, while dropping
  their cake

(a) You are an idiot. We're trying to keep a low profile and
Leigh Sales just threw half a strudel on the floor.

(L) It's just disastrous.

(a) Cherry strudel. I will eat the bit that's been on the floor
because I grew up on a farm.

- Crabb's car while Crabb drives Sales to work with some helpful driving tips from Leigh

  ⓛ Go straight. Straight. Go straight.

  ⓐ I'm going straight. Jeez.

  ⓛ You're driving slowly. It's like you're going to run over one of those little birds or something.

  ⓐ Hey, an elderly person was about to step out onto that street crossing, JEEZ!

- on a patch of grass next to the 10-lane freeway over the Sydney Harbour Bridge while waiting for a gallery to open

  ⓛ We did, amazingly for us, do a little audio check before it started and it seemed like it could sort of be acceptable.

  ⓐ Confirmed that it's really rubbish.

Let the listener be aware that as she said that, she took off her glasses in an incredibly pontificating manner, as if she was doing me a great favour.

classic episode 60

medieval contraceptive device

In which Crabb and Sales finally get their audio acts together by purchasing a professional apparatus on which to record their podcast, but within seconds it is given a questionable name. Later, the ignominies of using male-designed sound equipment are discussed.

a Is this thing on?

L Testing, one . . . two. One . . . two. Two . . . two. I think it is. Wonder if we can catch this audio.

a Yeah! First interruption is a plane coming over.

L This is a historic day on *Chat 10 Looks 3* because we – you might even be able to tell already – are coming to you with proper audio gear.

a That's right. It looks like . . . how can I describe what's currently spread out on my kitchen table? It looks like a medieval contraceptive device. [*Both cackle.*] And Leigh Sales, who has rather effortlessly glided into the position of production engineer, has just been using some very bad language and like, ramming things into plugs and saying, 'Why the fuck isn't this working?' while I sit back and have a cup of tea and enjoy myself.

L You should have seen me on Sunday when I got this stuff out of the packaging and had to work out how to use it. It was just absolutely diabolical. Chances are you'll never hear this anyway. Shit, have I pronged the wrong sprocket into the wrong [inaudible]? I say we plough on, because the timer seems to be clicking over to show that something's being recorded and those little bars are jumping up and down.

a Seriously, the AFP will be here in a minute. It's quite . . . it's quite *bomby*, isn't it? The whole thing.

well hello

Leigh

🅛 Clock the dirty look I'm giving Annabel Crabb as she snaps me trying to work out our new audio gear. I suspect if she'd turned her back, I would have given her the finger.

🅛 It comes in this little, sort of . . . what looks like a bulletproof box, and it's just full of cables and wires. Can I give a shout out to Rachel Corbett? She does a podcast called *You've Gotta Start Somewhere* and she came to interview me. It's basically about people in media and arts sorts of industries and how they've had their break. She's very professional because she's worked in radio. She had all this gear. I said, 'Rachel, can you give me some tips?' She was like, 'I would love to give you some tips because I have had it up to here with the audio on your podcast.'

🅐 Join the 98 per cent of our listenership who just have got the screaming shits.

🅛 I cannot even tell you how helpful she was. Well, you know, because I forwarded you the email – it was so detailed.

🅐 Hey, I didn't read the email because you're the engineer. I'm like, 'That's going straight in the bin.'

🅛 Rachel basically sent me a shopping list. She even named the shop. 'Go to this shop. Ask the guy for this.'

🅐 Ask for Ralph.

🅛 He'll be the guy with his pants hanging down and butt crack hanging out the top.

🅐 He probably plays the tuba.

🅛 So, thanks very much, Rachel. You rock.

sound
gear up
the fanny

In a subsequent episode . . .

L [*stalling for time while fiddling ineptly with the Medieval Contraceptive Device*]
Is this the time for you to take public your private rant about sound equipment
at events?

a We do have this thing, which is a terrible bitch session about how, whenever
you go to be on a panel at something or to speak at something, the sound gear
is always basically designed for a guy in a suit, right?

L I feel sorry for any sound guy who comes up to me because I'm pretty
much instantly defensive because I know what they're going to do is go,
'Have you got somewhere you can clip this thing onto, like a lapel? And
then can you clip this battery pack onto your waistband?' The whole system
is designed for men because it assumes that you're going to be wearing
some sort of pants with a heavy belt that can carry the weight of a battery
pack. And that you're going to have a suit jacket with a lapel that you can clip
something on, and it's going to be quite baggy so underneath it all you can
hide all the cables and the blah-de-blah. Every single time it happens I just
feel like, 'Oh, that's right. I'm getting a reminder here that panels and going
on stage is meant for men.'

a So any of you entrepreneurs out there – design a lady pack.

L I feel bad 'cos I've infected you with it too.

a I've become an evil bitch at these events. I was speaking at a women's
conference and the guy came up and did the whole, 'Where do we . . .?
Where's your suit?' I'm like, 'Hey dude, I'm wearing a dress.' So this guy's saying,
'We do have a headset-type one somewhere but we don't really . . . you've
gotta request that one specially.' I'm like, 'Did you not think that this women's

conference attended by 100 per cent women might be a good place for you to break out that special, by-request, it's-okay-for-ladies equipment?' Anyway, lovely guy. A bit shattered though, I suspect.

I once had to clip one of those heavy sound packs to my underpants in front of Bob Carr because I had agreed to go and speak at this thing like, seriously, six days after my baby was born. And I was really late because I had parked my newborn outside with an adult but I didn't have the right outfit on. And they were like: 'Quick, quick, quick, quick, quick. This has to go on somewhere.' So I just hoicked up my dress and clipped this pin to my underpants. **And I think Bob Carr was never the same after that. I don't know who was more horrified – me or him.**

L The worst one I've had was one where it was election night …

a So you were wearing an adult nappy?

L Wearing an adult nappy. For the ABC broadcast. It was that one where I was getting digitally penetrated by bar graphs. They wanted me to wear *four* battery packs, because they wanted backups for my microphone, but also for my earpiece. I went to the guy: **'Do you want me to be able to walk? I've got bar charts going up my jaxie as well. This will be a visual treat for the viewers.'** It's still on YouTube. It's the best vision ever.

A heavily mic'd-up Sales deftly avoids bar graphs going up her skirt during the ABC's 2010 election night coverage. *Picture: ABC*

classic episode 54

are you my driver?

It's Sales's somethingth birthday and the ladies have squeezed themselves in the priest hole in Annabel's office at the ABC to record an episode by alternating holding Leigh's phone up to their mouths. You can almost hear podcast producer Cathy Beale screaming from her home. Annabel has bought Leigh a delicious dessert-in-a-jar from nearby dessert bar Koi that 'looks like a science experiment in a terrarium', and as they eat it she glowingly recounts her interview with *Veep* creator Armando Iannucci. That's just a deft setup, though, to embarrass Sales with the Where's My Driver anecdote . . .

ⓐ So I interviewed Armando Iannucci on stage – CLANG! – last Wednesday. And on the Tuesday night, of course, you and I both went to see him at the Sydney Town Hall and afterwards had dinner with him.

ⓛ I think it speaks volumes for how much I love *Veep* that the dinner didn't even start until 10.15 pm. I'm normally in bed at this time and I haven't even ordered, I haven't even had my first drink.

ⓐ It was unbelievable. I felt like videoing the whole thing. It was like that bit where David Attenborough finally gets the footage of the snow leopard after the guy's been camping out on the mountainside for six months, and he gets two seconds of the snow leopard scratching its arse and then disappearing back into the snow. That's what it was like.

I was just waiting to see if you're gonna shut down Iannucci. 'Well, it's been a lovely night. Thank you, Armando. You're very clever.'

Anyway. I have a more treasured recollection of that night than watching you be out late, and that was . . . you know what I'm going to say, don't you?

ⓛ Yes, I do.

well hello

a So after the thing, we're all leaving the Town Hall to go to this restaurant. And I'm walking along with Sales, who, coming to the street, sees this row of cars and says to no one in particular: 'How are we getting to this restaurant? Do we just get in these cars?' Like, 'Are these our cars? Is that my car?' And our friend Bryce and I just are like, 'Ah, dude … they are just *cars waiting for the lights to change green*, like, what are you …?' Can you imagine?

L I was literally walking towards the first one because it was white. It looked like a sort of, you know, Uber-y type car.

a Can you just imagine if you actually jumped into the passenger seat of this perfectly defenceless civilian who's just listening to a podcast or thinking about having a sherry when they get home. And you're all, 'Hi. Yeah, take me to Hubert, please. And step on it, would you? I don't like being out late.'

L I just love that you've immediately said, 'Check your privilege!' And then on the way home you texted me and said, 'Seriously, the only other person I've ever heard use the phrase "Is that my car?" was Bob Hawke.'

a You're in that special little place where Bob Hawke's ego lives. Now enjoy it!

L I can't even really offer anything in my defence other than at the event we were just getting marshalled around everywhere.

a Like in an election campaign. 'Where is my bus? How do I get from here to across the road? I don't know!'

[*Leigh then goes on to open the rest of her birthday present: a T-shirt that says 'ARE YOU MY DRIVER?'*]

a Big thanks to our friend Gwen, who organised and had that made yesterday while we were in the budget lock-up.

L You told Gwen that story as well?

a Yeah, I've told everyone that story.

chapter 8

razzle dazzle'em

live shows

They say Fate is a cruel mistress and at this point Annabel Crabb might be wondering – is Fate's name Leigh Sales? Because Annabel could never have foreseen when she picked up the phone in 2009 to ask for tips on working at the ABC that a decade later she'd be forced to appear on stage in front of 1600 people dressed as Brian May, with a gleeful Leigh gussied up as Freddie Mercury dressed as a housewife.

Sales describes that opening moment of their live show at the Enmore Theatre in 2019 as one of the greatest of her life. Crabb remains purse-lipped.

So, how did a couple of chicks chatting into a phone morph into sellout events around the country at which two of Australia's most respected broadcasters routinely humiliate themselves even further?

let's have a crack

at this show caper

Chat 10 Looks 3 went live in 2017 after Annabel and Leigh saw the blokes from *The Dollop* podcast advertising a stage show and thought, 'Well, that can't be too hard, can it?' (Reader, it can.)

Sales secured two afternoon slots at Sydney's Giant Dwarf Theatre in Redfern, a venue so intimate and friendly that if the whole idea was a tits-up failure, it would be easy to never speak of it again. 'We only have to sell 100 seats to break even,' Leigh nervously reported to Annabel as the box office opened. But the shows immediately sold out, prompting a rush of blood to her head and a classically Salesian response: to then race off and book two shows at Melbourne's 1800-seat Comedy Theatre before Crabb could subdue her with a handkerchief full of chloroform.

Leigh

The mood half an hour before every live show: Crabb goes a bit nuts and Sales gets worried.

But then: how to entertain the punters? Crabb and Sales slumped into immediate self-questioning as to why anyone would pay good money to hear a couple of ageing hacks in armchairs crap on about what they're reading and watching.

Sales approached things in her usual manner: building a running sheet weeks in advance containing discussion topics and just happening to find several minutes in the schedule to shove in a show tune. Crabb, too, deployed her traditional approach: scribbling some material on the back of a piece of paper and then losing it in her handbag. They commissioned a stack of *Chat 10* merchandise from Gwen to sell from the foyer.

The Melbourne shows were first to come around. Sick with nerves, Annabel and Leigh almost didn't get there thanks to high winds at Sydney Airport and came close to buying overnight rail tickets as a contingency. On safe arrival, after a pleasant lunch at Leigh's new favourite cheerful Melbourne restaurant, the Spaghetti Tree, they went to see a Christian Dior exhibition at the NGV during which Sales *bought her new home at auction in Sydney over the phone* – just to ratchet up the day's tension a little more. Crabb opened proceedings at the Comedy Theatre later that afternoon by reading out an email she'd received overnight from Sales several days earlier that said, 'I literally woke up at 12.15 am completely awake as if a fire alarm just went off with the thought, "Oh my god, we've charged 1800 people $40 each and we literally do nothing but sit around talking and it's this Saturday. We have 5000 bird lapel pins."'

And now it was actually happening.

So yes, there was crapping on about books and stuff. But more to the audience's delight and Crabb's alarm, Sales burst into a song she'd penned about the *Chat 10* Facebook group, accompanied by her mate Chris on guitar (see page 64). Comedian pal Tony Martin popped up on stage to lend some credibility and was quickly sent back to his seat for being too funny ('This isn't your show, Tony. It's ours.'). Audience questions were taken and people who'd brought offerings of baked goods were thanked. And then it was, mercifully, over.

Annabel

a Leigh Sales and I find it improves our chemistry if we do trust exercises backstage

A month later at Giant Dwarf, awkward celebrity Sales insisted on making a grand entrance by dancing down the centre aisle of the auditorium, high-fiving the crowd, Ellen-style, while it dawned on Crabb – reluctantly shuffling along – that perhaps these gigs were *not really about her at all.*

Over the next few years the shows became a major plank of the *Chat 10* operation as Crabb and Sales played to more locations and bigger venues. Plaintive calls came from Chatters – come to Perth! Newcastle! Orange! Hobart hosted the first overseas-yet-still-interstate gig, aka the Lock Up Your Cheesemakers show. The Gold Coast event was held on the same weekend as the Gold Coast 600 Supercars race, thus providing an answer to what a Venn diagram of Chatters and petrolheads looks like. Brisbane got to see Bald Hills's favourite organ-playing Highland dancer in the flesh – and straight off the plane in her jeans and grubby T-shirt after another nail-biting flight delay almost had Leigh and Annabel miss the show entirely.

Over the years of doing the live events, *Chat 10* has worked with unfailingly professional (and patient) crews at big and small venues around Australia, folks who've marvelled at the excitement of the fans and quickly learned that the shows might require more white wine in stock and more loo paper in the Ladies'. They have also stepped in to handle crowd control at the signings afterwards that result in long queues of jolly Chatters armed with books and cakes snaking through their premises.

But, still, the question of how to entertain hundreds of Chatters by making it up as they go along would always gnaw away at the impostor-syndrome-riddled minds of Crabb and Sales during those 3 am staring-at-the-ceiling worry sessions, resulting in increasingly ludicrous ideas to pad out the time – sorry, give everyone a fun night out. Here's a few of the 'highlights' . . .

breaking free
at the Enmore

Backstage at the Enmore before Leigh emerged as Freddie Mercury and Annabel as Brian May.
Picture: Stephen Blake

In 2018 Crabb's partner Jeremy – the fellow in charge of The Details – booked legendary Sydney rock venue the Enmore Theatre. Feeling the weight of history, Sales was compelled to prove her heavy-metal chops on a stage that's hosted not only the Rolling Stones but also the Wiggles. Dressed as her interpretation of 'rock chick', Leigh strolled out with an electric guitar, strummed two chords that she'd taught herself for the occasion . . . and immediately handed it back to a roadie. Given the Enmore's requirement that there be an interval, Crabb and Sales invited special guests to paper over proceedings: the magnificent actor Pamela Rabe, and *Calamity Jane* musical star Virginia Gay, who gave a knockout performance.

But how would the Mild Ones top that at the Enmore show the following year?

Enter Queen-obsessed Leigh's relentless campaign to get a begrudging Annabel to dress up as Brian May to her worryingly convincing in-drag Freddie

Mercury, and re-enact the video to 'I Want to Break Free'. Crabb finally agreed 'because you were having a tough day', triggering weeks of Sales giddily sourcing the outfits, briefing her mates Christopher and Danielle on the hair and make-up requirements, and even popping into Sexyland ('the Bunnings of adult stores') to buy suspenders for her costume (a likely story). Fair to say the Enmore audience was agog when the hosts appeared on stage as Freddie and Brian, a sight that is probably still burned into the retinas of all present.

🅛 I just was so happy when Danielle stepped back from doing your hair and it was just the full, square, curly Brian May – it was just one of the greatest moments ever.

🅐 Yeah, it was a pretty awesome moment for me too, as you could imagine.

Full points to fabulous mystery guests Clare Bowditch and Marta Dusseldorp, who somehow managed to interact with Crabb and Sales as if the pair looked entirely normal.

enHansment
in Adelaide

Leigh

🅛 With Adelaide show-opener, the multi-talented Hans.

Their first Adelaide show was opened by the fabulous Accordion Hans ('You know me, I'll do any old shit gig,' he explained) before he went on to global supermega-stardom on *America's Got Talent*. 'There you go,' Annabel told the audience after he'd cranked out Madonna's 'Papa Don't Preach' in honour of Barnaby Joyce, 'you've actually had some proper entertainment now. We always get a bit nervous before these things 'cos we're like, "All we do is just sit on stage and talk – we'd better get in someone wearing sequins or who can sing."'

well hello

It's become tradition that Canberra hosts the end-of-year romp, where the switched-on audience at the ANU is treated to Annabel's brilliantly awful 'Twelve Days of Christmas in Australian Politics' song. Every year she fears there won't be enough idiocy from MPs to fill the ditty, yet every year she is proved horribly wrong. Otherwise, all Crabb and Sales do is sit on stage listing their favourite things of the year, teasing their host Brian Schmidt (see page 230) and talking rubbish. Yes, it is funny the things people will pay to see.

howzat!!!

sticky wicket in Melbourne

The annual Melbourne shows have evolved into a beast, with Jeremy recklessly booking two of the city's biggest arts joints, resulting in Crabb and Sales absolutely bricking it at the prospect of playing to houses of 2000+ Chatters.

At the Melbourne Convention Exhibition Centre (MCEC) in 2018 the audience was treated to an appearance by Facebook-famous Brett Kenny, of the Kenny Family Christmas Day Organisational Chart and a thoroughly inept attempt to recreate said chart with a *Chat 10* theme. They then watched on nonplussed as Sales – who'd recently interviewed Shane Warne and refused

Backstage at Hamer Hall, Leigh is making a mental note to add 'grand piano' to her lengthy dressing-room rider and Annabel is stress-testing the sticky tape holding the side of her Vivienne Westwood frock in place. *Picture: Miranda Murphy*

Chat 10 Melbourne Live Show – Org Chart

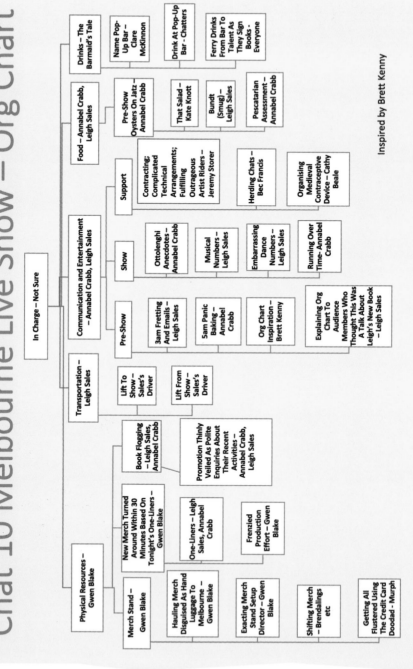

In Charge – Not Sure

Physical Resources – Gwen Blake
- Merch Stand – Gwen Blake
  - Hauling Merch Disguised As Hand Luggage To Melbourne – Gwen Blake
  - Exacting Merch Stand Setup Director – Gwen Blake
    - Shifting Merch – Brendalings etc
      - Getting All Flustered Using The Credit Card Doodad - Murph
- New Merch Turned Around Within 30 Minutes Based On Tonight's One-Liners – Gwen Blake
  - One-Liners – Leigh Sales, Annabel Crabb
    - Frenzied Production Effort – Gwen Blake
- Book Flogging – Leigh Sales, Annabel Crabb
  - Promotion Thinly Veiled As Polite Enquiries About Their Recent Activities – Annabel Crabb, Leigh Sales

Transportation – Leigh Sales
- Lift To Show – Sales's Driver
- Lift From Show – Sales's Driver

Communication and Entertainment – Annabel Crabb, Leigh Sales
- Pre-Show
  - 3am Fretting And Emails – Leigh Sales
  - Sam Panic Baking – Annabel Crabb
  - Org Chart Inspiration – Brett Kenny
  - Explaining Org Chart To Audience Members Who Thought This Was A Talk About Leigh's New Book – Leigh Sales
- Show
  - Ottolenghi Anecdotes – Annabel Crabb
  - Musical Numbers – Leigh Sales
  - Embarrassing Dance Numbers – Leigh Sales
  - Running Over Time – Annabel Crabb
- Support
  - Contracting; Complicated Technical Arrangements; Fulfilling Outrageous Artist Riders – Jeremy Storer
  - Herding Chats – Bec Francis
  - Organising Medieval Contraceptive Device – Cathy Beale

Food – Annabel Crabb, Leigh Sales
- Pre-Show Oysters On Jatz – Annabel Crabb
- That Salad – Kate Knott
- Bundt (Smug) – Leigh Sales
- Pescatarian Assessment – Annabel Crabb

Drinks – The Barmaid's Tale
- Name Pop-Up Bar – Clare McKinnon
- Drink At Pop-Up Bar - Chatters
- Ferry Drinks From Bar To Talent As They Sign Books - Everyone

Inspired by Brett Kenny

to shut up about it – insisted on directing Crabb in a harebrained, two-woman re-enactment of Warnie taking his 700th wicket. (Gripping audio for the podcast recording, of course – do tune in next time when they mime in frocks and heels all five hours and 53 minutes of the Djokovic v. Nadal 2012 Australian Open tennis final.) At least Chatters could discuss what the bleeding heck that was all about afterwards at *Chat 10*'s own pop-up bar, cleverly named The Barmaid's Tale by Clare McKinnon in a Facebook competition.

In 2019, at the venerable Hamer Hall, Crabb sought to divert attention from the lack of content by wearing a Vivienne Westwood gown with a structured corset that basically allows 'members of the avian community to see your rack', while Sales wore such a short frock that she issued a warning for people sitting in the front row.

pivot to video

Alas, plans to get around to more locations in 2020 were scuppered by nation-wide lockdowns, which required a shift to live stream days before a scheduled Brissie show. Thousands of Chatters tuned in for the Not The Brisbane Live Show chat over Facebook, despite internal concerns over Crabb's insistence on handling the technical logistics. Annabel broadcasted from her natty new kitchen as various children sauntered past, and Sales from her spare room with an array of awards oh-so-casually arranged on the shelves behind her. Audio quality akin to listening to handfuls of gravel being chucked into a bucket didn't derail the gratitude of many glum Chatters. And Gwen – on hand to help with the tech stuff – ripped out her alarming and now infamous Horse Impression … just as her dismayed mum tuned in from the UK. Sorry, Sheila!

Comparing iso-baking in one of several live chats Annabel and Leigh attempted after in-person events got canned. Later, they stepped up podcast production to cheer locked-down Victorians.

an apology to
Brian Schmidt

Informed readers are no doubt familiar with Professor Brian Schmidt AC as one of the world's leading astrophysicists – heck, the guy won the Nobel Prize for Physics in 2011 – and Vice-Chancellor of the Australian National University. He's also a pinot noir winemaker, an amateur bundt-baker and a huge supporter of *Chat 10 Looks 3* who's generously hosted the end-of-year live events at Llewellyn Hall in Canberra from early on.

Brian celebrates the greatest moment of his professional life (clearly not the Nobel): pulling off a perfect bundt dismount in front of 1300 Chatters. *Picture: Sara Rowley*

However, none of this has stopped Leigh Sales and Annabel Crabb from being unutterably mean to him every year at the Canberra Christmas show. It's an illness; they can't help it.

At the first event in 2017, an enthusiastic Brian made the critical error of revealing in his on-stage introduction that he was a 'former French horn player', leading to a torrent of sass from Annabel, who asked whether 'your euphonium isn't just a tiny tuba'.

In 2018, Schmidt arrived for what he no doubt hoped was a relaxing evening to conclude a year that included a kerfuffle over plans for a Ramsay Centre for Western Civilisation course to be homed at the ANU. Crabb and Sales helpfully spit-balled 'some other Ramsay centres', like the Gordon Ramsay Centre for Cooking and Swearing, the Alan Ramsey Centre for Journalism and Swearing, or the Ramsay Street Centre for Mid-Range Television Writing. So many ideas! Lucky, lucky Brian.

But in 2019, the Professor came triply prepared. He baked a lemon and poppyseed bundt and demonstrated a perfect tin dismount in front of a packed house. He complimented Annabel and Leigh on their new books. He even made the ANU's Head of the School of Music, Kim Cunio, *learn the tuba in one week* to play a musical intro for the show. And what did generous Professor Schmidt get for his trouble? INADVERTENTLY CALLED A WANKER.

Here's how it happened. Crabb asked Sales why she wasn't wearing her newly bestowed Order of Australia pin that night ...

a Since we last met here, Leigh's got more hardware on her lapel than the military has in its entire reserves.

L I forgot, but also – in this discreet room – I just would feel like a bit of a wanker.

a Brian Schmidt's wearing his tonight, by the way ... so I guess this is our farewell tour.

L He's, no, he's ... not wearing the ribbony one, he's just wearing, like ... less of a wanker one.

a I'm actually blushing for you right now.

We'd all like to take this opportunity to apologise to Brian.

We hope that he

a) invites us back; and

b) seriously considers our pitch for an ABC comedy-reality-drama: a deeply Australian show set in a university in a regional city – almost a bush capital, if you will – presided over by a genial, French horn-playing, Nobel Prize-winning, winegrowing fellow, working title *Schmidt's Creek*.

He's not wearing the ribbony one, he's just wearing, like ... less of a wanker one.

5 questions for...
the
Bum King

When Annabel and Leigh get organised enough to do a live show, they like to pick a charity to support with a percentage of the proceeds. And they tend to choose groups not because they're big and flashy but because they are organisations with good ideas about how to help people who tend to be forgotten. Or they're causes that just aren't that cool – because Crabb and Sales aren't that cool, either. For example: bums aren't glamorous, but *Chat 10*'s Melbourne shows have supported the medical research work of what Crabb and Sales call 'the Bum Unit' at Melbourne's Royal Children's Hospital, headed by Associate Professor Sebastian King – immediately nicknamed 'the Bum King'. His (very tolerant and funny) Majesty was dragged onto the Melbourne stage to be quizzed somewhat snickeringly about his unit's work, and now enjoys an odd level of fame he probably did not foresee.

1. You've had many significant achievements in your life, notably becoming a surgeon and also an accomplished cellist. But how much do those things pale in comparison to achieving high status in a shambolic podcast?

Since I was a young child I have always wanted to be a D-Lister. The fact that I have now been pulled up onto the *Chat 10* stage, asked about my anal fixations and then given a special apron with 'Smug Bum Doctor' tells me that I have I finally made it. That, and the fact that a whole bunch of my mates' partners are Chatters and get super excited that I know Leigh and Annabel. It's all downhill from here.

2. Are you ever recognised around the place as 'the Bum King'?

Occasionally I will run into families, in situations far removed from the hospital, and I will be given an update (so to speak!) of the most recent bowel actions. It can be a bit embarrassing, especially if I can't quite recall what was the original operation that I had performed. I also ask to be referred to as 'the Rear Admiral' – it's just that little bit classier.

3. Seriously, what exactly is what Crabb and Sales call 'the Bum Unit'? What kind of work does it do, and why is it important that it build a profile?
The Bum Unit is the Colorectal and Pelvic Reconstruction Service that I established at the Royal Children's Hospital in Melbourne. We look after children born with no bums, children born with bums that don't work, and children with severe chronic constipation. This is not glamorous work, but we all know how important it is to be able to go to the toilet properly and not be worried about being incontinent. My passion is to raise the awareness of these conditions for the patients and their families, and to help reduce the stigma associated with all conditions of the bum!

4. Is it true that you once attended the Academy Awards? How did that come about, and did you slip Sales's number to Idris Elba?
It is definitely true. I am an Oscars tragic, and luckily my sister is well connected and persistent. We had an amazing and very surreal weekend in LA. I did try to offer Leigh's number to Idris (or Ids, as I call him), but he was only interested in Annabel's number.

5. You are a huge fan of *Hamilton*. If you had tickets to *Hamilton* on Broadway, with Lin-Manuel Miranda making a one-time only return appearance, who would you take: Crabb or Sales?
Firstly, I would have to creep out of the house without telling my musical-loving daughter. Once that was achieved, I would definitely take Leigh – it would be great to hear her tell LMM how he could have improved the harmonies in 'Satisfied' and the rap in 'Guns and Ships'.

merch queen

Somebody stop Gwen Blake, stat

Serious question: can you even call yourself a mildly successful podcast operation if you don't have your OWN OFFICIAL FABRIC? Or branded reusable cups? Or beeswax food wraps or witty glasses cases or French-style egg decapitators?

No, of course you can't – and that's because your podcast isn't promoted by the merchandise juggernaut that is Gwen Blake, *Chat 10 Looks 3*'s branding queen.

Gwen – affectionately known by Crabb and Sales as 'Merch Bitch' or 'Bag Hag' – spotted a demand for *Chat 10 Looks 3* items and whipped up tea towels, tote bags and the famous fairy-wren pins to sell at the very first live shows in Melbourne.

Yep, there's a bit of merch for everything . . . Gwen modelling the 'smug bundt' apron.

A one-woman operation mostly run out of Gwen's spare room, the merch is also available through the *Chat 10* website (also done by her company) and at live shows, where you'll find Gwen womanning the sales table – helped by any of Annabel and Leigh's mates who weren't quick enough to come up with an excuse to get out of it – and haranguing Crabb and Sales to sign piles of aprons.

Oh, so your podcast doesn't have its own fabric? Huh.

well hello

These are just some of her well-designed, useful and where-possible-sustainable merch hits:

- 'Insults' tea towels, featuring an array of monstrous words that the ridiculous, cloth-eared wretches have hurled at each other
- 'To-do list' tea towels that read like Chatter bingo
- 'Smug bundt' aprons, signed if Leigh and Annabel have done what Gwen told them to
- 'Monster' bookmarks, revealing Sales as a filthy book-culler and page-folder
- Deeply unhelpful 'Where did you last see them?' spectacles cases
- Beeswax food wraps that had their virtue immediately besmirched by being nicknamed 'Crack Wax'– naturally, a wrap in which to store Chatters' Crack
- Assorted Chatter cards for sending during turbulent times, loaded with in-jokes and such inspiring quotes as 'You suck less than people think'
- An actual kilometre of signature *Chat 10 Looks 3* fabric, sporting loads of motifs such as books, bundts, music, specs, cabbages, cute fairy-wrens (both bird sexes covered, thanks) and other pleasing stuff
- At the time of writing, snow globes were not out of the question.

How do you spot another Chatter in the wild? They might well be wearing a fairy-wren lapel pin, which, despite her apparent annoyance at these adorable birds, was suggested by Leigh and created by Gwen. Around 5000 of these beauties are in circulation, popping up on the lapels (or frocks) of Chatters all over the place – bookshops, writers' festivals and even TV quiz shows.

Gwen also helps out backstage, wrangles book-signing lines, drives Crabb and Sales to shows, makes brilliant birthday presents and is so big in the Facebook group that Chatters ask to have their photos taken with her instead. Honestly, someone hit that woman with a tranquilliser dart.

5 questions for . . .
Gwen Blake

1. Hey neighbour! Pre-podcast, you were Crabb's buddy from up the road. Now you're Chatter royalty, as the producer of *Chat 10 Looks 3*'s merchandise, logos, graphics, photos, promotions, pop-up bars . . . it's a long list. How did that happen?

Crabb and Sales had both been mates of mine for a while. I could see their accidentally fantastic podcast gathering speed and had offered to help with graphic design if they needed it a couple of times but they wanted to keep it low-key and hassle-free, so we never did anything. Then one day, when things seemed to be gaining more momentum, Sales emailed me, saying, 'We don't even really know what we need but we figure a logo, the name in a font, some stuff we can use on merchandise or a website, etc.' Knowing how bonkers busy they both were, and how little they knew about branding, I ran a branding project for them and took care of sourcing, designing and ordering the fairy-wren pins. It developed organically from there and they trust my judgement – they hardly ever change or comment on anything my company or I create for them. They're the easiest clients ever!

2. Your day job is co-owning a successful packaging design and branding company. Have you ever had to promote a more hopelessly terrible brand name than *Chat 10 Looks 3*?

Haha. The thing is, most brand names are born from somewhere random and then end up encapsulating the products and brands they represent, often leaving their actual origins behind. *Chat 10 Looks 3* is just the same. It's weird to get used to but rolls off the tongue once you've known and lived with it for a bit. It's also coined the term 'Chatter' for a fan of the podcast, which has been an amazing development, giving listeners a feeling of belonging to the tribe. 'Hey, are you a Chatter?' seems to be a phrase often passed between random strangers – sometimes because they're wearing a fairy-wren pin. So, it's actually a genius name!

3. **How do you get your merchandise ideas?**
Sometimes they just leap out from the podcast with no effort from me at all – like reusable coffee cups and wax wraps, which were both talked about in episodes and then I followed up with the merch. It would have been criminal not to do either of those! The challenge in those cases is to quickly find a supplier and get them turned around while there's still buzz around the joke. Other ideas come from watching the Facebook group carefully and seeing what they're talking about and doing.

Ineggsplicably, Chatters went crackers for these egg toppers after Annabel went on and on and ON about hers at an Adelaide show. Sales can't use hers properly so it was promptly regifted.

4. **What's the wackiest thing you've created for**
Chat 10 and what's your favourite?
I reckon we've definitely set the world record for sales of egg crackers. I'm calling it! That's pretty darn wacky, as are tea towels full of creative insults, which sold heaps. We've _talked about_ underwear and candles that smell of ahem, Crack . . . there are so many hilarious things we could do, but we have to draw the line somewhere. These two women do have pretty important public roles, despite just being my rude mates 90 per cent of the time. I loved the cups, as it all just unfolded on the Facebook page after Crabb joked that 'Moral High Grounds' would be a funny thing to put on a reusable coffee cup. Someone on Facebook suggested I make them, then hundreds of others chipped in. I designed one and suddenly we'd sold more than a thousand cups and donated thousands of dollars to OzHarvest to buy meals for less fortunate Australians. That's the stuff I love – the stuff

that comes with real-time buzz and gives back to the community.

5. **You do loads of other organise-y things around the podcast and rumour has it you've physically put Sharpies in the hands of Crabb and Sales to get them to autograph bags and aprons. Can they even tie their shoelaces without your help?**
They can do it all; they're both ridiculously competent, as you'd expect. When they're getting ready for a show, I just want to take as much of the boring organisational stuff away from them as I can, so they can focus on being their hilarious selves and give everyone in the audience the best night ever. I have a really different professional background to them and I'm a control freak, so sometimes it's just easier for all of us if I take care of some things. It doesn't mean they couldn't do it if they needed to. Oh ... okay, yeah ... they're hopeless.

Gotta be careful what you say on the podcast. No sooner had Crabb made a gag about feeling superior for a reusable coffee cup than Gwen had cranked out hundreds of these Moral High Grounds cups.

And update your bloody Instagram! Gwen gives Crabb a few more tasks for her to-do list. *Picture: Leigh Sales*

well hello

conversation

the art of the CLANG

CLANG noun /klæŋ/

Definition: the sound of a celebrity's name being dropped
during a conversation. Used widely throughout the podcast,
either shrieked ('So, I interviewed Hugh Jackman the other
day – CLANG!') or quietly slipped into a sentence ('I ran into
Hugh Jackman at the supermarket – um, clang – and . . .').

Crabb and Sales have encountered a metric tonne of famous folk through their working lives. They'd have to be real sourpusses to not still get a thrill from meeting someone they admire, but how does one maintain one's cool in such hot company? Can one possibly avoid making an utter prawn of oneself? And, if you're, say, recognised in a restaurant as a mildly well-known TV personality and podcaster yourself, is it more awkward to be a clang-or, or a clang-ee? Annabel and Leigh have some experience in these areas . . .

L Do you have a strategy for when you meet famous people in real life?

a Well, I try to act cool, which is part of the universal and inevitable stumbling point, right? Because you're trying so hard to act cool that you end up acting nonchalant.

L Will you even say, 'I'm a big fan,' or do you just pretend that you're not a fan?

a I will absolutely always identify that I'm an admirer. You may as well start with an obviousness, I reckon.

L That's true. One of the most mortifying encounters I ever had was the first time I met Helen Garner, which was at the book launch of our mutual friend Michael Gawenda, who used to be the editor of *The Age*.

Michael had been the Washington correspondent for Fairfax when I was over there for the ABC, and we were really great buddies, and he was very close to Garner, and I used to talk to him all the time about her writing. I wanted to just pick his brains – what was she like, what's it like to edit her work – I just went on and on and on about her all the time.

Anyway, at his book launch, it was almost like when you're in the same room as someone you've got a crush on – their presence is magnified, and you're hyper-aware of every single thing they're doing – and so I just felt like I was in a constant state of, 'Oh my god, Helen Garner is in the same room.'

Over the course of the night I managed to sidle my way up to her, and I was just thinking the whole time, 'Okay, be normal, right? I need to be absolutely normal, not fawning all over her.' And so I did the opposite to what you said, I don't even think I acknowledged that I knew who she was.

Ⓐ Oh god.

Ⓛ But then we started chatting, and we were having a perfectly pleasant chat, and then bloody Michael comes barrelling up and goes, 'Helen, thank goodness you've met Leigh, she is your biggest fan, she never stops talking about you.' I was like, through gritted teeth, 'Michael, you've blown my cover, I was acting like a normal person.'

Ⓐ You were asking for it by going all 'ice-cool-Leigh-Sales'. You've just got to throw a bit of gush-er-oo-nie at the situation, which I note from your interactions with Paul McCartney that you've definitely done.

Richard who?

Ⓛ An interview's a different thing to seeing someone in real life because in an interview, of course they know that you know who they are. Also, over the years, I've come to the opinion: is there really anyone, even Paul McCartney, who doesn't like to be told that you think they're brilliant?

Ⓐ Sure. But you can even make a story of adulation go a bit weird by immediately panicking and confessing something embarrassing. Like, I went to a play in Melbourne with my daughter, and in the dinner break we found ourselves seated next to Richard Roxburgh and his family.

🎵 For some reason, I thought you were going to say Richard Marx, the '80s singer.

🎵 Richard Marx! I had a friend at school who was so obsessed with that song ...

🎵 [*immediately starts singing 'Right Here Waiting'*] Do you want me to get on the piano and knock it out?

🎵 Can we just break away from you epically embarrassing yourself, and return to my story here?

I immediately launched into an anecdote how about 10 years earlier, I'd been visiting my friend Rachel, who was general manager of Belvoir Street Theatre at the time. I had a suitcase with me and she said, 'Put that in my office,' and so I went barrelling in and there was Richard Roxburgh in her office, and I just did this whole 'Ooh, squeal, well, I'm just here with a suitcase, I'll just, errr, umm ...' and I abandoned the suitcase and ran out.

And so, with some sort of weird, self-destructive element – in which I couldn't in any way stuff the words back into my gob to stop them being heard by not only Richard Roxburgh but also his wife – I just went on and on and on, and he must be used to people gibbering at him because he adopted this handsomely supportive expression throughout the entire thing and couldn't have been nicer, as was his impossibly talented wife Silvia Colloca, who as I mentioned was RIGHT THERE.

🎵 The worst incident I've had like that was with Pamela Rabe. We were both at *The Book of Mormon* in Melbourne, and as we were leaving we happened to end up alongside each other. I was at the peak of my *Wentworth*-watching phase, and we went, 'Hello, hello,' and the gentleman

'Okay, be normal, right? I need to be absolutely normal, not fawning all over her.' And so I did the opposite to what you said, I don't even think I acknowledged that I knew who she was.

she was with said, 'Pamela is a real fan of your work,' and so I went, 'Well, I mean, she could not be as much of a fan of me as I am of her,' and then I just kept going the entire way, as we're shuffling out. 'I mean, and what about that episode when you did this? I was watching you and I just thought, "I've never seen anything like this," I mean, I just can't believe how good you are.' Mortifying. Somehow I bumped into her at something else not long after, *and I did the same thing.*

a Wow.

L And then she did a *Chat 10 Looks 3* live show with us in Sydney, and I felt like,

> **'Oh my god, I need to get a grip on myself' and when Rabe walks in, not do that for the third time.'**

In the D-grade celebrity crapper

L But hey, you finding yourself seated next to Richard Roxburgh reminds me of the time you and I went to a restaurant and then we heard the two women at the table next to us talking about you, and they hadn't realised that you'd just sat down. They were saying something completely innocuous, like, 'I really like that Annabel Crabb and her cooking show,' but we just snapped our heads up and looked at each other with the most abject horror, like, 'The people next to us are talking about you right now, and who knows where this could go?' You leant over and went, 'Hello, I'm right here.' And the look on their faces was just, 'Oh my god.' It was equally horrifying for both tables.

a I love that both of our immediate reactions in that split second was, 'We have to alert these women before they inevitably insult me and it becomes incredibly awkward.'

L I've been in public toilets when that's happened. Like, I've done a speech somewhere and then I'm in the cubicle, and they're talking about me while they wash their hands and I always think, 'I'm staying in here until they leave, regardless of what they're saying,' because it's just so mortifying for anyone to know you've heard them talking about you.

a It's really only an occupational encumbrance or complication for the sort of D- to Z-grade celebrity, isn't it?

L Oh, the A-graders have their own designated toilets, they're not in the public restrooms.

a When I did an event with Hillary Clinton, just even watching how her life worked – getting from A to B, getting inside buildings, getting out of buildings, having to be surrounded by this phalanx of not only security guards, but also people who were there to smooth her entry and exit into and out of any social situation – was absolutely bamboozling.

L Those really uber-famous people, the ones who are wonderful, like her and Paul McCartney, understand that 99 out of 100 people are going to feel flummoxed in their presence. What they do is to try to break the ice and put people at ease.

The first time I interviewed Hillary in Melbourne in 2010, her staff told me the schedule allocated three minutes for rapport-building backstage, so we could have a little chat. She led that rapport-building, really, telling me about how, when she'd last been in Australia in the late '90s when her husband was president and she was first lady, they'd gone to a function at Yarralumla and she discovered later that all the kangaroos on the property had been rounded up and relocated for the visit, so as to not pose a security risk to the president.

Sit back and let Sales tell you all about meeting Paul McCartney

L McCartney was similar in that he just allowed you to fan him, and acted like he hadn't been told eight million times how much his music meant to somebody. He responded with grace, like, 'That means a lot to me that you're telling me that.'

a While you batted your eyelids uncontrollably at him.

L I've interviewed people I'm fans of, but I think he was different because that music has been the soundtrack to so many things in my life. I feel like I can still smell my mother's record collection, with *Help!* and *Rubber Soul* and *Revolver* in it, and I think about my friend Tim from high school, and him introducing me to *Sgt. Pepper*, and I think about when I met my husband, and how we both used to love the Beatles, and listen to it, and sing along on road trips. The sheer hours that I've spent listening to that man's music, and the amount of pleasure it's given me – I feel I owe him so much. So, for me to meet him I felt the stakes were high, because what if I met this person and he's awful and then every time I hear *Rubber Soul* all I can think about is the time Paul McCartney was an arsehole to me?

> **Paul McCartney was adorable to me, and whenever I hear Beatles music now, I feel even more fondly about him. But that's a lot of pressure on Paul McCartney, isn't it?**

That every time you leave your house, you've got to be careful you're not going to ruin somebody's whole emotional experience.

a Isn't that fascinating – that obligation and sense of anxiety about disappointing people. Every encounter you have that's unremarkable to you may be one of the most remarkable interactions the other person has in their life.

L Did you ever see that video of Jay-Z on the New York subway, and that woman gets chatting to him and she doesn't know who he is?

a Oh, fantastic! No.

L How wonderful it must be when you're really famous and you occasionally come across someone who doesn't know who you are, because you genuinely can have a normal interaction. So Jay-Z's about to play a show at Madison Square Garden, but he's getting the subway to the show and he's being videoed because they're obviously going to do something with it later. This woman, who looks probably in her 60s, is sitting next to him and she goes, 'What are you getting filmed for?' And he says, 'I'm about to do a concert.' And she goes, 'What sort of music?' And he says, 'Hip-hop.' She goes, 'Uh-huh, would I have heard of you?' And he says, 'Maybe.' And she says, 'What's your name?' And he goes, 'Jay-Z.' And she's like, 'Oh yeah, I think I've heard of that name.' And she's just totally, completely nonplussed by it. It's the most adorable little clip.

a I can hear her kids screaming.

Please don't ask me that

L Famous people usually have been interviewed many, many times. `How do you approach interviewing somebody super famous?`

a Well, I think you do really have to modulate your impulse to ask them something they've never been asked before. It's understandable, because you want them to have a memorable time and also get something out of them that's new. But to be honest, people who are super, super famous have been asked just about everything before. Also, the audience probably wants to hear answers to the most obvious questions. I have in the past sometimes made the mistake of getting too deep in the weeds when I'm interviewing someone.

L Yep.

a I remember interviewing the actor and satirist Garry McDonald for a profile piece. I was such an interested superfan of his, and I did so much research, but I ended up really grilling him about his depression and about his relationship with his creative partner that broke down. At the end, he said, 'Oh my god, that was a real workout.' It was so unpleasant for him, because I was really, 'I know everything about you.'

L `It's like when I interviewed Margaret Atwood not so long ago, I was trying to show her, 'I know you're more than just` *The Handmaid's Tale*, I've read your whole body of work, Margaret Atwood.' And so my opening question was referencing a quote from the middle of her book *Negotiating with the Dead*. I mean, who is that of interest to, other than me showing Margaret Atwood how familiar I am with her work?

The farce is strong with this one

L When the first of those new *Star Wars* films came out, Harrison Ford was in Australia to do media. He was somebody I felt overwhelmed to interview, because I thought, 'If interviewing Han Solo doesn't go well, this is like messing with my own childhood.' What I needed to ask – because every single *Star Wars* fan would want to know the answer – was, 'What did it feel like to put the Han

Solo costume back on and walk onto the set of *Star Wars* again?'

ⓐ Or you could go with, 'So I found the novella you wrote in 1973.'

ⓛ 'Let's start by talking about your film *Witness*.' And so I just thought, 'You know what? I know he's been asked this a lot of times and I just have to hope that he's gracious enough to understand that.' And he absolutely was, he answered it exactly like you'd want him to. He just said, 'It was amazing, and it was overwhelming,' et cetera.

The other funny thing with Harrison Ford was he has a reputation for being pretty taciturn and could be a bit gruff and whatnot in interviews. So I was a bit worried about that. I thought, 'I'm going to have about one-and-a-half minutes with Harrison Ford before we're rolling to try to bust through his gruffness,' and my strategy was, 'He's an introverted guy, he's been travelling all around the world doing interview after interview, maybe the best thing that I could offer that might make him warm to me will be some silence.'

So after I said hi, I said, 'Look, you must be exhausted, I know you've had back-to-back interviews, while the crew tweaks the lights, would you like to take a minute to yourself to just sit here silently and not have to make small talk with me?' And I thought that was a masterstroke of likeability.

ⓐ The classic Leigh Sales Strategic Silence!

ⓛ But he goes, 'No, not at all, I'd love to have a chat.' And then I've realised, 'Oh my god, I thought he would take the silence and I've now prepped no small talk for Harrison Ford!'

ⓐ Ol' 'No-Plan-B' Sales. I know why this happened. If you were offered 90 seconds of silence, you would goddamn take it, so it's hard for you to possibly conceive of another carbon-based organism not taking that opportunity.

ⓛ Exactly. Especially after dealing with journos all day – good grief.

And who are you, again?

ⓐ In my experience, you can get around a lot of this by just never having heard of the incredibly famous person that you're about to interview.

It takes a lot of the stress out of it. When I was in London I got the opportunity to interview the Black Eyed Peas. My editor at Fairfax had been very keen for me to do this, and it was a sit-down with will.i.am. Anyway, I'm a bit of a music ignoramus, and when Jeremy got home from work that day I said, 'I've got an interview with some, I don't know, some quite famous music group, what are they called, the Black Eyed ... what, Beans?'

Ⓛ 'I think maybe they're the Black-eyed Susans?'

Ⓐ It's something food-related. And he looked at me with this sort of stare of incomprehension and contempt, and said, 'The Black Eyed Peas,' and I said, 'Yes, that's the ones, yes, interviewing them tonight, as it happens.'

Anyway, I had done all this research and because I'd been told that I was interviewing will.i.am, ==I'd looked at his past political activity and I had all these questions about that, and race relations in the US – I mean, everything except anything to do with their music.==

And the interview kept getting pushed back. In the end, it was about 11 pm and it's really weird, because the agent leaves me at the door of this hotel suite, and I walk in and then, immediately to the left of the door is this alcove with a bed in it, which has what looks like a naked woman in it, like with long, tousley blonde hair, and I think, 'My god, I've walked into this sex pad of some kind, this is quite rock 'n' roll.'

It turns out that I am actually interviewing their singer, Fergie, and this is her room. She climbs into a dressing gown, and comes and sits down with me, creating for me this terrible situation because I've prepared all these other questions.

Ⓛ For will.i.am.

Ⓐ Exactly.

Ⓛ So, did you say to her? 'And you are ...?'

Ⓐ I knew she was in the band, I knew a bit about her, but it was very funny and weird. Also, there was a giant bag of G-bangers on the couch next to her, a plastic bag of more G-strings than you would have thought necessary for one person, and I just wanted to ask about those, but didn't.

Ⓛ Not being a huge fan of someone definitely does help. I interviewed Patti Smith a few years ago, and while I know she's a massive punk rock legend I'm not personally a gigantic fan – so you're not constantly trying to put aside your own feelings about things.

BE the brand

L Have you got a wish list? 'Jeez, I'd really love to interview X, Y, Z?'

a Yeah, but some of them I don't want to meet for fear of not loving them. And writers, I'm increasingly of the view that I kind of prefer to read what they've written.

L Oh, 100 per cent, simply for the reason that you choose a career as a writer, and you're a highly successful writer, because writing is your preferred method of expression, not having to sit and be interviewed by somebody.

a That's why I think writers' festivals are such deeply weird events. I mean, they're terrific, some of my happiest times have been spent listening to people at writers' festivals, but also, it's kind of the luck of the draw, isn't it, whether someone who's a profoundly gifted writer will also be a great interviewee and performer in public. It's a cruelly unfair second hoop that writers have to jump through, particularly that now being at writers' festivals is the best way to pump up sales of your book, and thereby continue to be able to go on writing.

L It's like if you're a gifted athlete these days it's not really enough. You also have to be able to market yourself, and speak, and do all of that. Whereas presumably, in decades past, if you were an awesome cricketer that was enough.

a You can't just let it speak for itself now, because you've got to create this identity.

L You have to have a brand.

And now, the Warne story

L The ultimate goal in any interview with a famous person is trying to get to the *real person*, not their brand or public image . . . and that means we've arrived at a very happy segue for me here, to be able to bring Shane Warne into the conversation.

a Oh god. Right, yes, of course – we would always get to Shane Warne in the end.

L The thing I loved about interviewing Shane Warne – we did a big two-parter for *7.30* with him – is that—

a It was at your instigation, too. I remember being quite surprised years ago to hear that that Shane Warne was right up the top of your interview wish list.

L Not only is Warnie one of the greatest cricketers of all time, but also he's had a remarkably colourful personal life, and I think he's a genuine figure in Australian culture, like a Paul Hogan or a Don Bradman or a Bert Newton or an Ian Thorpe. Yet I felt that, with the exception of a couple of interviews with Michael Parkinson around the time Warne retired, I'd never seen him given a serious interview that treated him as both a significant sporting and cultural figure.

I also suspected he would be pretty good talent, because he seems to be the sort of guy who doesn't really have any airs and graces. I thought he would maybe bring an A game, and he really did. He sat down, and we were rolling, and I said, 'Shane Warne, nice to meet you,' and his reply was, 'Nice to BE met.' I thought, 'This is going to be absolute gold.'

Of course – we would always get to Shane Warne in the end.

I don't think I've ever interviewed somebody where they just seemed like they were being so honest, and had no filter, to the degree that there was this bit in the interview where he was talking about his difficulty meeting a partner—

a I remember this bit. You were like, 'Is that hard?' and he was like, 'It's so hard, Leigh.'

L He's saying, 'It's so difficult, because I get worried that if they don't have kids, they might want to have kids, and I've already got my kids and I don't want more,' and he's baring his soul. If I had been at a bar with him, I would have patted him on the arm and said, 'Shane, it's fine, you'll be okay, don't overthink it.'

But you don't do that in an interview, you're just trying to be professional and ask a question. I felt like I was floundering, and so I went, 'Ummm, do you ever wonder, errr …' and before I could formulate a follow-up question, he interrupted with, '… how will I ever meet anyone? All the time!' He was absolutely everything you want in an interviewee and I could not have been happier with that interview.

a Has he got this sort of syndrome where people who are very famous for a particular field end up being interviewed only by journalists also in that field?

L Possibly.

a They're not necessarily going to face the same questions as you'd ask them on *7.30* for a general audience. The context of an interview means so much about what you can ask them. That was one of the reasons why I always wanted to do a show like *Kitchen Cabinet.* You can ask people many, many different questions when they're sitting in their own home, and you're having a reflective interview that's not triggered by X happening in their portfolio, or Y news event. It's specifically an interview where you talk about them, and you give them an opportunity to talk about whatever they want, pretty much.

I would love to meet Shane Warne, because over the course of that interview with you, I just thought, 'You are hilarious and great.' When I was based in London, he was captain of Southampton and getting into all sorts of hilarious tabloid japes. I'd get asked to sit outside his house and stake him out every time he got himself into trouble.

It happened more often than you'd think, and so I used to sit there outside in a car with a photographer, playing Travel Connect 4, or periodically knocking on his door, and feeling like the lowest of the low, so I feel like we have that history. I never met him – I met his children a couple of times. Nothing makes you feel worse, or screams to you that as a journalist maybe you've reached the nadir of your reporting career, than knocking on Shane Warne's door and his poor, innocent kids are answering, and you're like, 'Hi kids, is your dad home?'

L This conversation has been most entertaining and leads me to believe that in our retirement, we'll have a lucrative money-spinner giving nightly talks on cruise ships about our celebrity encounters. Kill me now.

clangecdotes

Giles Coren,
aka Annabel's red shoes shame

Newton's Third Law states that for every action, there must be an equal and opposite reaction. And thus it is also with clangs: Crabb's Third Law states that for each triumphant, anecdote-worthy clang there surely is a failed, cringeworthy clang ... the ANTI-CLANG.

When Annabel was working in London, she lived around the corner from writer, journalist and author of savage restaurant reviews Giles Coren, whom she admires. They shared a house number – 47 – but on different streets, and so Crabb was often erroneously delivered his mail. 'I would just sort of pop it on his doorstep and run away cackling,' she recalls, but no further contact was made ... until Annabel was moving house. 'I had this fantastic pair of red shoes that were a bit worn down, and they were really good shoes. And I left them on Giles Coren's doorstep! I don't know why – I thought it was mysterious. And then I thought, "I'll watch his columns to see if he's mentioned receiving a freaky pair of red shoes." As I tell the story out loud now, it really does sound a bit creepy and weird. There was no note or anything threatening or anything like that.'

Years later, Giles Coren was writing a column on the London Olympics, and he had to cover the rhythmic gymnastics, and it was very funny. Crabb tweeted, 'Fantastic, this is the thing I love about the Olympics the most,' and he replied to her tweet. Crabb thought, 'Wing-a-ding-ding, I'm now having a conversation with Giles Coren!' She then said, 'So anyway, I used to live around the corner from you and I left a pair of red shoes ...'

Coren responded with, 'Wow, just wow.' Crabb never heard from him again. We don't know if he blocked her ... but we wouldn't be surprised.

Leigh was speechless at this story, when it was excruciatingly recounted in Episode 146. 'You're ... not really who I thought you were, actually,' she spluttered. Annabel: 'I'm questioning that myself.'

the Garner files

ⓐ I've got a horrible Helen Garner moment, too. When I was in London, James Button was the correspondent there and she was staying with him. James invited me over, knowing my Garner obsession, and I was just kind of speechless with excitement. I said, 'I'll bring dessert,' and took the worst dessert I've ever prepared. It was just a real dud. It was a variation on a cheesecake but it ended up like a liquid. It was like a really bad milkshake with crumbs. With jelly. Oh, my god – just the worst. I feel like at some point in the future, I will appear in one of those incredibly microscopic detail pieces she does, you know, 'The keen young reporter arrived with an inexplicable dessert.'

ⓛ She must watch *Kitchen Cabinet* and just not buy it. 'Clearly this is fake because I've eaten that woman's food and it ain't TV-worthy.'

The bitter chicory of abandonment

ⓐ Remember that time we got 'stood up' by Helen Garner at lunch? We were both so overwhelmed and really weird about it, because we had been totally looking forward to it so much, and then we just got the dates mixed up. And you went to the toilet ... and ran into Ian Thorpe.

ⓛ That was the funniest ever, because we were in such a state by the time I bumped into Ian Thorpe, and he's gone, 'Leigh, hey, how're you going?' And I've gone, 'Oh, Ian, I'm terrible. We've just been stood up by Helen Garner!' And Thorpe, he's just looked at me, and probably thought, 'Get this crazy bird away from me.'

ⓐ And when you came back to the table you said, 'What should we order?' And I said, 'Why don't we order the bitter chicory of abandonment?' And you said, 'I can't see it on the menu ... I'm sure they'd whip it up for us.'

Leonardo DiCaprio

what a coincidence!

Ⓛ Sorry. I've been so rushed today, I'm in a real hurry because I'm interviewing Leonardo DiCaprio ... CLANG.

ⓐ So, here's the context, right? Leigh's sitting in her office, literally waiting for Leonardo DiCaprio to call. Now. There have been – am I right, Sales? – over the past 10 days, a series of opportunities for us to record this final podcast. And you've been all like, 'No, no, I broke a nail,' or something else. Now I understand it that you, in your passive-aggressive way, have been orchestrating things so that we can be sitting in your office and get interrupted by a call from Leonardo DiCaprio.

Ⓛ To the degree that I just emailed my producer and said, 'When Leo's ready, can you please knock on the door and say "Salesy, Leonardo DiCaprio is on the phone ..."'

ⓐ '... and can you tell him I'm busy?'

Nigella Lawson

gets Crabb off to a flyer

Venue tannoy: Ms Lawson and Ms Crabb. This is your five-minute call. You have five minutes until the commencement of this evening's talk. Five minutes, thank you.

ⓐ C-LANG!

Ⓛ Love, that was one hell of a clang.

ⓐ I think I've really started this year right at the top of the leaderboard, clang-wise. Nigella is a lovely person. You know when you meet somebody that you're nervous about interviewing because you think, 'God, what if they just turn out to be some sort of awful beast'? Well, she was lovely. Very, very, very gracious. That's nice.

Ⓛ And it's the charm that she has. I mean, if people talk about Bill Clinton being charming, and 'he makes me feel like the only person in the room', like, what's her schtick?

a I turned up to meet her and she was straight over for a bit of a hug. And, 'Oh, gosh, I've been looking forward to this so much.' The woman's spent her time in Australia just being crawled over by all and sundry. I'd be surprised if she's ever had two seconds to put her head up and go, 'Holy shit, what's next?' But she was completely charming.

Sales's favourite
celebrity interview ever

L I had to interview Renée Zellweger this week.

L & **a** CLANG!

a Is she happy about sparking this entire meme on the internet about actresses who've interfered with their faces? I want to sit her and everybody from *Friends* down and have a talk to them about that.

L I had tricky questions like, what do you think is more of an indictment on society? The fact that people comment on the changing appearances of actresses, or the fact that actresses themselves feel the need to have plastic surgeries and they continue to look youthful? And then as soon as she walked in, she was so adorable and charming and delightful. Every person in the room just fell in love with her. She was so chatty to every single person and so funny and delightful. I just threw out every hard question. She played me like a fiddle. I just loved her. She's probably my favourite celebrity interview, ever.

stuck in the loo
with Colin Firth

L I always found it mystifying that you would pass up Hugh Grant for Colin Firth in *Bridget Jones's Diary* because Colin Firth in the film is the most humourless bore imaginable.

a No, I am in the other camp. I've personally been stuck in a toilet with Colin Firth. So I feel like we've got a special connection.

L CLANG! Amazing clang. I think you've told me that story before but remind me.

a I tell you every day and you keep forgetting. You refuse to be impressed by the crumbs of celebrity that I have 'cos you're just turning away Renée Zellwegers and Harrison Fords every day of the week. Anyway, look, I may have suggested a level of intimacy that did not occur. But I was in a cool club in Soho called Milk and Honey. I really was. This is some time ago. Anyway, I was really busting for a wee. And they did one of those kooky, charming, intensely annoying things where they labelled the toilets 'milk' and 'honey', if you please.

L So, I'm thinking honey is the women's. What would you go with?

a That's what I would go with too . . . not so much Colin Firth, as it turns out. So I'm watching a guy, and he's got that kind of uncertain look of someone who's looking at the toilets as well. And I see him heading off towards 'milk'. So I tentatively go into 'honey' . . . and there's Colin Firth.

L In honey!

a Yep, he's in honey, his pants are still on but he's looking around, and he's clearly just thinking, 'cos there's like, lady stuff in there, 'Oh, all right, uhhh . . .' And I then burst in, and it's the perfect situation because Colin Firth is frightened and he wants to leave, and I am standing in the door. So I have the power in this situation.

L Did you exchange any words?

a We did! I was so cool 'cos I didn't do, 'OH MY GOD COLIN FIRTH,' who I think is very handsome, I just said, 'Oh, hello.' I was really smooth. And he said – and I'm not making this up – he said, 'Oh, god, I've just made an incredible ass of myself, haven't I.' And I held up my end of the conversation for a bit and eventually let him escape and I went back to my friends.

the art of

the C-list group clang

🅐 Sales, you've probably never occupied this slot of the celebrity interviewing food chain. But when I was in London for Fairfax, I used to do a few movie profiles and interviews and stuff like that. And often in those cases, you'd have like a giant star with some film coming out. So you'd have a junket day at some hotel where the star would be in a room and you'd have TV and print reporters ushered in in 10-minute slots.

But if you're sufficiently unimportant that you don't qualify for one of those in-out-shake-it-all-about slots — it's like the collateralised debt obligation of the film interviewing world — there's also a pool interview where, say, six not-very-important writers from not-very-important countries get put in a room and the star will come in and be interviewed by all six of them at once. So then if you're a tiny newspaper organisation you can say, 'Scarlett Johansson *told me that* blah, blah, blah' – but you don't mention that you're also in the room with a Dutch newspaper or, you know, the *Federated States of Micronesia Daily*. And the funniest thing about those is that maybe that actor has done an ad series in that country, and that's all they're known for, like, 'I'm gonna be asking you about coffee.'

I met Paul McCartney?

Leigh rates Sir Paul as her best clang of all time and has told this story about 14 times in various iterations on the podcast – and clearly it wasn't enough to only mention him once in this chapter. So, we're going to mash this all into a hybrid everything-Sales-has-ever-gushed-about-McCartney clangecdote and

THAT WILL BE THE END OF IT.

Ⓛ We've discussed on the podcast before how it can be hazardous to meet people of whom you're a big fan because if they are unpleasant, for whatever reason, a little part of you dies. But meeting and interviewing Sir Paul McCartney for *7.30* was truly one of the greatest experiences of my life.

I am such a massive Beatles fan. I got onto the Beatles because one of my good friends from school, Tim, told me his favourite album was *Sgt. Pepper's Lonely Hearts Club Band*. I went through Mum and Dad's old vinyl collection and they had *Help!* and *Rubber Soul* and *Revolver* – but I didn't have *Sgt. Pepper*. I went and bought it and that put me on this lifelong Beatles thing.

I absolutely adore all of them, but particularly Paul McCartney. I saw him for the first time live in the US when I lived there in 2002. I cried from start to finish. Then in 2017 we get this offer: do you want to do his first television interview in Australia? He hasn't toured here for 24 years.

Ⓐ Do you need an oxygen mask or anything? You're a tiny bit breathy.

Ⓛ So I rang my friend Tim and said, 'I know this sounds like a really weird offer asking you to come away for a weekend with me. But do you want to come to Perth and meet Paul McCartney?' And he was just like, 'Are you joking?' We got to go and watch the rehearsal for the concert on the Friday night, which we both just couldn't believe – we were standing backstage in the wings watching Paul McCartney do 'Day Tripper' – and then I interviewed him on stage. At the end I said something like, 'I have never interviewed somebody of whom I am as big a fan as you and thank you so much for all that music.' I was nearly crying. And he said, 'Oh, love, give us a hug.' And then after a while he's like, *pat pat, pat . . .* 'Yes . . . okay, then . . .'

Ⓐ You start sniffing his hair a bit.

Ⓛ It was like, I had an internal hug going on the whole time because I was so happy. That's what I felt like for about three days. It was the greatest clang of all time. Even now, sometimes when I feel a bit sad I pull out the promo video for that episode.

oh my god

it's really
Monica Lewinsky

If Chat 10 had to choose a TV quiz specialty topic, the Clintons would be well in the mix. So, clanging Monica Lewinsky was next-level – but sparked some serious reflection by Crabb and Sales on her treatment by, well, almost all of us.

Leigh met Lewinsky at a Melbourne conference at which they were both speaking. Monica has become a global activist against bullying and public shaming of people, particularly online. They got to chatting at afternoon tea and then shared a car ride to the airport. So, what did one of the most intensely scrutinised people in history have to say? Nice try, but Sales ain't about to dish on that. 'I think there's nobody less on the planet who needs a person – a woman with whom they thought they were having a private conversation – to blab about it than Lewinsky does,' she explains. 'So I'm not gonna say anything other than that I just thought she was an awesome chick. I'll tell you one detail that was very telling: when we got to the airport, she said, "Can I give you some money for the ride?"' Bless!

Sales hosted a conversation with Lewinsky on stage in Sydney some months later and found her 'massively impressive'.

L I just feel so ashamed of her treatment; of what happened to her. And being the butt of so many jokes and for losing such a big chunk of her life to it. And she's a really smart, articulate, interesting, funny person.

a She had one of the most extraordinary transitions from nonentity to global fame. Probably the fastest ever. I can't think of anyone who was as unknown, and then became as globally known as she did. I think there's a lot of people for whom revisiting her and her experience is an uncomfortable feeling, because of the way we now look at what happened to her and think of the jokes, and we all kind of laughed at them. There was a prolonged political defence of Clinton from the left that I think probably skated over the politics of what had happened to her.

L That's right. When you hear her talk today about the impact that had on her and think about it in terms of that she was a human being at the centre of it, not just an almost cartoon figure.

well hello

jammin'

with Jimmy

Sales is, at her core, a '70s/'80s army brat from Brissie, and thus has Cold Chisel branded onto her brain. But she's also a fan of frontman Jimmy Barnes's writing. She loved his memoirs and reckons he's got a 'beautiful storytelling ability'. **(He's also a foodie, so that helps.)** So Crabb was immediately suspicious when Leigh revealed that she'd interviewed Barnesy and his wife, Jane, for *7.30* in a warehouse that *had a grand piano . . .*

L No, I'd actually thought, 'I'm not going to play the piano with Jimmy Barnes because I'm too massively outclassed.' Anyway, he asked, 'Can I get Jane to meet you? She's a fan.' So Jane did, and then she said, 'Let's do a song,' because they've been doing these amazing videos of themselves singing during lockdown and Jane's taught herself to play the guitar. And I said, 'Well, you and Jimmy do a song.' And she said, 'Do you play anything?' I said, 'A bit of piano,' and she goes, 'Oh, you do one,' and I said, **'I'm not playing with Jimmy,'** and she said, 'Come on, I can hardly play the guitar and I play with Jimmy all the time.' So I said, 'Well, what do we want to do?' And Jimmy said, 'Do anything.' And I said, 'What about a Beatles song?' and he goes, 'Sure,' and I said, 'What song?' 'Just any song,' he said. I said, 'Yeah, but like, what key?' He said, 'Any key,' at which point I thought, 'Well, clearly I'm not getting out of this.' So I sat down and started playing 'Something', which is off *Abbey Road*. And you know what? Because it just happened spontaneously there was no time to be nervous or for overthinking. So it was actually just fun and enjoyable. Whereas, if you'd said to me that morning, 'You'll get to do a song later today with Jimmy Barnes,' **I just would have had diarrhoea all day.** It was just so delightful, and it was just one of those moments where I thought, how privileged am I to just get to sit here and listen to Jimmy Barnes sing a song while I play along . . .

a . . . and he pretends that you are really great.

chapter 9
watch

A revolt against lists

Hello, Annabel Crabb here. I'm leaping in with a poorly organised stream of consciousness because I know, with a dreaded certainty, that Leigh Sales will already have filed her lists of favourite TV shows and movies, colour-coded for whether or not Idris Elba is in them. And frankly, I tried to keep up for a bit with the book lists, but now I'm out. My brain doesn't work like that. I'm the sort of person who can crap on indefinitely in conversation but when asked a question point-blank such as 'What is your favourite movie?' every film I've ever seen flees my memory immediately and I can think of absolutely nothing beyond ridiculous stuff like *Arthur 2* or *Splash*.

The first time I was on Richard Fidler's radio show *Conversations* I was being interviewed beforehand for a producer, who said, 'You've worked in politics for all these years, you must have some wonderfully funny stories. Perhaps you could share some?' At which point my brain became like the Serengeti before the rains – absolutely arid and devoid of any life whatsoever. I could not think of a single interesting thing I had ever heard or seen.

So instead of lists, I'm going to set out what I've picked up over the years about what is now so charmingly called 'content consumption'. Meaning: TV, streaming, movies and podcasts. Things that you receive passively, rather than reading or hauling your arse to a theatre or gallery.

For me, TV and streaming is the first thing to go when I'm busy. I'm always really cautious about getting invested in a new series, for instance, because I know it'll mean 12 hours out of my life that I can't spare. For Sales, though, I reckon TV is actually in some ways a time-saving device. (Stay with me, I know this sounds like a pretty creaky theory.) Leigh gets home from work at, let's say, 8.30 pm. She's totally wired, as anyone would be at that hour if their entire working day was spent building up to 30 minutes of live television, asking questions to people who often don't want to answer them, while keeping an eye on the clock and remembering not to swear.

I reckon when Sales comes home and watches TV it allows her brain to

well hello

decompress in quite a time-efficient way. Particularly when it's TV that is completely unlike the TV she makes. Half an hour of *RuPaul's Drag Race* can quite efficiently return her brain to normal after half an hour of Paul Keating Mansplain, and render her ready for that 9 pm bedtime.

So yeah, I'd say that the two of us have different viewing habits.

Mine are driven by circumstance. There are some key preconditions that dictate the sort of thing I'll watch.

- **Extreme levels of stress and overwork:** No TV at all. Feel too guilty that I should be doing something more productive.
- **Stress levels moderate:** Reruns of *30 Rock*. Guaranteed laughs, plus no sinkhole of addiction, as I've seen them all before. Ditto *Veep* or old episodes of *The Larry Sanders Show* (to my mind still the best TV comedy series ever made). Alternatively, for some reason: true crime documentaries. I don't know why, but when I'm stressed, I find it relaxing to learn about the depravity of the human spirit. I also enjoy watching back episodes of *The Heights*, the ABC's own excellent in-house soap opera.
- **Stress levels low:** This is when I feel okay about jumping into a new series. Things I've loved over the past year: *Good Girls* (which includes Christina Hendricks and Retta – one of my favourite TV actors of all time – as suburban mums sucked into a life of crime). Retta is also in *Parks and Recreation*, which I started watching this year, an entire decade after the rest of the world, and realised how great that series is. *The Crown* (come for Olivia Colman's Betty Windsor, stay for Gillian Anderson's Maggie Thatcher). *Succession* – I would really like to erase it from my brain so that I can watch the whole thing again.

- **On a plane:** Being on a plane grants you a licence to watch stuff you ordinarily wouldn't. This is the only setting in which I will watch big-budget schlock.
- **At home alone:** Afforded the opportunity to watch anything I like, considering the needs of no one else, I will invariably spend the entire evening scrolling through various streaming platforms finding nothing that really suits my mood then fall asleep watching *Mad As Hell*. No uncertainty whatsoever about my Home Alone menu, though. Macaroni tossed with peas, crumbled feta and torn up mint, with olive oil, lemon and black pepper. Toasted pine nuts on top, if I can find any.

The truth is, with TV as with music, I am very guided by Jeremy. I'm the books lady. Podcasts, however, are another story. Unlike with TV, I never feel guilty for 'wasting time' on them. This is because they fit into the cracks of life – walking to school to pick up the kids, catching the train to work, shopping, errands, driving. You can do something else with your hands and your eyes while you listen: cooking, or cleaning, or administrivia. You can listen any time, and pause when you need to. Plus, I've also found that a really good podcast – the kind whose next episode I just cannot wait to hear – can function as an incentive to exercise. I have gone out for a run just so I can listen to a half-hour episode without someone interrupting me to ask where their sneakers are. And I really don't love running.

Podcasts that are always in my feed: Slate's *Political Gabfest*, largely for the wonderful presence of Emily Bazelon. *This American Life*. *99% Invisible*. I love a podcast that looks at forgotten bits of history and brings them to life. I loved *Debutante* by Nakkiah Lui and Miranda Tapsell, and *Revisionist History* by Malcolm Gladwell, and also *Cautionary Tales* by Tim Harford. For a reminder that humans are good, *Too Peas in a Podcast*. *Side Door*, the fascinating podcast about little-known curios at the Smithsonian (listen to the episode about the E.T. Atari game – the worst video game ever made!). *The Eleventh* (the ABC's podcast about the Dismissal) is brilliant, as is Rachael Brown's *Trace: The Informer*, about Australian lawyer and supergrass Nicola Gobbo.

Anyway, enough from me. Leigh Sales's Culture PowerPoint begins in 3, 2, 1 …

chat 10's top 10s

Spoiler alert! Here are Leigh's favourite TV shows and movies about which she will never stop banging on.

Salesy's top 10: telly

10.
Anne of Green Gables
(the 1985 version starring Megan Follows)
This was one of my favourite childhood books and the Canadian television version is about as perfect an adaptation as you could see. The only thing I didn't like about it was that truly hideous dress with puffy sleeves that Matthew gave Anne. But don't get me started on Matthew . . . oh, dammit, too late, I'm howling already. Lucy Maud Montgomery is such a treasure of Canadian literature that I suspect they must have gone all out to make the most flawless version of this treasured novel they could. Well played, Canadians, well played.

9.
Borgen
An incredibly addictive Danish political drama, charting the election of the country's fictional first female prime minister, centrist Birgitte Nyborg. I spent the whole time going, 'Why can't we have a political leader like her?' You get to watch her evolve from an idealist into a canny, pragmatic politician and witness the compromises she must make in her professional and personal lives. First rate.

8. *Olive Kitteridge*

A four-part adaptation of the novel by Elizabeth Strout, starring the incredible Frances McDormand in the title role. I've rarely seen something on screen pack so much emotional punch using so little dialogue. As with *Anne of Green Gables*, this is an adaptation that does full justice to the wonderful source material (that just happens to be on Salesy's Top 10 fiction list, what a coincidence).

7. *Veep*

This is so funny that you constantly have to pause your device because you are laughing so hard, and the pace is so fast that unless you stop, you will miss the next three or four gags. Julia Louis-Dreyfus is hilarious as America's first female vice-president, Selina Meyers. It's worth watching purely for the brilliant comic partnership between her and Tony Hale, who plays Gary, her aide-de-camp. The ensemble cast riffs off each other brilliantly.

6. *The Office* (the British version)

This is hard to watch because David Brent is so excruciating. There's something so recognisable in him and I think what makes it tough viewing at times is that perhaps we fear we're seeing ourselves. Maybe we are David Brent and, like him, we just don't realise how awful we are! Among my favourite moments are the episode where he brings his guitar to work and the one where Neil from the other office shows up and is effortlessly handsome and charming, to Brent's barely suppressed fury. It's a perfect piece of work.

5. *Friday Night Lights*

I really had to be talked into watching this, given it's about a high school football team in Texas. But it has so much heart! I missed the major characters, Coach and Tammy Taylor, like they were real-life friends when I came to the end of the five seasons.

Worth watching purely for Connie Britton's perfect hair, which is always the star of anything she's in. Worth also watching for Tim Riggins – and from those of you who've seen it, can I get an amen.

4. *30 Rock*

This is like comfort food. Like many great sitcoms, once you know the characters you can dip in at any episode, in any season, and it requires nothing from you. All it does is make you laugh and laugh. It's the story of a fictional comedy show at NBC, where the head writer is Liz Lemon, played by Tina Fey, and the network CEO is Jack Donaghy, played by Alec Baldwin. After my father died, I kept *30 Rock* on high rotation. If I ever met Alec Baldwin, I would cry and thank him because he is so hilarious; he got me through. *30 Rock* also has one of the best and most satisfying final episodes of any show I've loved.

3. *The Bureau*

This French spy thriller follows the lives of an elite group of undercover agents. It's sophisticated and intelligent, and if you get distracted and miss a couple of subtitles, you're in trouble. But the reward is huge; it took over my life when I watched it. The characters unfold brilliantly over the seasons. It is SO addictive that I recommend only starting if you are certain you have about 50 hours of television viewing time that you can immediately accommodate.

2. *The Americans*

Anyone who has listened to the podcast knows how helplessly infatuated with this show Crabb and I were. We even devoted a whole episode to droning on and on about it. It has some similarities to *The Bureau* – it follows two undercover Russian agents operating in Washington DC in the 1980s. One of the key differences is that *The Americans* has a sense of impending doom right from the start, whereas *The Bureau* gives you some hope that the key character may be able to hustle his way out of a tricky situation. *The Bureau* lets the tension wax and wane, *The Americans* never lets up. At times, I wondered if I was actually getting any pleasure from watching *The Americans* because the anticipation of inevitable tragedy was so relentless. Keri Russell and Matthew Rhys as the Russian spies are utterly superb. In the final episode I was crying almost from the start – not because of sadness, but because the writers had ratcheted the tension up so high that my nerves were completely shot. Even hearing the theme music now sets me on edge. Brilliant. Cannot adequately express how much I loved it.

1. *The Sopranos*

I've watched this entire series three times from start to finish. I never tire of it and I never stop marvelling at what a work of genius it is. So many bingeworthy shows that have come after it owe a lot to *The Sopranos*. With repeated viewings, I've become surprised at how funny it is – in a very black way, of course. The relationship between Tony and Carmela Soprano (James Gandolfini and Edie Falco) is so real that it still amazes me that they were acting. As everyone knows, the ending was highly controversial, but I loved it (and personally, I'm in the camp that believes Tony was whacked at the restaurant). The other thing that strikes me with this show is how fully realised it is from Season One, Episode One. It doesn't really evolve and find its feet as some shows do; it's fully formed from the start. The supporting cast is glorious and I particularly found Tony Soprano's mother and his nephew Christopher the most wonderfully written and performed characters. The violence in *The Sopranos* means it's not to everyone's taste, but seriously, if you've not seen this, run don't walk.

Salesy's top 10: films

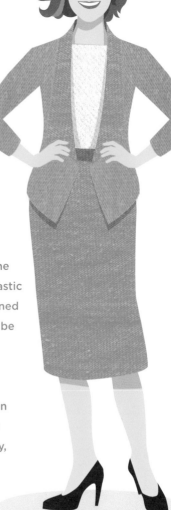

10. *Austin Powers: International Man of Mystery*

Stop with your judgement. Why is this on my list? Because it is bedwettingly funny and because I still reference it all the time. DO I MAKE YOU HORNY, BABY? YEAH! I would love to spend this paragraph quoting my favourite moments ('I have one request, and that is to have SHARKS with frickin' LASER BEAMS attached to their HEADS'; 'A chaste man who died of a disease that bore all the hallmarks of syphilis') but I know you'll find that really, really tedious – so just go and pour yourself a glass of wine on a Friday night and watch it. Special bonus points for the use of Quincy Jones's 'Soul Bossa Nova' in the opening sequence. It's groovy, baby, YEAH!

9. *American Beauty*

It's many years since I've watched this and yes, I know Kevin Spacey is cancelled. But I thought it was amazing when I first saw it. Annette Bening having the crying fit in front of the vertical blinds; the rose petals falling over Mena Suvari; the dancing plastic bag. I don't think a great film deserves to be consigned to the dustbin because the lead actor turned out to be an obnoxious tool.

8. *A Chorus Line*

Fans of the original musical consider the film version a travesty. I hear what they're saying. I can't believe they cut 'Hello 12, Hello 13, Hello Love' so horrifically,

and the bastardisation of 'Let Me Dance For You' –
shoehorning it into the Zach/Cassie relationship, rather than
letting it be about Cassie's need to perform – is so wrong.
BUT. When you're a kid growing up in Brisbane, you're not getting
to go to Broadway to see *A Chorus Line*, are you? This was as
close as I got and I LOVED it. I could sing every word and I reckon
I watched it at least once a week for a couple of years. If we're
talking musical films, *Chicago* is way better, but I have a nostalgic
soft spot for this one.

7. *Tootsie*

Dustin Hoffman is of course fantastic but Bill Murray steals every
scene he's in. It's so funny, but also so poignant. I also love the
Dave Grusin soundtrack.

6. *Misery*

I've never read the Stephen King novel so I've no point of
comparison but I consider this a perfect little film. It amazes me
how well it marries horror and comedy. I also love how sparse it
is – it has perfect structure; is short compared with films these
days; has a beginning, a middle and an end; and is generally one-
and-a-half hours bloody well spent.

5. *Anvil! The Story of Anvil*

A wonderful documentary, ostensibly about two guys who
were heavy metal rockers in the 1980s and had one hit album,
but can never let go of their dream. When it starts, you think
perhaps it's going to be a pisstake of them but it turns into the
most wonderful, reverential and moving exploration of friendship.
The defining thing about these two guys' lives turns out not
to be their music, or their quest for stardom – it's their lifelong
friendship. Their families are also marvellous in the love and
support they offer.

4. *Die Hard*

Listeners of the podcast may be surprised to not see this as my number one, so well known is my love of it. Seriously, what's to not love? You won't have a better two hours. I adore Bruce Willis but the person I revere is Alan Rickman. These characters both became models for many subsequent action films – John McClane as the reluctant hero and Hans Gruber as the super-smart, cultured baddie you're sort of rooting for. When it became such an epic hit, the makers of *Die Hard* must have seriously kicked themselves that Gruber died in such an incontrovertible way at the end of the first film. If I'm flicking around the TV and this is on, I find it hard to not settle in.

3. *Office Space*

On here purely because a week does not go by that I am not spouting lines from this film. It is the story of Peter, a guy who decides he's going to keep showing up at work, but not actually work anymore, a move that gets him labelled 'a straight shooter with upper-middle management written all over him'. This film left me with two things that bring me endless happiness: a) the discovery that the red Swingline stapler really IS the world's best stapler (I love stapling things with mine!), and b) the joy of saying 'PC Load Letter, what the fuck?' literally any time a piece of technology that I'm using won't work, to the great mystification of most people around me. It is always wonderful if somebody within earshot laughs and gets the reference. I know they are a kindred spirit.

2. *Muriel's Wedding*

God, I love this film so much. I'm always surprised when people consider it a comedy. It's a tragedy, with a few funny bits. I know it's weird to feel an affinity for actors who play characters you love, because they're just actors playing roles, but I have always had the greatest affection for Toni Collette and Rachel Griffiths because of this film.

The use of ABBA is inspired too – ABBA songs have such a melancholy tone to them that fits beautifully.

Many scenes from this stick in my head – Bill Hunter telling the family they're all 'bloody useless' as the camera pans around the table at their faces; the mother's cracked heels in the supermarket and the way she watches a cup of tea in the microwave; the burned lawn at the end. If I'm at a table and we stand up to leave but somebody has an unfinished drink, I like to say, 'Wait, let her finish her Orgasm,' which gets plenty of funny looks.

1. *Singin' in the Rain*

I don't have words. Just the most flawless film ever made. A total joy bomb. Quite rightly, the scene of Gene Kelly doing 'Singin' in the Rain' is the most famous, with Donald O'Connor's 'Make 'Em Laugh' a worthy second. It's hard to single out a favourite bit but I love the 'Broadway Melody' in the middle, particularly the arrival of Cyd Charisse sashaying around in that little green number – surely one of the greatest film entrances EVER. When you watch this film today, it's incredible how contemporary it feels. There is so much charm on screen in this, I just smile like an absolute fool from start to finish. I hope I see this on the last day of my life.

well hello

classic episode 6

50 shades of giggling

This episode, along with the first, is the one Chatters often recommend to friends reluctant to try the podcast. Possibly *not* what they'd expect from two of the nation's pre-eminent journalists, but it's Crabb and Sales's best film review work ... and easily the most R-rated. It was only Episode 6 but things had already slid rapidly downhill from the lofty cultural premise of *Chat 10 Looks 3.* (This episode is eclipsed in insanity only by the time they went to see the movie version of *Cats* – but no one wants to revisit THAT.)

Deciding that they were 'in a rut' of just watching and reading things they liked or were interested in, Leigh and Annabel headed out to catch a matinee viewing of the film adaptation of the erotic novel *Fifty Shades of Grey.* They were quickly reduced to puddles of cry-laughing their way through surreptitiously buying the tickets ('Can we get those in a brown paper bag, please?'), watching the movie and then podcasting about it in the foyer afterwards. What follows is a HEAVILY edited version of the conversation to remove long stretches of giggling, weeping and Sales's hideous, phlegm-filled bark of a cough that surely destroyed every sex scene for the other cinema attendees.

Ⓛ [*Wishing she were in dark sunglasses and a hat*] So, what did you make of the film?
ⓐ I think I'm not cut out for that sort of thing. I just couldn't stop tittering. I would be bad, I think, at BDSM of any kind – role play, submissive, dominant – because the sniggering factor would just be too much.
Ⓛ Well, I just think my erotic fantasy is to be in a hotel room alone and that's it. We've got five children under eight between us. The idea that you'd waste a hotel room on anything but sleep ...

a Like what was that, a 140-minute film? I would accept just watching Ryan Gosling do the dishes real slow.

L There was some sort of device . . . 'the duster', we called it. And I said to you, 'It looks like he's doing the mopping,' to which I think you said something like, 'Now there's an erotic thought, having someone do your mopping.'

a Just half an hour of mopping things. During a particularly childish interval during the film, every time there was a new shot, I was just identifying the phallic object in it. It was sort of like when you see a Wes Anderson movie and you're kind of like, 'Oh, that's symmetrical.' I'm like, 'That looks like an art postcard I once wanted.' In this one it's a bottle of wine.

L Elevator shaft.

a Tap. Oh, yeah.

L I think, for me, there were two genuinely erotic moments in the film. The first was the opening, which reveals his immaculate walk-in wardrobe. That was really titillating. I was like, 'I'll have one of those, thank you.' And the other one was they had that pavilion owned by his parents with the indoor pool and the greenhouse sort of thing.

a Always wanted one of those.

L Definite turn-on for me. The other thing that's my problem with these sorts of films is that I know you're meant to suspend disbelief and whatnot, but he has this red room, which is his play room. I kind of think: who cleans it? Who cleans the red room?

a I assume that that would be something the submissive would get around to at some point.

L Good point, actually.

a I mean, they didn't dwell on those aspects of the contractual agreement, but I assume that if anyone's going to be slopping out that red room, it ain't going to be him, is it? Right?

L And she's fallen into the lap of Seattle's most experienced sexual predator. You say it was like a cartoon. It was your classic 'young, innocent girl with a beast' story, basically. And 'I can't show you my true self, because I'm a beast'. So it was Christine and the Phantom and it was Beauty and the Beast and all of that.

well hello

a But whose fantasy is that? I don't know. It feels like a guy fantasy, obviously, because there's this sort of dewy-eyed, lip-munching hottie who just happens never to have had her knickers off before, but has just gone, 'My clothes fell off. I would really like you to hurt me badly. That would be great. Let me get in your plane.'

L The other thing that, and again, I know you're meant to suspend disbelief when you come to the films. But so, for example, that moment where she reveals that she's a virgin and I think he's already shown her through his little torture dungeon by then, hasn't he? I think so. Not for a moment does she go, 'Hang on. I'd better check with my girlfriend.'

a I might phone a friend.

L Yeah, I might phone a friend. Often in these sorts of films where women are the protagonist, one of the things that strikes me – because, frankly, I know a bit about women and about friendship between women – I think that you run a lot of stuff by your friends, particularly major decisions. And the fact that she didn't go home to her flatmate and say, 'Wow, I'm really into this guy, but I've got to tell you, just between us, because he swore me to secrecy, he's got like a dungeon full of mops and dusters.'

a So let me get this straight, Sales, your problem with this film is a plausibility issue? I just could not see that coming.

L And I realised at a certain point that what I was waiting to happen was for him to be revealed as Batman. Because he was this rich dude and he had a lot of boy toys and he had a secret, and he had a manservant like Alfred. Taylor, this one's name was. And he lived in something that looked a little bit like a lair. And it was like my filmic expectations were being violated, because I've seen that film and it's *Batman*.

a Okay, we're all very confused about this film, aren't we? I don't know. The whole thing feels like a man fantasy, but it's wound up being this female fantasy.

L But tens of millions, hundreds of millions of women have bought it. So we're missing something here.

a Is that kind of a surrender of control? Maybe it's just that a whole bunch of women read it who are just really sick of having to make decisions about . . .

L . . . everything.

ⓐ So maybe the idea of some insane hunk who just keeps you in your own little freak room in his palatial apartment and annoyingly plays the piano . . . oh my god, the piano. You liked the piano, and I could tell your panic word was not far away when he just sort of kept going off playing the piano. But I mean maybe that's the fantasy, not having to remember to get milk or something like that. I mean, and having obviously this hunky boyfriend who periodically materialises in your flat when you don't want him to be there.

ⓛ There was a lot of stalker overtones, with him just showing up at places. She goes to visit her mother in Georgia and he just shows up there. The piano stuff . . . so, for the listeners who maybe haven't seen the film, he frequently – in the middle of the night after they've had sex – goes downstairs and plays some classics on the piano. And there was actually one scene where she came out of the room, draped in a sheet, and I'm sure this was an unintentional effect, but she sort of walked across in front of the grand piano. And she looks so much like Liberace.

ⓐ Wow. Your mind was really wandering over the course of that film.

ⓛ In the mid '90s when I was the arts reporter for the ABC, I ended up going to all sorts of things that I just would never normally choose to go to, but it was really good because I feel like it taught me a little bit more about what I like and what I don't actually like.

ⓐ And [adopts 'sexy' voice] *where your boundaries are.*

ⓛ *Where my boundaries are.*

ⓐ Sorry, I'm just never going to stop talking this way the rest of my life and it's your fault.

ⓛ What's my safe word going to be?

ⓐ I don't know. 'Malcolm Turnbull.' Sorry. I'm just being an idiot.

ⓛ Well, I think it's good sometimes to push yourself out of your comfort zone and see something that you wouldn't normally see. Cigarette, Crabb?

ⓐ Actually, I really have to go home and cook the kids' dinner.

well hello

Sales on *The Clock*

In the six years that we've been doing Chat 10 Looks 3, god knows I've had a few obsessions. There was *The Americans* and my endless campaign to convince Crabb to watch it. There's Helen Garner, of course – barely an episode passes without at least a glancing reference to her. 2020 may have been the year of That Which Shall Not Be Named everywhere else, but at *Chat 10* it was the year of *Hamilton*, and our relentless mentions undoubtedly irritating indifferent listeners. But amid everything I've loved during *Chat 10*'s history – all the wonderful books and films and podcasts – one piece of culture stands out to me. It is the experience about which I've thought the most, and for which I have the greatest awe, and it is Christian Marclay's contemporary film art montage *The Clock*.

The Clock is the result of a painstaking process of compiling short clips from thousands of different films, traversing countries and decades. Each minute of *The Clock* includes a shot of a clock, or a watch face, or an allusion to the time of day (for example, a character will say, 'What time is it?' And somebody will reply, 'It's 12.14.'). The time on screen always correlates with the exact time in real life, so if a character says 'It's 9.28', it's actually 9.28 wherever you are watching it. The piece runs for 24 hours on a loop, meaning there's a shot to match every minute of the day. At museums and galleries where *The Clock* is shown, a fixed number of three-seat couches are set before a large screen. You cannot book, you must queue to attend, but once inside, you can stay for as long as you like.

At the end of 2018, I was in London and *The Clock* was screening at the Tate Modern. I was enjoying the blissful feeling of an almost empty holiday schedule, with nowhere in particular to be and no obligations. Every day I'd wake up and automatically think,

'I'd better get up and get moving so I can get everything done.' And then I'd remember with joy, 'No, actually, you don't have to do a single thing. You can lie in bed all day if you want.' *The Clock* was not something I'd planned to visit in London. I'd previously seen 45 minutes of it at Sydney's Museum of Contemporary Art and while I had thought it clever, it didn't make a lasting impression. But for some reason, this time I thought it something that might be worth a less hurried look.

Unexpectedly, I found myself completely intrigued by it and I returned to the Tate Modern almost every day. Sometimes I would hop off the Tube and duck in for 45 minutes first thing in the morning. If I was on my way home after a day exploring, I might drop in at 5 pm. I arrived one day at 11.30 am as I wanted to see what would happen at midday. Another time, I stopped by at 7 pm before dinner to check the early evening mood. I felt compelled to watch as many different windows as I could. I would have loved to have gone at 3 am to witness the melancholia that apparently grips the film around that hour,

but I had to draw the line somewhere.

Going repeatedly to *The Clock* was the most astonishing labyrinth of an experience. On the first viewing, I was mostly driven by curiosity. Could Marclay and his team REALLY have found a shot of a clock in a film, or a reference to a specific time, for every single minute of the day? And how did they edit it to stay perfectly on time, so that 11.22 in real life was 11.22 on the screen, but didn't eat into 11.23? Some times of day are simple – you could have filled the entirety of midday with shots of Big Ben chiming in different films. But one can only imagine the heartbreak close to the end of the process, when somebody was searching for an elusive 5.46 am reference, only to stumble across a second shot of 5.47. It was breathtaking to consider *The Clock* from this technical level alone, including its seamless audio.

Later, I found I was able to pay attention to other things. Themes emerged at different times of the day. Obviously, 7 am was full of alarm clocks going off. 9 am had schools starting and 3 pm had them out. 5 pm: people leaving work.

well hello

7 pm onwards: women constantly being disappointed by men not showing up for dinner. There were also unexpected periods of tension. At a quarter to the top of the clock, a race against time would often begin – people dashing to make a meeting, trying to not miss a train, or rushing to meet a deadline. And then once the hour struck, there was great relief and resolution, as if a wave had crashed on the shore.

For the initial period of any viewing I was acutely aware of time passing. You cannot help but notice it, because every minute is marked on the screen. A regular film condenses time so that an hour can be conveyed in a few seconds; *The Clock* does the opposite. After a while, I stopped being hyper-aware of every minute and would realise that 20 or 30 had passed and I'd been completely absorbed. While *The Clock* itself unfolds in real time, the content selected for the screen drastically compresses time. You can be watching twentysomething Jack Nicholson at one instant and 10 minutes later he's aged 40 years in a different clip. Or you can see old Paul Newman and half an hour later time is rewound and you're seeing young Paul Newman. It is strange and somewhat rattling.

By my third and fourth viewings, I became pre-occupied with figuring out when to leave, and how others judged the same thing. Many people would leave at the top or bottom of the hour, or on the quarter hour. That seemed too obvious to me so I would set myself rules such as, 'I'll go at 5.11.' I never needed to check my watch, of course. But then 5.11 would come and I'd think, 'Oh, I just want to see 5.12.' It's a slippery tunnel from which it's difficult

I would have loved to have gone at 3 am ... but I had to draw the line somewhere.

to climb out. I started using other charms to motivate my departure: 'The next time Julia Roberts appears, I will leave.'

By my final viewings of *The Clock*, I was so acutely aware of the passage of time that even outside the film I was fixated on watching how long the queue took to move and what people did to occupy themselves as they waited. Were they impatient? Chatting? Looking at their phones? How long did people tend to stay once they got inside? When I left, it was discombobulating to step back into real life. There had been a surreal, dream-like quality to the film experience, and so stepping outside felt like groggily waking up. I was vigilant for references to time on screen for months afterwards. If a cutaway of a clock or a film character mentioned the time, I'd think something like, 'Oh 2.34 pm – that would have been a handy one!'

I've thought a lot about why this particular artwork made such a huge impact on me. Crabb has a running joke on *Chat 10* about how heavily my professional life at *7.30* is dictated by the clock. The program's title is a time reference, for heaven's sake. From about 7.15 pm, literally every minute of my time is accounted for and there can be no slippage. I walk into the studio at 7.23 pm. If I arrive at 7.22 pm, Mick, the floor manager, will remark that I am early. If I come at 7.24 pm, he will note that I'm late. If it's 7.25 pm, he is antsy. If it's 7.26 pm, every staff member in the control room is in a heightened state of anxiety and I've done the team a disservice. I mark up my notes for interviews by the minute so I know where to be by what time, and what subjects should drop if I can't fit in everything once the clock starts. I am counted down second by second for the end of interviews or stories.

> **Crabb always says that I have an in-built timer that causes me to attempt to wrap up podcast episodes of *Chat 10* around the 29.30 mark ... roughly the same duration as an episode of *7.30*.**

Oddly enough, attending *The Clock* was an escape from the tyranny of time that dominates my life. I would never normally have the opportunity to go every day to a repeated viewing of a work of art I enjoyed, without any pressure to

well hello

hurry along. It felt like luxury, and the art itself was by turns funny and interesting and touching. Sometimes I wanted to laugh at the sheer audacity of what Christian Marclay had pulled off.

I was intrigued to see what this Russian doll of an artwork's next revelation would be. That's partly what kept luring me back. The whole experience was mysterious, compelling and addictive. I hope that someday, in some city somewhere in the world, I will be able to sneak in that 3 am viewing after all and see what lies under the next layer.

chapter 10
cooking & music

Crabb on cooking

peace, joy and a baked apple

If you ever get the opportunity to incorporate your hobby into your day job and get away with it, you should take it.

When I first had the idea for the ABC series *Kitchen Cabinet*, it was mostly driven by curiosity about whether politicians would talk differently (and more normally) if you took them out of a TV studio or from behind a desk and put them in their own kitchens. But I'd be lying if I said it wasn't a tiny bit driven by the sparkling possibility of being able to claim vanilla beans as a legitimate tax deduction.

Ten years later: have I ever actually claimed a vanilla bean (or any gastronomic accoutrement, for that matter) as a work expense or deduction? Of course I haven't. I'm a disorganised schmuck trailing a broken-hearted skein of underutilised taxation accountants in my wake like Donald Trump trailing ex-wives and unpaid construction workers.

But cooking brings me joy, and to my professional life it brings a modicum of peace.

Here's why I love it:

1. It's generous. This means I can shroud my selfish desire to spend time on my hobby with a convincingly philanthropical cover story. I'm cooking because it's X's birthday! I'm cooking because Y is sad! I'm cooking for the children and that makes me a good mother so CHECK M8, haterz!

2. It's useful. At the end of cooking there is food. So even if it doesn't go the way you expected, you're still meeting someone's basic human need in the final wash-up. Even if that human need turns out to be for a lasagne baked into a simulacrum of a parched drought plain because you were multitasking and forgot about it. You'd be surprised how adaptable human needs can be.

3. It's absorbing in a way that journalism isn't. When I'm cooking, I feel as if I'm using a different part of my brain. Making a dish requires process and attention, but it's not the same kind of process and attention that writing a story demands. Some of it is repetitive – pleasingly so. I love peeling potatoes and shelling boiled eggs.

4. It's predictable in a way that journalism isn't. So long as you have the right ingredients and an approximation of the time required to make a recipe, you should end up with a result that is at least in the ballpark of what you had in mind. This experience is so comedically dissimilar to journalism that I find it restful. Plus a cake doesn't ring you up afterwards and cuss you out for not adequately characterising its motivation.

5. It feels like there should be five reasons, so I should add that I like to eat, and the best way of making sure you get to eat what you want is to be in charge of the cooking. People often say to me, 'Your children must be so handy in the kitchen!' Shamefully, I don't get them to cook enough because my cooking is better and I don't want to eat wonky food. I'm not proud of this.

Obviously, you can expect some problems when you incorporate your hobby into your day job. In my case, it has produced an army of helpful people on social media who urge me to 'stick to cooking' when they dislike something I've written or want generally to express the view that I'm an idiot. And fair enough. As we all know, cooking is an activity widely undertaken by the feeble-minded, and my being interested in it is a virtual guarantor of shallowness in a way that an interest in sport, films or obscure alt-rock bands, for example, definitely is not for male journalists, politicians or economists.

To be honest, the bigger problem for me is the extent to which my cooking life actively sabotages my work life. I don't know how else to put it. More regularly than should probably be the case for a normal person, my food tries to kill my laptop.

It happened even while writing this book.

I was at the ABC on a Tuesday afternoon when I realised it was getting late and there was nothing at home ready for dinner. This is a rare failing on my part. The only sector of my life in which planning even has a pulse is cooking; I wake up every morning thinking about what's going to be for dinner.

So I had a great idea: duck pancakes. Now, I know this sounds complicated but actually it's not. Out the back of the ABC are a couple of excellent Asian supermarkets that sell frozen pancakes. And there's a hole in the wall where you can buy a BBQ duck (or, more upsettingly, half a duck) hacked into pieces by a calm man with a cleaver. I already had cucumbers and some hoisin sauce at home. So: duck pancakes for dinner. Quick result.

All went to plan for a while.

Duck Man quickly dismembered half a duck for me and snapped it wordlessly into a takeaway container, which I secreted in my bag along with the frozen pancakes and an extra litre of Kewpie toasted sesame dressing (a little problem of mine we needn't discuss right now).

I raced home, unpacked everything and microwaved the pancakes. (I love microwaves, by the way. I know there are people who worry that it's the Government Controlling Your Brain but I would never do without one because you can make prawn crackers and pappadums with no oil, not to mention defrost duck pancakes. Plus, if you drink as many cups of tea a day as I do, you're always coming across a tepid half-cup that could use a little reheat. Yeah, I hear you judging. And no, I don't care.)

As I unpacked my bag, I noticed a little bit of oil on my laptop. I wiped it off and proceeded with duck pancake preparation. No drama. The duck went . . . I want to say swimmingly, but that sounds disrespectful.

It wasn't until the next morning when I plugged in my laptop to a power source that a problem made itself apparent. It wouldn't charge. The socket seemed a tiny bit oily. I did some useful things like sticking a rolled-up tissue in there, and Jeremy did some useful things like standing around and saying, 'What do you mean, you haven't been saving things to the cloud?' while the laptop gasped out its final breaths. Actually, to be fair, Jem did eventually emit a heavy sigh and sit down to evacuate things from where I'd saved them on the laptop (the cyber equivalent of shoving things under the bed) and copy them to where they're apparently supposed to live (a 'cloud' location in which I will never, so long as I live, believe or trust).

All that was left to do was make an appointment at Apple's Genius Bar so we could get on with the next step of the process, which is telling a person half your age that you've killed the only device upon which you every day rely to make a living, and, what's more, that you've done that using duck fat.

I'm used to the ritual humiliation of such visits.

I vividly recall another crisis years ago in Adelaide, on a work visit that I kicked off with a celebratory 600 ml of Farmers Union Iced Coffee, South Australia's favourite drink. Having decanted it into a glass, I sat down to write an overdue column and promptly knocked over the glass, directing a lethal stream of delicious fluid into the laptop's innards.

In case you have any plans of your own in this department, please be assured that commercially produced iced coffee is about the worst thing that you can pour into your device. It combines dampness and stickiness to an unmatchably debilitating degree; to a laptop, it's like a bleach martini with an oleander garnish.

The young man to whom I presented myself as a supplicant on that occasion didn't even speak. He gazed at me with a combination of disbelief and (I like to think) horrified respect before confirming, with a

I say 'cooking-related laptop misadventure' but, to be fair, that formulation engages a degree of euphemism. A simpler way of putting things would be to say 'I cooked my laptop'.

decisive shake of the head, that the situation was well beyond repair.

I've killed laptops multiple times. I've left them in airports and on the roofs of cars, and I even once left one on a road in Cyprus while covering the evacuation of Australian citizens during the Israel-Hezbollah War in 2006. But probably the stupidest cooking-related laptop misadventure happened in 2008.

I say 'cooking-related laptop misadventure' but, to be fair, that formulation engages a degree of euphemism that would make a management consultant's PowerPoint beat faster. A simpler way of putting things would be to say 'I cooked my laptop'.

How? Reader, it was inadvertent, though a strong whiff of contributory negligence permeates the tale.

We had been on holiday in South Australia and I hadn't taken my laptop along. For complex reasons (a rococo blend incorporating heavy notes of 'personal stupidity' and 'inadequate home and contents insurance') I had a habit of hiding valuables in the oven when we went away. It is not something I do anymore.

I think you can probably imagine how this rolled.

Upon our return from holidays, fuelled by a joyous sense of homecoming and relief to be back in my own kitchen, I decided to make an apple pie, and preheated the oven while happily peeling apples (see above reference to mindless, repetitive kitchen tasks) and rolling pastry.

Until, of course, the mysteriously acrid smell of what turned out to be a baked Apple Macintosh iBook filled the air. I yanked open the oven door and emitted a howl so terrible that Jeremy, outside retrieving the bins, raced inside, assuming something terrible had happened to the baby.

These laptops do fight hard, I'll give them that. When the Baked Apple returned to room temperature, it still worked. Whatever you PC people want to say about Macs, you do have to respect a machine that is prepared to rise groggily to the occasion after 30 minutes in a moderate oven. Its keys were fused together, and it had grill marks on the bottom like a nicely done focaccia, but it bravely surfed the net and assisted in the evacuation of key files before ultimately succumbing the next day.

All in all, I'd say that, yeah, the whole incorporation of cooking into my working life has gone pretty well apart from the above-recounted instances.

It's really the addition of children that has sometimes pushed things over the edge. Like the 2013 season of *Kitchen Cabinet*, which kicked off when I was on maternity leave with my newborn third child and learned that the filming was going ahead earlier than planned due to certain unavoidable scheduling factors. Coincidentally, my third child, Kate, was unusually clingy (read: could not be put down, sleep without uninterrupted skin contact from a parent, take a bottle, travel in a car, sleep at all for more than 20 minutes), so when the call came, I was sufficiently unhinged by lack of sleep to think that embarking on a multi-state cooking-and-filming tour with a baby who liked to be worn 24/7 was a manageable idea.

Highlights of that season involved:

- Catching trains, trams and buses everywhere so that we could service Kate's need to be held.
- My heroic colleague, producer Madeleine Hawcroft, strapping Kate to her chest in a sling every shoot and wearing a remote earpiece so she could listen to the interview. Next level.
- Feeling weird in Adelaide at the end of a 10-hour shoot with federal MP Nick Xenophon, culminating in the cooking of octopus over a charcoal grill, and realising that I had mastitis. If you go back and look at that episode, you can actually see my right boob starting to look weird at about the 25-minute mark. GOOD TIMES!

As you are probably reflecting right now, little of the foregoing can be blamed on food. Mainly these misadventures can be attributed to the haphazardness of the author. Which also forms the basis for my final reason for loving cooking, which I just remembered.

Cooking for other people is a compensation for haphazardness. When you feel bad about being short on time or away, or being unable to think of anything useful to say, cooking for someone is the hopeless person's way of saying 'I care about you'. And if you can nail that, well, it's a start.

icons of chat 10:

Annabel's boyfriend

aka . . . *Yotam Ottolenghi*

Crabb and Sales kicked off the very first episode of *Chat 10 Looks 3* with an almighty and typically awkward CLANG – Yotam Ottolenghi! – and really just haven't shut up about him since.

Unwitting yet terrifically accommodating poster boy of *Chat 10* Yotam Ottolenghi, with a couple of groupies.

Annabel revealed that she'd blagged her way into a publicity dinner with the Israeli-born chef and restaurateur, at which someone asked, 'What's your most shameful ingredient or food you like eating?' Crabb recalled, 'For me, it's an instant answer. I really love tinned smoked oysters. It was a high-stakes call, because it is in some ways an embarrassing thing. But he just looked at me and I think a crackle of electricity did sort of, well, go forth between our eyes, and he said, "No, you too?" And then for this incredibly pleasurable three to four minutes, we're just firing back and forth things that we like to do with smoked oysters.'

Sales: 'I'd like to hear Yotam's take on this. He's like, "This crazy woman accosted me and like, *smoked oysters.*"'

Henceforth known as Annabel's boyfriend (Not Really . . . Not Yet), Yotam unwittingly became a major recurring character in the podcast as Crabb and Sales cooked from his books religiously and discussed what they'd produced. And hundreds of Chatters did likewise – including foundation Chatter Caroline Braithwaite, who worked her way through every recipe from *Simple* and posted the results in the Facebook group (we've not the heart to tell her he has a new one out).

His cauliflower cake went gangbusters in the group and people made pilgrimages to Chatter Ground Zero, aka his various restaurants. The level of detail in his delicious recipes was alternatively loved and lovingly mocked, including one Chatter declaring that her friends referred to him as 'Yotam Oh-So-Lengthy'.

Yotam-mania hit its peak in the CLANGtastic 100th episode (which Sales really wanted to call 'Wow, We've Actually Made 100 Episodes Of This Turkey'), when Ottolenghi generously arrived IN PERSON to become *Chat 10 Looks 3*'s first and possibly only special guest on the podcast. 'I just owe it to you, Annabel, because you've been my serial interviewer for so many years,' he explained.

A magnificently good sport, he handled it with aplomb when Crabb and Sales lost it with excitement and explained how he'd become a Chatter icon. He talked about what he read, watched and ate; the success of *Simple*; how he dealt with critics; the Aussie cookbook he uses a lot and how he was into swedes and turnips; and why he left academia (phew).

Finally, he revealed what he'd cook for himself at home alone: and put down the pomegranate molasses, people, because it's ...CHEESE AND CRACKERS! Smoked oysters were left unmentioned.

Despite Ottolenghi politely failing to embrace Crabb and Sales's idea for an Australian roadkill cookbook, it was remarked later by Leigh that he was 'a great example of how excellent it is when you meet someone you've long admired and they are exactly as delightful as you always hoped they would be.' Crabb agreed. 'I know. That would have been frankly awkward if he'd been a jerk.'

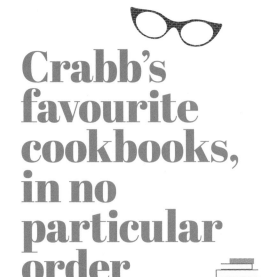

Crabb's favourite cookbooks, in no particular order

because she does not crave order like that raging list-slave Sales does

- ### *Best Kitchen Basics* – **Mark Best**

  This is pretty much my ideal cookbook. It's stylishly designed. It's superbly written. It's funny and clever. And it's full of things you would never, ever think to do yourself. Make 47 egg yolk tagliatelle, for instance. I cannot tell you how satisfying that is as a project. Why 47? Why not 48? Is he allowing the cook to drop one egg from the four dozen? I have no idea, but I like it a lot. I made the tagliatelle to calm myself down after my oven caught fire halfway through making pavlovas for a friend's birthday. Tiny little egg custards served in eggshells? I'm here for that too. It was Best who alerted me to the existence of the French egg topper, the device that neatly decapitates eggs, leaving a smooth-edged shell. I bought one and then raved about it at a *Chat 10* show in Adelaide and next step of course was Gwen sourcing hundreds of them for merch purposes.

  I know I'm digressing here, but this development gave me an unlikely moment of triumph in a subsequent conversation with Amanda Vanstone. Amanda is a cooking enthusiast and will sometimes ring me with a particularly urgent tip. It's hilarious; she just starts talking as soon as I answer. 'Got a pen? Okay. Take a kilo of crabs. Uncooked. Right? And a block of butter. Half a bottle of sherry . . .' (This conversation happened, I promise you.) Anyway, she rang me and said, absolutely apropos of nothing (she hadn't been at the Adelaide show and she doesn't listen to our podcast), 'Hey, have you ever heard of these French egg cutter things?' to which I was able, miraculously, to reply, 'Oh yeah. I have 450 of them to hand right now, actually,' which is the only time I've really felt like I've been in an exchange with Amanda where I've held all the cards. Extremely satisfying.

The other incredible thing in Best's book is his recipe for kingfish ham. Yep. Fish ham. It takes several weeks and involves setting fire to things on your stovetop. I warmly endorse it.

• *Community* – Hetty McKinnon

The Asian kohlrabi coleslaw is what made me want this book the second my friend Sue Dale showed it to me. I've made it many times. It's still superb. The whole book is superb. And it's a gateway drug to Hetty's subsequent books, *Neighbourhood, Family*, and *From Asia With Love*. I love Hetty's backstory – she set up Arthur Street Kitchen from her home, making large quantities of a single salad each day and biking portions around to recipients in her neighbourhood. You can tell from reading her books that you'd absolutely enjoy being her friend. I met her when she returned to Australia to launch *Family*, her third book, and she is exactly as nice as I'd always thought.

• *The Cook and Baker* – Cherie Bevan and Tass Tauroa

I love that The Cook and Baker (it's a bakery) sits in Bondi Junction amid paleo outlets and raw food joints. The book version is a big, buttery explosion of excellence and I could not love it more. Leigh Sales makes the Oaty Ginger Crunch a lot and it's very compelling. But don't overlook the Cheddar and Sweetcorn Scones. To do so would be a PROFOUND error.

- ### *Strudel, Noodles and Dumplings* – Anja Dunk

  As a person who grew up in South Australia's mid-north, which is infested with German bakeries, I'm a mad fan of yeasted cakes, quark and ingenious uses for stone fruit. Anja Dunk's book is an utter delight. She even has a recipe for quark! There are more noodles and dumplings than you could poke a Bienenstich at. It's beautifully designed, and Dunk does her own photography, which is top-shelf. Anyone who can photograph her own knife rack this beautifully is an automatic friend of mine. Try the Yeasted Plum Cake. And the Turmeric Noodles with Lemon and Poppyseed Butter? Ah, yes please.

- ### *The Cook's Companion* – Stephanie Alexander

  Goes without saying, really. This book does what really great cookbooks should always do: shares knowledge generously and in a way that's easy to absorb. There's a reason millions of households have this volume. And that reason is that people's homes aren't set up like restaurants. Most kitchens don't stock a whole gamut of fancy ingredients all the time. What they do have, every so often, is a load of eggplant that someone dropped over. Or cumquats from a tree in the backyard. Or more zucchini than you know what to do with. Stephanie's revolutionary ingredient-based structure means that you can immediately find five things to do with the ingredient you have, and a list of things it goes with. It's genius. And it's never going to stop being useful, no matter how food trends change.

- ### *Plenty* – Yotam Ottolenghi

  This is worse than choosing a favourite Garner book. *Ottolenghi* – the original book – was the one I read first, when my friend Beck sent it to me. But I've religiously bought all the others as they were published. I've listed *Plenty* here because of two things I cook out of it very regularly: the Caramelised Garlic Tart, which is a magical dish, and the Tomato and Marinated Mozzarella dish, which incorporates fennel seeds in a completely inspired way. But obviously, yeah, you're going to need all the Yotam books.

well hello

- **_The Bread Bible_ – Rose Levy Beranbaum**

  I bought this book when I was living in London and it's
  the reason I'm now good at baking bread. Beranbaum
  is an absolute stickler for detail. She creates recipes with
  extremely precise proportions (down to the gram, even
  for water), so it's reassuring for the beginner. And this
  book has everything from yeasted cakes to bagels to
  challah to crumpets. Her Rosemary Foccacia Sheet is
  like a weird miracle – a wet, soupy batter that you beat
  in a mixer for 20 minutes with a tiny amount of yeast,
  driven only by Beranbaum's assurance that at the
  20-minute mark it will 'suddenly metamorphose into
  a shiny, smooth, incredibly elastic dough'. And it DOES!
  And a few hours of rising later, you end up with a chewy,
  airy focaccia. This recipe is absolutely worth the price of
  admission, but stay for the butter-dipped dinner rolls.

- **_Asian After Work_ – Adam Liaw**

  Picking up this book at a friend's mum's house was
  my first proper introduction to Adam Liaw.
  I wasn't watching _MasterChef_ back then,
  but I was immediately drawn to his
  writing style and his cheery capacity to
  make complex dishes accessible. His Faster Master
  (quick master stock) is a real breakthrough if you love
  the idea of a master stock but don't have room in your
  house/brain for another entity with complex emotional
  and practical needs. Once you pick up this book,
  you'll swiftly collect the full set of Liaw's work.
  I certainly did. He's brilliant. And very funny
  on Twitter and Instagram, too, in case you're
  not already following him.

I bought one and
then raved about
it at a _Chat 10_
show in Adelaide
and next step
of course was
Gwen sourcing
hundreds of
them for merch
purposes.

- ***How to Eat*** – Nigella Lawson

  Look, Nigella Lawson's had more kilometres of copy written about her than all the other authors on this list put together. But the reason her books sell bajillions of copies is that she's a terrific writer, who is moreover possessed of a relentless and broad-minded curiosity about food. And the right kind of generosity – for her, food should always be about others. I share her suspicion about the oversupply of cookbooks that are about the author eliminating this or that from their diets, or cultivating a healthier gut and so forth. I mean, don't get me wrong, they are useful in their place, but to me a cookbook should first and foremost leave you better equipped to surprise and delight the people you love. *How to Eat* is full of great recipe ideas and kitchen tips. I have made the Chocolate Raspberry Pudding Cake about 500 times.

- ***Salads*** – Peter Gordon

  I love Peter Gordon. My friend and cookbook co-author Wendy Sharpe introduced me to his London restaurant The Providores and gave me this book, which I love because it confirms that anything can essentially be a salad, and boasts some seriously inventive combinations. Gordon's not vegetarian but cooks a lot of meat-free stuff. He's a Kiwi and you can see his Pacific influences. My favourite recipe from this book is the Kumara, Baked Spiced Ricotta, Spinach and Roast Grape Salad with Olive and Caper Dressing. Once you know that you can roast grapes, the world is a different and better place.

well hello

Sales inventions

L One of my favourite things to do on the podcast is mention to Crabb that I've made something from one of her cookbooks but then casually drop in that I've made a few switches to the ingredients or method. There's something about this that she finds particularly annoying and that's why I do it. She gets this look on her face like she's trying to be tolerant but just below the surface she is intensely irritated. Because of that, I now specifically read her recipes scanning for things that I can alter and, let me tell you, it's not that hard, given her penchant for illogical choices, like pine nuts on a lemon cake when it's obvious to everybody that toasted flaked almonds would be far superior (personally, I consider pine nuts an accompaniment for a savoury dish, such as hummus or salad).

In this book, I choose to share with you the Sales Inventions, cultivated to enhance taste, improve ease of cooking and shopping, and to annoy the hell out of Annabel Crabb. All in all, an excellent use of my time and yours.

I shall start with her Pea and Mint Tarts which, must be said, are outstanding and I make all the time. But you can pretty much vary them with any ingredients you choose. On the next page is my personal favourite: goat's cheese, sundried tomatoes and basil.

Sales 'improves' Crabb's pea and mint tarts by omitting the peas and mint

Pea and mint tarts

Makes 36

280 g (10 oz/2 cups) frozen peas, thawed

250 g (9 oz) feta, crumbled

handful of mint leaves, shredded

finely grated zest of ½ lemon

pinch of chilli flakes – optional

2 eggs

300 ml (½ fl oz) sour cream

80 g (2 ¾ oz/¾ cup) finely grated parmesan

4 sheets ready-made puff pastry, thawed if frozen

150g goat's cheese, chopped

150g sundried tomatoes, chopped

Handful of basil, chopped

Method

1. Preheat the oven to 180°C (350°F) and lightly grease three shallow 12-hole mini-muffin or patty-pan tins (or make and bake these in batches if you only have one such tin).

2. In a bowl, mix the ~~peas~~ tomatoes with the ~~feta, mint and lemon zest~~ goat's cheese and basil. If you're making these for grown-ups who like things a bit hot, you could definitely add some chilli flakes at this point. In a small jug, whisk the eggs, sour cream and parmesan, then season to taste with pepper (don't worry about salt, which will be supplied in sufficient quantities by the ~~feta and parmesan~~ goat's cheese).

3. Now, lay out your pastry on a lightly floured surface and cut out rounds about 8 cm (3 ¼ in) across – you should get about 9 rounds out of each pastry sheet. You could re-roll the odds and ends but I wouldn't really recommend it, as overworked pastry gets a bit dense and shrinky. Press each round into a hole in your prepared tin, creating an instant tart case.

4. Load each tart case with a heaping tablespoon of the ~~pea and feta~~ tomato, goat's cheese and basil mixture, then pour in enough of the egg mixture to fill them about two-thirds full.

5. Slip the tarts into the oven and bake for about 15 minutes, or until puffed and golden. Check the base of the tarts to make sure that they are well browned and crisp, not pale and flabby, then cool on a wire rack.

To transport
Pack the cooled tarts into a basket or tin and get going.

L I really cannot tell you the entertainment I'm getting writing notes to append to your recipes. I cannot believe I'm being paid for this shit.

a OMFG how can you be so vindictive AND such a loser at the same time? You should be donated to science.

L Working this exchange immediately into the book.

a Is there no creative vein in my life to which you will not at some point attach your predatory fangs.

L Also going in.

a In which case, edit to read, 'into which you will not sink your predatory fangs'.

L All also going in. We may make our word count just by exchanging insulting text messages.

Sales 'improves' Crabb's chocolate pomegranate cloud cake by banning the pomegranate

L This is a fantastic cake, I'm not gonna lie. But, in my humble opinion, as with pine nuts, pomegranate belongs in salad. I don't mind pomegranate ice cream, but using pomegranate seeds on this cake screams, 'I've got a good basic chocolate cake going on here and now I'm going to make myself look like a try-hard by adding a weird ingredient that's going to give you the complete shits when you discover it's out of season.' There's nothing wrong with strawberries, people. They're plentiful, they're welcoming, they don't make your kitchen look like a crime scene. At Christmas, you can also throw a few mint leaves on this cake and the red and green makes it look festive. You're welcome.

Chocolate pomegranate cloud cake

Makes 1 x 23 cm (9 in) cake

250 g (9 oz) dark (70% cocoa) chocolate

125 g (4 ½ oz) unsalted butter

6 large eggs

175 g (6 oz) caster (superfine) sugar

300 ml (10½ fl oz) thick (double) cream

2 teaspoons icing (confectioners') sugar, ~~seeds from ½ pomegranate,~~

and grated chocolate, ~~to decorate: edible dried rose petals – (optional)~~

Punnet of strawberries, chopped

Scattering of small mint leaves

Method

1. Preheat the oven to 180°C (350°F) and line the base of a 23 cm (9 in) springform tin.

2. Grate or chop the chocolate. Melt the butter in a small saucepan over gentle heat, then remove from the heat and stir in the chocolate – don't stir it too much; if there are any stubborn unmelted bits of chocolate after a few minutes, briefly return the pan to the heat. Once the mixture is smooth and glossy, set aside to cool slightly.

3. Separate 4 of the eggs and set the whites aside. Using an electric mixer, beat the yolks and the other 2 whole eggs with 75 g (2½ oz) of the caster sugar until really creamy – this may take 3-4 minutes on high speed. Gently fold in the melted butter and chocolate. In another bowl, whisk the egg whites until they're just frothy, then slowly add the remaining 100 g (3 ½ oz) of caster sugar while whisking. (Obviously, an electric whisk is almost essential here. Or a tag team of whisking assistants.) Keep whisking until the mixture holds soft peaks.

4. Add a big spoonful of the whisked egg whites to the chocolate mixture to loosen it, then carefully fold in the rest, keeping as much air in the mixture as possible. Pour into the prepared tin and bake for about 35 minutes. With this cake, it's better to err on the side of undercooking than overcooking: it should have risen, and then collapsed, and be no longer wobbly around the edges. Don't bother with a skewer, because if it comes out clean, you have overcooked the thing!

5. Leave the cake to cool in the tin; it will sink before your eyes and look as if a meteorite has hit it. But don't worry – we'll be needing a crater to hold all that delicious whipped cream. Speaking of which, whip the cream with the icing sugar (here, err on the side of under-whipped so it is velvety rather than stiff and grainy).

6. When the cake is completely cool, run a knife around the edges to loosen the cake from the tin. Then, very, very cautiously, un-spring your cake from the tin and slide it from the base onto a serving plate.

7. Spread the cream over the top and sprinkle with the ~~pomegranate seeds and grated chocolate~~ strawberries and mint leaves. ~~For something really special, dapple your creation with a few rose petals, torn into teeny pieces.~~
   Seriously, who has time for this shit. ↗

Sales 'improves' Crabb's passionfruit curd by simply ignoring a key part of the recipe

L I absolutely love passionfruit. When they're cheap, I buy bags of them, pulp them and put the juice into ice cube trays so I always have some at hand. I consider the seeds to be a wonderful part of the passionfruit. Hence, my utter contempt for this recipe, which calls for the passionfruit to be strained. What sort of monster ...?

Passionfruit curd

Makes about 700 g (1 lb 9 oz/2 cups)

110 g (3 ¾ oz/½ cup) caster (superfine) sugar

4 whole eggs

2 egg yolks

125 g (4½ oz) unsalted butter, cubed

pulp from 8 passionfruit, ~~strained~~ No, no, no. Seeds in.
Otherwise, you might open the fridge and think it's lemon curd.
Keep the seeds and there's never confusion. And it tastes better.

juice of ½ lemon

Method

1. In a heatproof bowl set over a pan of simmering water, whisk the sugar, eggs and egg yolks together until pale.

2. Now whisk in the butter, cube by cube, and keep whisking over the heat: the butter will melt and the mixture will gradually thicken to a nice, custardy texture.

3. Finally, whisk in the passionfruit pulp and lemon juice and wait for the curd to thicken up again, then immediately transfer it to a bowl (if using straightaway) or sterilised jars, covering the surface with plastic wrap so it doesn't form a skin as it cools.

Sales goes fully rogue and completely reworks Crabb's spiced cherry Eton mess

L Look, I ate this. It was fine. I just felt like maybe it would taste better after spending a night in the fridge getting to know itself. But the meringue isn't going to tolerate that kind of antic, is it? So what I did was turn this into a trifle. My changes are too expansive to simply amend her recipe, so here, just have mine instead.

Spiced cherry Eton mess

Serves 6

500 g (1 lb 2 oz) fresh pitted cherries or 2 × 420 g (15 oz) tins
pitted black cherries, drained, syrup reserved

55 g (2 oz/¼ cup) caster (superfine) sugar

125 ml (4 fl oz/½ cup) rose wine or cherry juice – if using fresh cherries

juice of ½ lemon

2 long strips orange zest

1 vanilla pod (bean), split and seeds scraped

1 cinnamon stick

2 star anise

1 teaspoon cornflour (cornstarch)

300 ml (10½ fl oz) thickened (whipping) cream

2 tablespoons maple syrup

250 g (9 oz) mascarpone, at room temperature

250 g (9 oz) Greek-style yoghurt

10 meringue nests or 150 g (5½ oz) meringues

100 g (3½ oz) slivered almonds, toasted

Method

1. Cut the cherries in half. If using fresh fruit, put the cherries in a nonreactive saucepan with the sugar, wine or cherry juice, lemon juice, orange zest, vanilla seeds, cinnamon and star anise. Bring to a simmer and cook for 5 minutes, or until the fruit is soft. Make a paste of the cornflour and a tablespoon of water.

Add this to the pan, then bring to the boil and cook, stirring gently, until the liquid thickens. Transfer to a bowl and chill.

2. If using tinned cherries, put 125 ml (4 fl oz/½ cup) of the syrup in a nonreactive saucepan with the sugar, lemon juice, orange zest, vanilla seeds, cinnamon and star anise. Bring to a simmer and cook for 5 minutes. Make a paste of the cornflour with a tablespoon of water. Add this to the pan, then bring to the boil and cook, stirring constantly, until the syrup thickens. Stir the cherries through the thickened syrup, then transfer to a bowl and chill.

3. Whip the cream with the maple syrup, mascarpone and yoghurt until it forms soft peaks. Spoon the cream mixture into a large bowl, then break up the meringue into 1–2 cm (½–¾ in) chunks and crumble them over the top. Using a large metal spoon, give the meringues and the cream a few turns to mix, then add the cherries and fold just a couple of times to leave ribbons of syrup and fruit running through the cream and meringue.

4. Pile the lot on a plate or just serve from the bowl. Sprinkle the almond slivers on top. This may not be entirely traditional, but no jury would convict.

To transport

Take the meringues in their packet, the cream mixture in an airtight container and the chilled cherries in their syrup in another. Don't forget the almonds. You'll also need a bowl big enough for folding, and a big spoon.

well hello

SPICED CHERRY TRIFLE
- MY RECIPE, DEC 2016.

2 tins pitted cherries (reserve the juice)
1/4 cup caster sugar
juice of 1/2 lemon
2 long strips of orange zest
1 vanilla bean pod, split & seeds scraped
1 cinnamon stick
2 star anise
packet of sponge finger biscuits
2 flakes
1/2 cup toasted flaked almonds
250g cream cheese (at room temperature)
2 egg whites
2 tbsp caster sugar
1 cap full of brandy.

Put 125ml of the cherry juice into a saucepan along with the sugar, lemon juice, orange zest, vanilla, cinnamon & star anise. Bring to a simmer & cook for 10 mins until flavours infuse. Cool & add brandy.

Whisk the egg white to peaks. Beat in caster sugar, then cream cheese. Gently fold through the cherries.

Dip sponge finger biscuits in juice & make a layer in a bowl. Spread with cream cheese mix. Alternate, ending with cream cheese.

Top with crumbled flake & toasted almonds.

Sales gets pretty rude actually about Crabb's Kefalograviera, fried egg and rocket rolls

L Frankly, I don't even think I need to explain why I'm amending this, do I? You know already. Who on EARTH is going devote part of their busy day to run around, popping into the 7-Eleven and beyond to check if they've got Kefalograviera? I mean, what even is it? I thought it was the bloke who won the Wimbledon Men's Singles in 1983 until I consulted the World Wide Web (it's cheese, apparently). Friends, there's no posh cheese that's ever been able to outrun bacon in a dish like this. Never has been, never will be. This is just a wanker's bacon and egg roll, if you ask me. I'm pleased to note, however, that she's using crusty bread and not brioche. I thoroughly disapprove of the trend towards brioche buns for sandwiches and hamburgers. If I want two slices of cake with my meat patty, I'll ask for it, thanks.

~~Kefalograviera,~~ Bacon, fried egg and rocket rolls

1 tablespoon extra-virgin olive oil

6 eggs – the fresher, the better

~~250 g Kefalograviera, cut into 5 mm slices~~

6 crusty bread rolls, split in half

good-quality mayonnaise

2 generous handfuls of rocket leaves

juice of 1 lemon

6 rashers of bacon

Even easier: If you have no Kefalograviera in your orbit, use haloumi. Good for most things. Or of course you could use chorizo, sliced thickly on the diagonal and browned in a hot pan. You won't need any oil for this task, as chorizo is plenty oily.

well hello

Method

1. Heat a heavy-based frying pan over medium heat and add the oil.
    One by one, crack the eggs into a small bowl and slide them into the pan –
    ideally, you should be able to cook 3 eggs at a time. Fry them for about
    2 minutes on the first side, or however long it takes for the white to reach a
    flippable consistency. ~~Lay a slice of cheese over the egg, then flip it with a~~
    ~~deft movement so the Kefalograviera ends up under the egg. If this degree of~~
    ~~hand-eye coordination eludes you, position the cheese in the pan and flip the~~
    ~~egg onto it. Increase the heat slightly so as to give the cheese a good browning.~~
    Cook some bacon. Set it aside.

2. Meanwhile, toast the split rolls lightly and smear with mayonnaise.
    Toss the rocket leaves in the lemon juice, then stack a small handful on
    one half of each roll. Put the bacon in the roll.

3. Slip each egg into a warm roll, then do the other 3 eggs. Serve the rolls
    on a decorative platter.

a couple of smug bundts

How a bundt in the oven birthed a Chat 10 catchphrase

The bundt cake is an astonishing piece of engineering when perfectly executed, sporting a central chimney and fluted sides down which a glistening glaze or icing can trickle. A flawless dismount when de-tinning is key, and Crabb watched Sales pull this off in an episode of their mini-show *When I Get A Minute* on the ABC in 2016 using a method that reveals much about Leigh's orderly approach to cooking . . .

The joy of a perfect dismount.
Picture: ABC

L So the cookbook that I'm actually using the most currently is the one you gave me for Christmas.

a Oh, isn't that nice!

L *The Cook and Baker* – it is so great. Everything in it is absolutely delicious.

a [*Finds handwritten list of some kind, tucked into back cover*] Look at you with your little 'list of things I'm gonna make' . . . you're so organised.

L I do it whenever I get a new cookbook. I read through it – it's very enjoyable. I write down on a piece of paper the page numbers and everything that I'd like to cook, and then I methodically work through the list and then I write on the recipe and say, 'How did it turn out? Was it underwhelming? Did it need more of something?'

🅐 [*Gently shakes head.*]

🅛 Today I'm cooking from the new Nigella book *Simply Nigella*. What I'm making is a pumpkin bundt cake, which I must admit is the third thing I've made from it from my list.

🅐 Oh my god. This one has a list too.

🅛 Of course it does.

🅐 You are SO CRACKERS.

🅛 Anyway, I bought myself a bundt tin for Christmas.

🅐 It always sounds rude, doesn't it. There's just something about it.

🅛 You are so immature.

[*Bundt cooks.*]

🅛 [*Takes tin out of oven.*] It's good to go, baby. Except . . . I'm a little concerned.

🅐 Why? Looks good.

🅛 [*Examines underside.*] Well, the cake's cracked. I'm actually glad it cracked. You know why?

🅐 What is it, Pollyanna?

🅛 Because if I tip this thing out, and it just goes *pffft*, and it's a disaster, people will relate to that. And so then I think you could have a television show where you did that and go, 'It didn't work out. Now, whip a bit of cream through it, throw some peaches on top . . . and it's Eton Mess.'

🅐 [*Pretends to take phone call.*] Oh, hang on a minute – it's for you. It's Channel Nine.

🅛 So, you know, you have to leave it in for about 10 minutes because it'll hopefully shrink away from the edges a little bit.

🅐 And then it'll just go plop out of the tin.

🅛 That's what we're hoping.

🅐 And then you'll dust it with this lovely icing sugar. Do you want me to continue the difficult sifting task?

🅛 You know what I want to see you do in the opening titles of *Kitchen Cabinet*? Instead of, like, you know, gentle bits of flour dusting, I want to see actual real cooking like 'ARGH, DAMMIT!'

Another impossibly smug bundt by Sales.

ⓐ Actual crying.

[*Annabel and Leigh spend another few minutes discussing the genius of* The Katering Show, *and the emasculation of Daddy Pig by Peppa and the endlessly capable Mummy Pig.*]

ⓛ It's time for my reveal. Okay, so how do you actually do this? [*Taps around tin with knife.*]

ⓐ You really don't have a lot of faith in this.

ⓛ Much like a doctor on *ER*, I just want to give it every chance of survival that I can.

[*Sales turns perfect bundt cake out of tin. Shrieks, does little dance.*]

ⓐ I feel like your whole family should come running down from the stands like in *MasterChef*. That is actually bloody impressive.

ⓛ That is a bit of a smug bundt, isn't it?

ⓐ It's a total smug bundt.

Far be it for me to have to explain another law of physics to you.

classic episode 63

it's a redacted!

Annabel Crabb. She's a sweet-tempered cake-maker in an amusing apron, right? Slow to anger; almost impossible to enrage. Her rarely seen wrath is reserved for Big Things – like injustice, cruelty or discovering 20 minutes before school time that it's Harmony Day today and everyone's supposed to be wearing orange.

White-hot fury is just not in her nature. *Or so we all thought* until Episode 63, in which Annabel tells of her faulty oven catching fire at an inconvenient time and such is her apoplexy that she goes on a rant at the manufacturer, whose name shall be redacted.

a 'I was cooking a quite ambitious large pavlova situation for our friends Gwen and Stephen, who have a joint birthday party. I was working up to a real multi-egger double pav in the initials of their names. So I'm preheating the oven to 150°C – not even a hot heat – and I'm just puttering in the kitchen and I can start smelling an odd smell and I can hear this 'pop, pop, pop', like a really muffled popcorn-popping sound. And then I looked at the oven and the thing was on fire inside. So I turned it off and it just sort of died a lonely death.

'And then I was overcome by this surging wave of rage because that oven is not very old – three years old, maybe. Now, I won't name the brand – let's just call it a limey pile of junk, because it has failed me on several key occasions before. The last time it shat itself was my daughter's birthday. Its fan has blown or its thermostat or whatever or it just won't get hot. And I just think, 'Ovens, you've got one job. It's to get hot. We're not trying to put a person on the moon here. Just "apply heat to food" is what I need you to do.

'So I flew into an insane rage and went on a giant rant at the manufacturer. I'm not a vengeful person, but when you take away my oven, you change me. I really am quite reliant on cooking for my peace of mind. It's like meditation for me and if I can't do it, then I become psychotic. Really fast.'

Sales, sensing an opportunity to belt out a tune – sorry, 'soothe her friend' – naturally turns to the piano to write a comforting little song to the tune of the Cole Porter classic 'It's De-Lovely', ploughing on regardless despite Crabb's insistence that 'this is the only possible way that you could make this whole experience worse for me'.

It's a [BLEEEEP]!

The guests are here
The glasses clink
But now my oven is on the blink.
It's a trash pile, it's a lemon
It's a [BLEEEEP].

I understand
The reason why
You hate this oven
'Cos so do I.
It's a shit heap
It's a fire trap
It's a [BLEEEEP].

I can tell
At a glance
That you bought
This crap
Stuck in a trance.
I can hear
Nigella Lawson
Murmuring, 'Hello,
Let this dog go.'

So let's be clear
My chickadee
Next time opt for
Smeg or Miele.
It's disaster. It's a nightmare.
It's a hopeless joke. It's a scare bear.
It's just useless, it's nutty, it's pathetic, it's dumb,
It's a [BLEEEEP]!

an over-rooted cake

L Let me paint a scene for you, Chatters. So I'm in the priest hole with Annabel Crabb. She's provided some carrot cake. Just very delicious.

a Is it good?

L I haven't eaten the icing yet. Is it cream cheese?

a Sure is. Otherwise you're just camping out . . . as Paul Keating always says about carrot cake. Also, there's a little bit of an orange zest in the cream cheese frosting for you. Yeah, you get that for free. So the story of this carrot cake is that I had some cream cheese frosting left over and I was building a cake to take it, because I hate to throw out frosting.

L You know, I made a salad this week. I had leftover tofu and I just went looking for a salad that took tofu so I could just get that out of the fridge.

a I like that starting place. And so I did that thing where you google 'best carrot cake' or something like that, and I found a Good Food thread called 'Australia's best carrot cake recipe'. Now obviously this is highly, highly subjective, but I went ahead and I baked the winner. It turns out the winning recipe is by Angelique Lazarus, who is one of the women who put together that cookbook called *Monday Morning Cooking Club*, which I actually have cooked a bunch of things out of and I really like the book. This is a carrot cake that plays all the hits. It's got your crushed pineapple in there – controversial to some, but A-okay by me.

L Look, I'm just gonna make a bold call.

a Oh yeah, what?

L There's not enough carrot in it.

a There's, like, FOUR CARROTS in there!
I went over! I over-carroted! It is an OVER-ROOTED CAKE.

L I can barely taste the carrot and I hardly see it.

a Wow. Tough crowd.

L But it is delicious, nonetheless.

a So you'd make it, but change the recipe?

L I wouldn't call it a carrot cake. It's a walnut cake, with hints of carrot.

a Well – they're pecans, for starters.

L I guess I don't know what I'm talking about. Root carrots. I don't have anything against quality roots.

a Do you know why you're annoyed by roots?

L Why? Tell me.

a Because it's an extension of your 'tuber' problem.

L Gawd. Is the quality of the gags in this thing going to pick up today or not?

This is what it's like hanging out with her:

'Podcast, podcast, podcast, cake, Hamilton, podcast, Hamilton, podcast, cake, cake, kohlrabi, podcast, kohlrabi, cake, Hamilton.'

and now, Sales's music thing we reluctantly let her have

The year I turned 10, my mother caved in to my pestering for music lessons – organ lessons, to be specific. A few blocks from our house lived a keyboard teacher, Leanne, who was prepared to take me for six dollars for half an hour, once a week. On the appointed day, I would put Mum's money and *The Complete Organ Player: Book 1* by Kenneth Baker into the basket of my red pushbike and pedal down Bald Hills Road to Leanne's modest, low-set brick house, which sat close to where the bitumen petered into a dirt track leading to the South Pine River. I would coast up the driveway, lean my bike against the wall and wait outside until the boy before me, Michael Rossi, finished his lesson.

The music room was at the front of the house. Every week as I stood patiently, I would listen to Michael's showy style – his left hand pecking out Latin rhythms; his right hand whizzing up and down in glissandos or darting off the keys to make quick-change organ stops; his feet busily dancing over the pedals. He was Leanne's only male student, and her favourite.

'Michael Rossi can really play,' she would sigh.

At the end of his lesson, I always expected the front door to fling open to reveal someone resembling Liberace. Instead, a short boy would stroll out, his music tucked under his arm, brown hair neatly parted and shirt tucked tightly into his shorts. My feelings for him landed somewhere between envy and reverence.

The centrepiece of Leanne's music room was what we called 'The Conn' – an electronic organ built in America by C.G. Conn Instruments, a manufacturing powerhouse of its day, long ago swallowed by Steinway. The Conn looked like a kind of musical spaceship. Three dozen colourful buttons were arrayed in a semi-circle around three keyboards. It had 13 pedals and an electronic drum section, offering everything from foxtrot to ballad.

Leanne was in her early 20s, newly married but with no children yet. She was a grown-up, but not the kind with whom I was familiar, like parents or teachers. She was in that brief sweet spot of early adulthood: old enough to have independence and answer to nobody, but not yet ground down by life's responsibilities and disappointments. As far as I was concerned, she was the most fun grown-up ever. It never felt like I was there for anything as serious as a musical education. Even practising felt like part of an exciting game we were playing together. I never wanted to front up for my next lesson at Leanne's without having mastered the task she had set me. I didn't fear her, or worry that I would get into trouble; I simply liked her so much that I didn't want to let her down. I wanted to stay in the game. Today, as an adult myself, having had many instructors in all sorts of things,

> **I realise that only a great teacher makes you forget you're doing the work of learning.**

Leanne quickly saw that I was driven and that the harder the challenge, the more I would strive to meet expectations. Initially, all I was interested in was playing the notes accurately from beginning to end so I could move on to the next piece (and perhaps usurp Michael Rossi as teacher's pet). I paid no attention to the dynamics written on the sheet music – the symbols that indicate whether to play loudly or softly. An organist's right foot sits on a large, rectangular volume pedal and my preferred position was flat to the floor all the time, regardless of the musical notation.

well hello

'God, I dread the day you get your driver's licence,' Leanne would grouse after she had yet again shouted over my thunderous playing. 'More expression!'

Leanne was an inspired motivator because she had no musical snobbery. If I took an interest in classical music, we would open a book of Bach music. If I mentioned that I liked a certain song in the Top 40, I would arrive the next week to find that she'd jotted down an organ arrangement to match my skill level. When I wanted to switch to piano, we did. During the decade or so that I attended lessons, we became close friends. In my teens, the half-hour classes turned into an hour, and afterwards I would hang around her house. She had two toddlers by then with a third not far off, and we would talk about music and school and life.

Leanne had a great record collection and I remember the day she pressed an orange double album into my hands and told me to take it home. It was Stevie Wonder's *Songs in the Key of Life*, still one of my all-time favourites. When I showed up for my next lesson, infatuated with Stevie's brilliance, Leanne had, of course, turned it into an occasion to learn something new. If I wanted to play Stevie Wonder and drop the Chopin piece I was halfway through, sure, she'd go along with that, but was I aware that Wonder's preferred keys had four or five flats? And did I think I could figure out an E flat minor ninth chord on the second inversion with an augmented fifth and a G natural on the bass? Or, if I thought it too difficult in that key, did I prefer to sight-transpose the sheet music up a semitone to E minor? If not, Leanne would shrug, no problem, we can go back to the Chopin. She was forever dangling the kind of treasure that could only be grasped if I followed her map on a quest well out of my comfort zone.

One of the most intriguing characters in The Last Dance, the Netflix documentary about the American basketballer Michael Jordan, is Chicago Bulls coach Phil Jackson. He's an impenetrable tower of a man whose presence pervades the entire series, even though he says very little. Jackson leads the Bulls to six NBA championships and wrangles the team's forcefully individual characters – Jordan, Dennis Rodman, Scottie Pippen, Toni Kukoč. Their faith in him borders on the religious. Jackson's strategy, like Leanne's, was to carefully study his charges, paying close attention to their personal drives, and adapt his methods to suit each person.

The coach's memoir, *Sacred Hoops*, is a surprisingly dull mixture of sports psychology, Christianity and Zen Buddhism. Only one piece of wisdom from the book stuck with me but it did so in a profound way. And here it is. Perhaps you have a favourite teacup. You might love it and have a sentimental attachment to it. You might dread the day it breaks and imagine how sad you will be not to have it anymore. Jackson's advice is to imagine that the cup is already broken, even as you are drinking from it. Let go of the hope that it will never break and believe it has already happened. Once you do that, your focus will shift to appreciation of the cup as you sip your tea, acutely aware that it is yours only temporarily. Jackson believes this awareness grounds you in the present and releases you from worry about things outside your control.

The broken cup has come to mind almost every day since I read *Sacred Hoops*. Like anyone, I have moments when I find my job hard going. Sometimes I close my eyes and channel Phil Jackson, imagining a time when I won't be immersed in daily news, experiencing its crazy twists and meeting its interesting personalities. Suddenly, my job doesn't seem so burdensome. My mindset switches to how much I enjoy what I'm doing and how enormously I will miss it when it's gone. Similarly, when I'm irritated at someone, I imagine what it would be like if that person left my life permanently. Usually the annoyance melts away and is replaced by gratitude for the things I like about them.

Music holds me in the moment in a similar way. When I sit at the piano, I must concentrate on reading the music, counting the beat, making my fingers cooperate, using my foot on the sustain pedal, listening to see if the notes floating on the air sound correct. It takes so much focus that it's impossible to think of anything not immediately before me. I don't have leftover mental capacity to fret about what I could have done better at work or to concoct fantasies of tense conversations about imagined slights.

Some people might consider that a form of meditation, but my best description is that it's like taking a holiday from myself; a break from my brain's nonstop ticking and whirring.

I sometimes wonder if this is how Annabel Crabb feels about cooking. When I bake, I sense I'm using the same parts of my brain as when I play the piano: I'm following instructions on a page, translating them into actions with my hands, using rhythm to beat or sift, bowing to precision by gliding a knife across the top of a cup of flour or slicing fruit to identical widths. At the end of the process, the hope is that the parts work in harmony to make something beautiful.

Grounding myself in the present through piano or baking comes almost automatically. Using the broken cup method is harder, because it's difficult to believe that some things are already lost to you when they're right there in front of you. Accepting the impermanence of an object that doesn't matter that much, like a cup, is straightforward. Embracing the inevitable end of things that are extremely important to you is confronting. Beyond losing my family and closest friends, the very hardest thing for me to consider broken and gone is my ability to play the piano. I know it will almost certainly be the case one day if I'm lucky enough to grow old. I dread it – although if I listen to Phil Jackson, I should replace that dread with acceptance. It's hard, because

without the chance to play music, my life would be diminished. Without the chance to listen to it, my life would be intolerable.

Phil Jackson's stoic courtside demeanour is similar to what I often strive for as a television current affairs anchor. I have a professional obligation to convey authority, and an anchor should also seem reassuring and reliably calm, regardless of what's going on. A viewer at home might feel rattled by the day's events but they should expect the person on screen to help them make sense of what's happened and to restore their faith – as much as possible – that things will be okay.

Performing that role requires the constant suppression of normal emotion. One of the reasons I can do it most of the time is that I am naturally reserved. That stiff upper lip, plus years of practice at swallowing down tears or anger at tragic or shocking news, has come at a cost. My emotions, particularly sad or negative ones, are buried deep beneath the surface and it can be difficult for me to let them out.

The antidote to this is music. Playing it allows me to express complex feelings without the discomfort of verbalising them, and listening to it distracts me and makes me feel better. It is the key that unlocks the vault in which I keep grief and frustration and all the other emotions I repress all day.

At the height of the lockdown, I left my house one day for a permitted walk. I selected a playlist and Bach's Prelude and Fughetta in G Major wafted through my earbuds. Within a minute, my eyes filled with tears. I couldn't immediately identify the feeling the music had released and was surprised to realise it was relief. I wondered, from what is this music relieving me to the extent that it's made me cry?

As I walked and listened, it struck me that the trigger was the order in Bach's music. His compositions are constructed like intricate mechanical devices, the themes and patterns delicately spinning against each other like the cogs in a watch. Through his precision, Bach offered me beauty and predictability in a world drowning in ugliness and uncertainty. It was soothing to be met with stability amid chaos. Without Bach in my ears, there was no way I could have experienced relief, nor could I have articulated that my spirit craved it. The music met a need for order that I didn't even realise I had.

Music's influence on the brain is well documented, perhaps most famously in the book *Musicophilia* by the neurologist Oliver Sacks. He explores the way music can alleviate various psychological and physiological complaints, from depression to Parkinson's disease. Music stimulates many sections of the brain simultaneously (including visual and motor receptors, as well as auditory ones). There is no 'music centre' – the kind of brain activation depends on the songs played as well as the individual's preferences and memory. An MRI will show different parts of a person's brain lighting up at hearing their favourite music, compared with the unfamiliar or disliked. In a 2020 profile in the *New Yorker*, the composer John Williams mused on the way the motifs from his epic *Star Wars* score trigger intense emotions in many people. The opening brass of the main theme pushes serious nostalgia buttons.

'It's a little bit like how the olfactory system is wired with memory, so that a certain smell makes you remember your grandmother's cooking,' Williams explained.

Music from our youth, or any skill we've spent a lot of time honing when young, is held in the cerebellum, the region of the brain that stores muscle memory. It's what an athlete uses when they say they're in the 'zone'. Skills in this part of the brain, like driving or teeth brushing, can feel like autopilot. The power of muscle memory means that a patient deep in the grip of dementia may be unable to recognise loved ones but can still respond positively to music from their past.

When I play the piano these days, I am lazy and I mostly rely on the knowledge ingrained in my muscle memory. Luckily, for my requirements, that gets me by. I can still read music adequately and I can pick out tunes or chords by ear. But when I observe what's happening to my technical skills, I am acutely aware of that broken cup. A friend thoughtfully gave me some Bach sheet music for my birthday after I told him that listening to the composer had comforted me during lockdown. When I sat at the piano, opened the book and attempted to play the first piece, I realised how much ability I'd lost through years of not practising scales or methodically working on difficult pieces. My left hand sounded like it was being controlled by somebody dangling it from the end of a stick. Even after repeatedly practising a difficult bar, I had only a 50-50 chance of executing it correctly when I played the piece from the start. If I left it more than two days before having another go, I would have scant finger memory when I returned. This was confronting because I recognised the piece as something I could have played with ease 20 years ago.

It would be easy to tell myself the comforting lie that it would all come back if I just returned to some regular practice. I believe that will never happen, for the same reasons all of us lose our grasp on things we used to be able to do: insufficient time, lack of motivation, the effects of ageing, too much stuff to binge-watch on television. As upsetting as that is, my chief consolation as I lose my playing ability – which, I hasten to add, was mediocre at best – is that I hope, until the day I die, I will be able to listen to others do what I never could.

When I was in my 20s, I'd often fall into a funk when I saw a brilliant musician – like when I went to see the cellist Pieter Whispelwey play with the Australian Chamber Orchestra. I was jealous and despondent for days afterwards.

In my late teens I had bought a cello and taken lessons for a while but decided it was too hard and quit. Watching Whispelwey filled me with self-loathing for my own failure. The cello cup was broken and I knew it for certain.

But somewhere along the way, my attitude changed. Now when I see a brilliant performer in any pursuit, whether Pieter Whispelwey on the cello or Michael Jordan on the basketball court, I think, I can't do that, but thank god somebody else can. I'm thrilled to witness their magnificence.

When I was a teenager, I had a conversation with Leanne about whether I should carry on sitting music exams in order to obtain my 'letters'. She asked if I thought I would make music my career. I was fairly certain I wouldn't but said I wasn't totally sure.

Leanne said something like: you could try to make music your career but it's hard and even a lot of extremely talented musicians can't pull that off. And if you do somehow succeed, music becomes a job – and at times nearly everyone hates their job. If music is your work, then what will you turn to for relaxation and joy? If you choose something else as your career, music will always be your escape. Your love for it will never be dampened. She advised me to think about it carefully, and if I decided I didn't want to pursue music, then why bother doing any more exams? I had enough pressure at school. Why not learn piano purely for pleasure? I'm grateful for that advice every day. I never sat another music exam. Leanne was absolutely right that music would become my joy and escape. The way she taught me ensures I have enough skills to get by for what I am and was always destined to be: an enthusiastic hobbyist who loves hacking around on the piano, singing nonstop around the house and boring people witless by banging on about things like how tight the brass is on *Sinatra at the Sands*.

Many people talk of how much they hated being sent to music lessons as a child. They grew up to detest classical music and retained nothing of what they learned. For me, it was the opposite. When I contemplate the things for which I'm most grateful in life, one is that my parents parted with the money for music lessons and instruments. Another is that I arrived in Leanne's front room as a child who loved music – and the way she nurtured and respected that love meant that when I left her as an adult, it was powerfully intact.

oh god, not *Hamilton* again

One of the indulgences of having your own podcast is being able to bang on about pretty much whatever you like for as long as you like – at least, until your listeners rebel. And so it was with *Hamilton*, which Leigh and Annabel discussed so endlessly that some fed-up Chatters actually started to complain.

Despite relentless badgering by fans of the show, Leigh initially declined an opportunity to see *Hamilton* in New York, blaming its bigger-than-Broadway ticket price and her conviction that she wasn't going to like 'a musical about a Treasury Secretary told in hip-hop'.

And yet the nagging wore her down, so she saw it. And loved it. So she started to nag Annabel. Who listened to it. And loved it. And then saw it. What follows is about a bajillion words uttered about *Hamilton*, ruthlessly edited. And if *Hamilton*'s not your bag ... go have a cup of tea while we get this over with.

ⓐ When we first started doing this podcast five years ago, and I'd never heard of *Hamilton*, someone wrote to us and said, 'You've got to see *Hamilton*! Like, get across it.'

ⓛ I feel like, basically, a group of people the size of the population of Romania has badgered me to see *Hamilton*.

ⓐ And you would be, I imagine, possibly the only person in history ever to go and see *Hamilton* in a grumpy mood.

ⓛ I had one free night in London. There was one ticket left on this Saturday night so I thought, 'Okay, I'm going,' and then I got there and I was grouchy and jet-lagged – 'I'm tired, I'm not going to like this, blah, blah, blah.' And then

I was full of self-loathing because I was like, `You are such an entitled moll` because look at you, you've got the money to go and see one of the world's great shows.' Everyone except me was so excited. And so I thought, 'For god's sake, Leigh, have a look at yourself and bloody, you know, stop it.'

ⓐ `'Force down Beluga on a cracker and a glass of champagne.'`

ⓛ Anyway, it started and then basically from the opening minute, it was unbelievable, it was so good. And that's with so many people telling me, 'It's so good, it's so good,' I was thinking there's no way it can be that good. It was *that* good. It was effing unbelievable. At the interval, I was texting various people who'd really bullied me, and going, 'Oh my god, this is insane.' And since I loved it so much, there were certain tunes that as soon as they came on, I just thought, 'Well, I'm gonna be singing that for a week.' And so I got the soundtrack, and I've since been going through the book of it, to understand . . . my mind was boggled when I was watching it. `Like, how did Lin-Manuel Miranda get this out of his head onto paper? But even more, how did they get this off paper onto stage?` The thing that was incredible too – it was an absolute revelation – was how well hip-hop lent itself to a musical, because hip-hop's basically a narrative and a musical is stories told through songs so hip-hop works brilliantly. Alexander Hamilton was this immigrant to New York who was this sort of scrappy, you know, sort of brash dude and so his vibe fits really well with hip-hop. And of course, everyone on stage was just so unbelievably talented.

ⓐ Note Sales is now Salesplaining why this is so good. `This is possibly the most annoying outcome from this entire annoying experiment.`

Fast forward to the live show in Newcastle a few weeks later, which opened with a snippet of 'My Shot', one of the numerous hit songs from *Hamilton,* and now both Leigh and Annabel are massive pains in the bum about the whole thing.

ⓛ I can't believe how fast you got addicted to it. We recorded the most recent podcast and then about a week later you texted me and went, 'I am addicted to *Hamilton*,' and I don't think you've ever previously listened to or watched anything that I've recommended.

well hello

ⓐ Oh, come on. I gave it four years and then I watched *The Americans* and I was suitably apologetic about that. But also my 13-year-old daughter has memorised several songs now and is working through the entire 41-song program.

It's so clever. And I just feel so embarrassed that years after it's appeared, I'm like, 'This is amazing!' I mean, I like to read Booker Prize winners 20 to 25 years after they've won, just so that nobody can accuse me of being influenced by fashion. But I started listening to it in my headphones while I was on a slightly busy day and I found myself pacing along to it and just feeling complete joy, because somebody has executed something so perfectly. The ambition of some of the rhymes that they pull off and this sort of frenzied fusillade of genius. I mean, I think I have one good idea for a line or rhyme or whatever, and I kind of recycle that indefinitely. But this production is just genius after genius after genius.

ⓛ I might have said this on the last podcast, sorry if I'm repeating myself . . .

ⓐ You probably did, it's going to get annoying.

ⓛ . . . when I saw it, and then when I've listened to it subsequently, a song would come on, and I'd go, 'Well, I guess that's the showstopper, isn't it?' Like, you know, 'My Shot', which we just walked out to, I thought, 'That's the showstopper. Wow, it's early in the show.' And then every song would come on and you'd go, 'Wow, another showstopper.' It's just basically a whole show of showstoppers.

ⓐ But also it's a sort of story that never gets made into a musical. I mean, *Hamilton* is the story of America's first bureaucrat. He designed the financial system and the banking sector, but also manages to be this real hound dog and the whole thing is this extraordinarily sticky story even though it ostensibly is not really the fodder for a hit musical.

And a few episodes later, just when *Hamilton*-ambivalent ('*Ham*bivalent' . . . we'll get our coat) Chatters thought it was safe to go back into the podcast . . .

ⓛ Have you listened to it enough yet that you have a favourite song?

ⓐ Every single morning, without a word of a lie, I wake up with a different

Hamilton song in my head and I also think that the only thing getting our family through this enforced togetherness phase is that we are just constantly singing *Hamilton*, and weirdly enough, every morning is a different song. It might just be 'Wait for It' or it might be 'Here Comes the General'. Every day is different.

🅛 You know, I can just see, like, around the country, all the Chatters going, 'Oh god, not *Hamilton* again.' And have any rhymes particularly grabbed you?

🅐 A hundred million of them, but there's a Cabinet rap at some point, where – you'll be pleased to hear that I've also been emailing the executive producer of *Insiders* with all of these links and saying, 'So I think you could easily do a package to this *Hamilton* song. I mean, next time that Barnaby Joyce runs for the leadership – which, let's face it, will be in about 3.5 seconds, it's got to be, you know, "I'm not throwing away my shot", right?'

🅛 Cut to *Insiders* headquarters: 'Goddammit. I knew if she kept hanging around Sales this long this was going to happen eventually.'

🅐 I keep hammering him with these suggestions. 'When are these colonies gonna rise up like COAG . . . the next COAG story – sex that up with some *Hamilton*. You're welcome.' And he's like, 'Hi, thanks for your suggestions. See you soon, I hope to see you . . . around.'

Readers, we have done you a favour by cutting possibly hours more *Hamilton* gibber. Which brings us neatly to this admission from Crabb:

🅐 We are total party bores right now. We're in the corner with the pinot gris going, 'And what about that line where, you know . . .'

🅛 This is where you're like, 'Enough of the *Hamilton*.'

🅐 The whole party's just edging away into the garden to smoke furtive cigarettes and whine about us. I am actually worried about the *Hamilton* thing now, because actually it's in my brain, the whole time.

🅛 Same here.

🅐 And I wake up in the morning and it's on a loop in my brain.

🅛 It is the stickiest thing I've ever listened to. I think that a song from *Hamilton* has been pretty much playing in my head constantly for the entire year.

🅐 It's a bit worrying. I think I'm a bit too far in.

A few weeks later, Sales has some Big News.

If your phone rings right now and it's Barack's people, I'm gonna actually hurt you in a bad way.

🅛 Annabel, I'm not sure if you caught it . . .

🅐 Oh, what is that, Leigh?

🅛 . . . but I interviewed Lin-Manuel Miranda last week.

🅐 Did you?

🅛 The composer of *Hamilton*.

🅐 I'm just gonna take a picture of how big and dumb the grin on her face is right now.

🅛 I would say the number two and three people on my interview wish list would be . . . Ricky Gervais would have been number two and Lin-Manuel Miranda would be number three. Number one is Barack Obama.

🅐 If your phone rings right now and it's Barack's people, I'm gonna actually hurt you in a bad way.

🅛 'Oh, Barack, hi. Yeah, great, I could do that. No problem. Okay, good, squared away.' So within the space of one week, I interviewed both Ricky Gervais and Lin-Manuel Miranda from their homes; it was crazy.

🅐 People are doing it really tough right now, Leigh Sales, they don't want to listen to your triumphalism and your privilege.

🅛 Anyway, Lin-Manuel was, as you would expect, absolutely delightful.

🅐 I know, because we all put off watching *MasterChef* until after 7.30, which – I'm sorry, love – never happens.

🅛 Did your kids enjoy it?

🅐 Oh yeah. They loved the preceding stories about, um, health regulation. No, they all watched because they knew what was coming up – they knew there was a treat at the end.

🅛 So our friend Gwen . . . her son, Samson, like all of our kids, is unscratchably addicted to *Hamilton*. And when Gwen told him I was interviewing Lin-Manuel, she took a photo of Samson's face.

And it was such a great photo, just wonder and thrill. And I thought, I'm going to use that as a way in to discussing how fans of *Hamilton* feel because there does seem to be an extreme level of passion and joy around it, and I thought his face captured it. Anyway, when I held up the photo to show Lin-Manuel, he gave a great answer, which he began by saying, 'I remember when I used to be Samson.'

Ⓐ Cue Samson's life just being completely fulfilled ...

Ⓛ Samson's head exploding.

Ⓐ ... at the age of 10.

Ⓛ I thought, 'That's lovely that he recognises that that will mean something to the child if he says their name. He said, 'I used to be Samson. I remember when I was young, and I would be watching musicals and they get in your DNA and you have to know every single thing about them.'

Ⓐ He's obsessed with *Rent*.

Ⓛ How he described it ... the way that, when you love one, you just become so obsessed by it and you're singing it with your friends and all the rest of it. It just perfectly captured, I think, why people do love musical theatre so much.

Samson Blake's mind being blown at Lin-Manuel Miranda saying: 'I used to BE Samson.' *Picture: Gwen Blake*

Salesy's top 10s

(that nobody asked her to compile)

musicals

I'm so glad I was asked to compile this. The first thing that sprang to mind was the list of my least favourite musicals – *The Pirates of Penzance*, *West Side Story*, *My Fair Lady* and, most of all, *South Pacific* ('Bali Ha'i' truly makes me want to gag). All the rest of these I'd happily sing from start to finish, any day of the week. And I do.

10. *Fame*
I was in love with the idea of going to a performing arts school after I saw the TV series of *Fame*, which is actually far inferior to the film. There's a wonderful song called 'Out Here on My Own', sung by Irene Cara in the film. I do love something in the opening titles to the TV show – and I believe in fact I may have barked it at Crabb during some podcast or other. It's the monologue that the dance coach, Debbie Allen, delivers: 'You got big dreams? You want fame? Well, fame COSTS. And right here is where you start paying. In SWEAT.'

9. *Annie*
Literally as soon as I wrote down the word 'Annie' I started singing, *'It's a hard knock life for us, it's a hard knock life for us.'* Now I'm already singing in Carol Burnett's drunk voice, *'Little girls, little girls, everything about them is. . . little.'* Yes, I could go on like this all night. Come for the great songs, stay for the bonus Tim Curry as Rooster.

8. *Grease*

This holds a special place in my heart because I played Sandy in Aspley State High School's Year 11 production of this masterpiece. Let's just say I was more comfortable in her prissy stage than when I had to deliver the line, 'Tell me about it . . . stud.' Childhood Friend Mandy was regularly press-ganged into playing Sandy in the primary school playground to my Danny and was then roped into the chorus while I took centre stage in high school. Amazingly, she's still friends with me (although CFM's take on this would be worth pursuing).

7. *Hello, Dolly!*

In the least surprising revelation from me ever, I love Barbra Streisand and I loved the film version of *Hello, Dolly!* with her in the lead role. I saw Bette Midler in the Broadway production in New York in 2017. She was fantastic and it was so incredible when she came onstage. The love and excitement in the room and the feeling that you were in the presence of Broadway royalty was incredible. The song 'It Only Takes A Moment' is my favourite, sung in the film by Michael Crawford of *Some Mothers Do 'Ave 'Em* fame. You might also recognise it from the film *Wall-E*.

6. *Little Shop of Horrors*

Unfortunately, this musical has dated really badly because of the domestic violence subplot. There's almost no way of getting around that without a complete rewrite (otherwise, what's Seymour's motivation for feeding the dentist to the plant?). The songs are so great, though – as with *Annie*, I'm already sitting here singing. '*Look out, look out, look out, look out!*'

5. *Hamilton*

Okay, this is the last thing I'll say about *Hamilton*, which goes straight into this list with a bullet at number five. Sometimes, if you see an old-school musical it feels like a fantasy thing, because people break into song. But, like *A Chorus Line* (see the next page), *Hamilton* is actually a quite gritty, sort of realist-type thing that did something new with the genre and felt really contemporary. It feels like you're watching a real story getting told. Well, a real story in which people break into song and dance every now and again. That's realistic in my house.

4. *The Rocky Horror Picture Show*

I truly think Tim Curry makes the greatest entrance in film history – that tapping foot in platform heels as the elevator descends. And then that number 'Sweet Transvestite' – oh good god, you are basically plastered back in your seat, he absolutely KILLS it. Really, it is such an utter tour de force that the rest of the film sinks after it. He is just so superb. I love this whole soundtrack. I'm a big fan of 'There's A Light' and I regularly prance around the house in my squeaky Columbia voice singing, *'It was great when it all began, I was a regular Frankie fan'* (the opening to 'Rose Tint My World').

3. *Chicago*

I love the stage version and I also think Rob Marshall made a cracking film. I regularly sing 'When You're Good to Mama' to my kids. They love that, and 'Cell Block Tango'. There are so many winning numbers in this musical. I love every character and every song.

2. *Singin' in the Rain*

It's my favourite film but only my second-favourite musical. It makes me SO happy, it's the greatest feelgood thing ever. Gene Kelly doing 'Singin' in the Rain' is absolute bliss, but I also can't get enough of Donald O'Connor doing 'Make 'Em Laugh' and Debbie Reynolds doing 'Good Morning'. Absolute 100/100.

1.

A Chorus Line

So if I love *Singin' in the Rain* so much and it's my favourite film, why is it not my favourite musical? Simply because *A Chorus Line* was really the musical that tipped me into hardcore love of musicals. It was a truly ground-breaking piece of work at the time it was written. I don't imagine I could have a better night at the theatre than watching everybody in gold top hats dance in unison and sing 'One'. There was a wonderful documentary made called *Every Little Step* about the real-life auditions for a New York production of *A Chorus Line*. I saw the production that was the basis for that doco, which I found quite thrilling.

albums

This was a really difficult thing to do (you're welcome) and I'm sure that once it's in print, I'll go, 'WHAT, I can't believe I forgot to include [insert omitted album here].' But these 10 certainly do represent some of my broad musical tastes and I can't say I'd like to see any of them swapped out.

10.

Live in Chicago – Kurt Elling

I can't remember how I was introduced to Kurt Elling but he has the most phenomenally smooth jazz voice. The energy on this live recording and the musical interplay among the band members is really something else. I particularly love the way 'My Foolish Heart' devolves to very soft and sparse and then Kurt uses a vocal crescendo to bring the band back in full throttle. The cover of 'Smoke Gets in Your Eyes' is also worth the price of admission.

9.

Watershed – k.d. lang

I am a huge k.d. fan and it was a tough choice between this and *Hymns of the 49th Parallel*, which would probably be a lot of people's favourite. Her voice packs such an emotional punch and I like the country influence in her music. I saw her live at the

State Theatre in Sydney about a decade ago and she was utterly masterful. Tears were pouring down my face when she sang 'The Valley'.

8.
Liquid Skin – Gomez
This band has wonderful musicality and works so well as an ensemble. They are really inventive with their sounds and songwriting. Ben Ottewell, one of the singers, sounds like a man who's drunk a bottle of whiskey and smoked a packet of cigarettes every day for 70 years – but he looks like an economist from the Treasury department. I've seen Gomez many times and you won't see a better live band. My favourite track on this album is 'Las Vegas Dealer', which is in 5/4, and has a great beat that the audience always claps along to in a live show. It really goes off.

7.
Brahms' Piano Concerto No. 1 (The recording I listen to is the Berlin Philharmonic with Krystian Zimmerman on the piano and Simon Rattle conducting)
I am hesitant to say I have a favourite classical composer but Brahms is certainly up there. His music is very lush to my ears and it strikes some sort of deep emotional chord with me. It's in the same ballpark as Beethoven but I don't find it anywhere near as painfully sad. The second movement of this concerto is exquisite. I first heard it performed live by the pianist Emanuel Ax with the Chicago Symphony Orchestra and I've never stopped listening to it in awe since.

6.
Tapestry – Carole King
My mother owned this album and it was a favourite of mine from childhood. I don't know what it is about those '70s folk rockers but they can do an awful lot with a few chords and a bit of guitar.

5. *The Bends* – Radiohead

A flawless masterpiece. I've often wondered if – when the band sat back for a listen to this from start to finish in the studio, after they'd added their final touches – Jonny Greenwood and Thom Yorke looked at each other and said, 'Mate, fuck, we have just made one of the greatest albums of all time.' Or at that stage had they tinkered with it so much that they weren't sure how good it was any more? Or do they still hear it today and think bits of it are flawed? Hopefully I'll get to interview one of them one day and ask. Among many brilliant songs, 'Fake Plastic Trees' is special to me.

4. *Sinatra at the Sands* – Frank Sinatra, with the Count Basie Orchestra, conducted and arranged by Quincy Jones

As with the Kurt Elling mentioned earlier, this is a live recording that makes you feel as if you are in the room. Along with Frank's inimitable style, he's accompanied by the Count Basie Orchestra, helmed by the legendary Quincy Jones. I mean, HELLO! You can tell that Frank and the band are having the greatest night. From the opening cymbals, to the voice of the announcer, to Frank coming out and saying, 'Wait a minute, who let all these people into my room?', it just makes my heart soar.

3. *Temple of Low Men* – Crowded House

It was a hard call between this album and *Woodface*. I opted for this because I like its melancholy note. Neil Finn crafts incredible songs. Along with the Beatles, he really has provided the soundtrack to a lot of my life, from teen years onwards.

2. *Songs in the Key of Life* – Stevie Wonder

My music teacher Leanne introduced me to this double album when I was a teenager and I have been an epic Stevie Wonder fan ever since. It's amazing how cool this album still sounds today. I'm not sure what we were doing listening to this album at organ lessons. I suspect the song 'I Just Called to Say I Love You' may have been a recent hit and that Leanne wanted to show me that it wasn't really reflective of Stevie's catalogue. A true genius and trailblazer.

1. *Abbey Road* – The Beatles

Yes, I know I'm a cliché and that I was always going to have a Beatles album in first place. I could have peppered the rest of the list with other Beatles albums but I figured best to limit myself to one. It was a tough call but I chose based on which album I listen to most frequently and it's this one. 'Something' would be in my top five Beatles songs. I intensely dislike 'Octopus's Garden' (and pretty much all Ringo Starr songs) but the medley that used to be the old B-side of the album is SO GOOD.

bum-acne tuba players

If ever an entire professional group had grounds to lawyer up for defamation, *Tuba Players v. Leigh Sales* would be a zinger of a test case for the courts. Sales first revealed an unprovoked disdain for tuba players in an early episode, unleashing this shocking takedown while discussing her enjoyment of the stage show *Calamity Jane*:

🅛 Virginia Gay was Calamity Jane. She was incredible, the whole thing was great. There was a tuba solo. It was quite a young, good-looking guy, which changed a sort of stereotype in my mind that I have about tuba players, which is that they're all fat dudes with bum acne.

🅐 The fact that you even have a stereotypical tuba player view is deeply unsurprising to me and so weirdly disturbing.

🅛 Don't you think that's what 'tuba player' says, though? In the same way that 'cello player' says 'romantic, beautiful-looking female'...

🅐 ...pre-Raphaelite beauty, perhaps?

🅛 Exactly.

🅐 And tuba player just says: 'I've got acne on my bum, should you care to ever attend one of my bare-arse performances'? Wow, you are a woman of very eclectic tastes.

🅛 I apologise to any tuba player listening.

🅐 And I like the casual brutality of your review: 'Oh, the tuba player who was actually handsome' and 'whose arse was not covered as far as I know with suppurating acne.'

L I haven't maligned the entire brass section or anything, it's just tuba players.

a All you trombonists? You're all fine, you're free to go. French horn? No problem, off you pop.

L Trumpet? Not a problem.

a Tuba? Not so fast.

Oomph! Tubists were caught unawares by this vile slander. Chatters were stunned! But, as Crabb put it, 'like a dog returning to its own vomit', Sales *doubled down* in later episodes to honk their horns further . . . and bore Crabb senseless with music nerd talk in the process.

But then – an epiphany! Sales finally found new respect for tuba players, after many people sent her a video from the US of 'white supremacist nimrods' at a protest being ridiculed by a total champion marching alongside, playing comical tuba music. 'It's the greatest thing ever; that your contribution to the race debate in America is just to lend a tiny bit of your own ridiculousness to really mess up someone else,' she backhanded.

Leigh has now transferred her derision to viola players.

conclusion

right, let's wrap this thing up now

During live shows Sales tends to throw Crabb a lot of this look above, which she calls 'Affectionate Tolerance'.
Picture: Stephen Blake

ℒ **I never dreamed the first time that we sat here recording on my phone, exactly as we're doing now, that this was what it would become.** If somebody had said to you, 'It's going to be a thing listened to by hundreds and thousands of people and have a massive group and do big live shows around the country,' . . . you'd never have thought.

ⓐ It's bizarre.

ℒ But also I think – to be a bit overly deep about it – that it does show how sometimes you can do something and it opens up in a direction that you never thought possible. The idea of mapping out your life – 'I'm going to do this and then this is going to happen' – that's not usually what actually happens. **This has ended up being quite a significant part of our working lives** but it didn't start out as us trying to make it a significant part of our working lives.

ⓐ No, absolutely not. It makes me think that people at TV or radio networks who have the job of finding people who work together well on-air and have chemistry or whatever – that's a really hard job. This whole thing that we do has grown really organically. And has been also just 100 per cent fun because of that. No pressure.

ℒ **Do you ever wonder if we'll still be doing this when we're 70?**

ⓐ I never think about that. It never really feels like something that needs a long-term plan. I think one of the most enjoyable aspects of it is that we get to hang out with each other a bit, which, to be honest, if we didn't do a podcast, I'm sure we'd be kind of like, 'Must catch up with Crabb.' And never do it.

ℒ Oh, definitely.

ⓐ But because we put aside time, we do have quality time together.

ℒ I can imagine us doing it when we're 70.

a God, imagine how annoying you'll be by then. You'll have all your normal, completely bizarre human tics, but exacerbated by age.

L I'll be down to, 'This must be recorded in 21 minutes, 30 seconds.'

a Exactly.

L When I think of us when we're 70, it feels like we could easily still be doing it just because it's so fun. At that point, the live shows will be in clubs and RSLs and I'll be wearing, like, a big colourful muu-muu.

a Sure. Could we do cruises?

L We will have a really bad cabaret kind of show.

a You'll insist on playing the piano, badly.

L It'll be full of retirees. All women wearing three-quarter-length pants and oversized, colourful shirts.

a A hundred per cent. We'll have a lanyard, there'll be a lanyard. What will the merch look like by then? Probably incontinence pads. Gwen can just put a fairy-wren on them.

acknowledgements

The first and biggest 'Thank you' goes to the Chatters – that amorphous and kindly bunch of people with whom we've become friends over the past six years. Your generosity to each other and to us is something to see. Thank you especially for the extra help many of you gave us by subscribing in 2020; you've helped keep the podcast and community free to anyone who wants to be a part of it.

Thank you to Phil Willis, aka Brendan, for helping us shape this debacle into a podcast and website. Thank you to Cathy Beale, aka Brenda 1.0, for expanding it into a community with the thoroughness and discretion that only a really top-flight librarian can manage! Thank you to Bec Francis (Brenda 2.0), who manages the ever-burgeoning shambolia of *Chat 10* over a range of social media platforms with generosity and sound judgement.

And thank you to the Brendalings – those Platinum Chatters who go the extra distance to keep the Facebook group orderly and kind, and whose smiling faces we look forward to seeing at live shows. Here they are, past and present at time of writing:

Alice Best, Caroline Braithwaite, Jane Britt, Emma Christian, Sarah Lulu Faith, Yvonne Green, Bronwyn Hayward, Kerry Hogan Ross, Genevieve Hughes, Kristy Hunter, Paul Kenny, Rebekah McAlinden, Emma O'Malley, Katie Pepper, Trish Pepper, Sonia Sarangi, Reb Schoates, and Deepa Srinivasan.

We're much obliged to Antony Stockdale, who produces the podcast and manages advertising and is moreover an endlessly pleasant and funny person to work with. And Jeremy Storer, who already has his hands full living with Crabb but somehow now also finds himself doing the taxes for *Chat 10* and producing live shows around the country, both of which he makes look easy.

Thank you to everyone who's ever appeared in our shows; all the patient and slightly nonplussed crew at the various venues around Australia at which *Chat 10* Live has played; all the Chatters whose stories we included in this book; and all the celebrities we clanged, especially the awkward ones.

To the team at Penguin Random House: what a pleasure you made this book, beginning with the single most impressive book pitch we've ever seen and